DOING WHAT MATTERS

DOING WHAT MATTERS

How to Get Results That Make a Difference—The Revolutionary Old-School Approach

JAMES M. KILTS
Former Chairman and CEO of the Gillette Company

WITH JOHN F. MANFREDI AND ROBERT L. LORBER

CROWN BUSINESS
NEW YORK

Published in the United States by Crown Business, an imprint of the Crown Publishing Group, a division of Random House, Inc., New York.
www.crownpublishing.com

Crown Business is a trademark and the Rising Sun colophon is a registered trademark of Random House, Inc.

Library of Congress Cataloging-in-Publication Data

Kilts, James M.
Doing what matters : how to get results that make a difference—the revolutionary old-school approach / James M. Kilts, with John F. Manfredi and Robert L. Lorber
Includes index.
1. Management. 2. Organizational effectiveness. 3. Success in business. 4. Executives—Biography. I. Manfredi, John F. (John Frederick). II. Lorber, Robert L. III. Title.

HD31.K4674 2007
658.4'09—dc22
2007010065

ISBN 978-0-307-35166-1

Printed in the United States of America

Design by Robert Bull

10 9 8 7 6 5 4 3 2 1

First Edition

To my mom and dad who taught me everything that matters

—James M. Kilts

To my family, the ultimate in people who matter

—John F. Manfredi

To my late business partner and friend, H. Kef Kamai, who worked with me through the Kraft years with Jim and who always understood how to Do What Matters, both in business and in life

—Robert L. Lorber

CONTENTS

DOING WHAT MATTERS

INTRODUCTION

"I THINK YOU'RE GOING TO GET FIRED"

Years ago, I started learning the importance of "doing what matters" when my mother called me to the phone saying: "It's the foreman at the plant. There are no more cartons. They're shutting down the line. I think you're going to get fired."

At the time, I held an entry-level position at the General Foods Kool-Aid plant in Chicago to put myself through the graduate business school at the University of Chicago. I was responsible for ordering supplies and simply forgot to order cartons for one of the beverage lines. I called the salesman from the box company at home that evening and pleaded with him for cartons. That same night, I helped load a truck, brought the cartons to the plant, and, fortunately, kept my job.

That simple lesson about doing what matters—*what you must do to be successful in business, and, as important, the things you should ignore*—has been central for me as I eventually moved from plant assistant to CEO.

WHAT HAPPENS IN THE REAL WORLD?

Whether ordering cartons for the production line or managing big businesses, as I have for the past twenty years, the simplicity of the *Doing What Matters* approach works. That was certainly the case when, as the CEO of Kraft Foods, I was in charge of a $25 billion plus company that had operations all around the world. The same was true at Nabisco, whose brands were global icons—Oreo, Ritz, Chips Ahoy!, Planters nuts, Life Savers confections, and many others. And most recently (2001 through 2005), the *Doing What Matters* approach was put to the test as I headed one of the best-known and most profitable consumer product companies in the world, the Gillette Company.

But while I have a lot of business experience, the idea for *Doing What Matters* didn't start to gel until I spent the time between leaving Kraft and joining Nabisco as a visiting lecturer and executive in residence at my alma mater, the University of Chicago's Graduate School of Business. Working with the students was a thrill, both in the classroom and in informal get-togethers. They are among the best and the brightest, and they absorb vast amounts of management theory, principles, and applications. However, a recurring question throughout the year was "What happens when school is out and I enter the real world of business? With so many options and so much data available to me, how do I, as a manager, decide and do what really matters?"

That's when I started to think that while knowing a lot is great, knowing *how* to use that knowledge is what matters in business. Maybe I could help translate knowledge into the basis for useful action. Perhaps my work experience could link the school learning—the principles and theories about business—with the old-fashioned, tried-and-true, practical applications of what really matters in business.

Over the next eight years, my mind and energy shifted from the halls of academia to the more white-knuckled experiences of helping to lead Nabisco and Gillette out of serious business nosedives that threatened their very existence. However, during those years, the question of deciding on, and then doing, what matters was an ongoing consideration for me.

RECONCILING "REVOLUTIONARY" WITH "OLD SCHOOL"

For example, the seemingly contradictory subtitle for this book, *How to Get Results That Make a Difference—The Revolutionary Old-School Approach,* came from those experiences. Old school means the fundamentals, and the importance of always having them front and center. Are the cartons ordered? If not, then the line shuts down.

But the fundamentals *alone* aren't enough, unless they're applied to the warp-speed environment you operate in today. Let's say that you've inherited a sales force that's gone through a $50 million reorganization, but is still on a trajectory to crash and burn, as was the case at Nabisco. You must take radical action quickly—before the moment of impact.

You not only have to sort out what you should pay attention to and what you should ignore, you must do so with *revolutionary* speed and decisiveness. Yet, even with disaster staring them in the face, people from the lowest to highest levels in many organizations often prefer to "rearrange the deck chairs." They'll give lip service to stepping up performance, but in practice go about business as usual.

That was certainly the case at Gillette. Its position as the number one maker of blades and razors was virtually unchallenged in all regions of the world. Its manufacturing capabilities were unparalleled, and its engineering, research, and new-product development were unmatched within all consumer products.

Not only had Gillette invented the safety razor and the double-edged blade, it had also commercialized every major advance in wet shaving for over a hundred years. And in recent years, the Gillette development machine seemed to be working better than ever. The Mach3 shaving system that was introduced in 1998 was a runaway success that generated more than $2.5 billion in sales during its first three years—a premium-priced, exceptionally high-profit product that men all around the world loved.

WHERE'S THE GROWTH?

So what was the problem?

Start with *net sales, net profit,* and *net earnings* stalled at *zero growth,* with Wall Street and the Gillette board of directors convinced that the worst was yet to come. Yet in 2001, as the new Gillette CEO, the first outsider to run the company in more than seventy years, I was told by Gillette's vice president of human resources that 65 percent of the managers had received performance ratings of *exceeds expectations* or *outstanding*. And Gillette was not just in a tailspin. It was caught deep in a circle of doom.

My job was to turn things around, and do it without having the luxury of time. Yes, we had to preserve what was important—world-class brands of the highest quality, great traditions of unmatched innovation and technology, integrity, and respect for people. But I also was there to lead the revolution by using the past as a starting point. Old-school approaches would be built upon, adapted, and, at times, totally transformed and overturned so Gillette would return to its glory days and its managers would be among the most prized in business.

Let's take the performance measurement system as an example of what had to be done. Like many companies, Gillette used the five-grade system of *Does Not Meet Expectations, Needs*

Improvement, Meets Expectations, Exceeds Expectations, and *Outstanding.* Perversely, the worse a company does, the more likely it is that more people will be graded higher. Managers don't want to demotivate people in bad times, so they move them up the scale. That's why two-thirds of Gillette's managers were at the top of the performance scale despite the company's ongoing decline in performance.

Over time, the system has little meaning and actually hurts performance. *Doing What Matters* uses a numeric system that goes from 1 to 100 percent. Yes, it's back-to-school. You can get a score of 53 percent or 99 percent . . . and everything in between. Every single percentage point becomes meaningful, not just because of personal pride, but also because scores are shared with all peers! The *Doing What Matters* system grabs people at an emotional level, let's them know exactly where they stand, and gives them a desire to excel and change—now!

The revolutionary old-school approach was never more needed than with innovation and product development, even though Gillette excelled at *big-bang* innovation. The successes included the twin-bladed Atra system, which was replaced in 1989 by the first independently spring-mounted, twin-bladed Sensor for Men, followed a year later by Sensor for Women. Less than a decade later, came Mach3, the three-bladed cartridge with a two-to-one performance preference over Sensor.

CRACKING THE NEW-PRODUCT-DEVELOPMENT CODE

This type of game-changing product development—big-bang innovation—is the Holy Grail for all consumer product companies. It provides a competitive advantage that almost always leads to accelerated growth and profitability. Gillette seemed to have cracked the code.

On the surface, Gillette's well-established approach to making the highest-performance products and offering them globally at a premium price to shavers whose brand loyalty was unwavering seemed to be working flawlessly. Unfortunately, the opposite was true.

Big bang at Gillette was the province of a small priesthood of big brains. Revolutionary change required everyone to be concerned and involved with innovation. But how do you create revolutionary change, yet not make the mistake of throwing the baby out with the bathwater? Part of the answer is the three-tiered process of Total Innovation (TI).

You don't eliminate big-bang innovation, which is essential. You add two more layers—*continuous improvement* and *incremental innovation*—and make a pyramid. And you expand the base of innovators from a small group of researchers, developers, and engineers to everyone in the company from top to bottom, regardless of rank, function, and expertise—or lack of it. Everyone participates in Total Innovation.

Cost cutting provides another example of how *Doing What Matters* is both revolutionary and old school. Cost cutting is commonplace, but it's usually employed during a time of crisis, as an effort of last resort. But the globalization of business means you are competing with low-cost providers from every nook and cranny of the world. The *Doing What Matters* approach calls for ZOG—Zero Overhead Growth. It makes eliminating unnecessary costs a way of life—a strategic imperative—not something that's just short-term first aid.

NEW MIND-SET SIMPLIFIES PROBLEMS

Let's look at some other transformations of the old-school approach.

- Breaking down barriers and getting people from different units and divisions to communicate with one another is usually an elusive quest. The *Doing What Matters* unique approach has people lining up to share plans and exchange information.
- Many hardworking, well-intentioned managers slide into cycles of dismal underperformance. The *Doing What Matters* approach can help people and companies avoid entry into—or facilitate quick escape from—the *Circle of Doom.*
- Formulas abound for choosing good people. The *Doing What Matters* practices not only gave my companies great bench strength, they also groomed CEOs and senior leaders for several other Fortune companies.
- Many experts focus on the importance of your first one hundred days in a new position. In *Doing What Matters,* we'll tell you how you can use day one—the first day on the job—to set the stage for your future success.
- Strategic plans take great effort and resources to prepare, but often wind up gathering dust. The double-A version in *Doing What Matters* guarantees action and accountability and makes your strategic plan an essential, everyday guide to business.

Doing What Matters is not just techniques, but an entire mind-set for taking complicated problems and making them simple. Using illustrations and anecdotes from my experiences with Gillette, Nabisco, and Kraft, *Doing What Matters* sets the foundation for moving forward in an uncertain world where maintaining the status quo is a recipe for failure.

It reignites ways of becoming excited about the fundamentals so you can beat the competition and create value for shareholders by getting people to change and advance together.

THE RIGHT TEAM FOR THE TASK

Now let me tell you a little about my coauthors—John Manfredi and Bob Lorber. They're not your typical coauthors. In other words, they're not people whom I've just teamed with to write this book. They have been part of the process that led to the thinking in this book—John as one of my executive staff members for more than eight years and Bob as an outside consultant and adviser.

My relationship with John actually goes back more than thirty years, when I was in product management and he was in product publicity at the General Foods Corporation. And in recent years, he has worked with me day in and day out as we developed and implemented the plans that turned around Nabisco and then Gillette. Bob Lorber has worked with me and members of my executive teams from my days at Kraft and again at Gillette. In addition to being a great teacher and coach, Bob, along with Ken Blanchard, cowrote the bestselling book *Putting the One Minute Manager to Work*. So we are the authors.

HOW IT ALL COMES TOGETHER

Before we start, let me discuss how we've organized the book. It has four sections.

What Matters for Leaders The first section deals with the fundamental analysis that is the basis for managing a business and the personal attributes that are critical for leading one.

Fundamental analysis helps you work your way through a lot of myths and misconceptions about management. It provides you with a rock-solid foundation for setting your targets and establishing your objectives. In brief, it gets you on the right road for doing what matters.

Personal attributes gets you right into what matters for leaders. Based on the knowledge gained from years of hiring, training, developing, promoting, and, of course, sometimes terminating people, I identify four attributes that are predictive of successful leaders: intellectual integrity; emotional engagement/ enthusiasm; action orientation; and a solid understanding of business and people. We devote a chapter to each of these attributes, explaining how they influence the performance, culture, and ultimate success of business activities.

Avoiding a Plunge into the Death Spiral The second section deals with the process and procedures that make all the difference in leading and managing an organization. Selecting the right team and then gaining their understanding of the leadership process that guides the company is critical. Not all people in business have to be students of business. But you must have a good grasp of how to run an organization, or it's just not possible to lead one. To highlight the importance of all this, we'll see how what we call entering the Circle of Doom can plunge a company into a death spiral.

Point/Counterpoint—Long-Term Versus Immediate Needs The third section shifts to one of the most difficult areas in business, especially in today's environment. It's the vision and long-term planning that are essential for all organizations. How do you balance the need for short-term performance yet at the same time define a vision and long-term strategy that lets everybody know where you're headed? It's something that often creates a lot of uncertainty and tension within organizations. And it's absolutely imperative to get it right.

Face-to-Face with the Media and Politicians The fourth and final section covers two areas: one tends to be the least familiar and, in many ways, scariest for people in business—politicians and the media; the other looks at a number of the lessons that

I've learned throughout my career. Though different, these areas are bound by their underlying theme, which is the importance of doing the right things.

Now let's get started with *Doing What Matters*.

Jim Kilts

SECTION I

FUNDAMENTALS,
ATTITUDES,
AND
PEOPLE MATTER

CHAPTER 1

HOW DO YOU KNOW WHAT REALLY MATTERS?

One of the first phone calls I received when news broke about my becoming Gillette's new CEO was from a Boston-based business associate. "Jim, I know a lot of Gillette executives, and my advice is *go slow*." Gillette people don't like outsiders, he said, which is why the company last had an outside CEO seventy years ago, and he failed miserably. "Give people time to get to know you before you start changing things," my friend said. "It's the best approach you can take."

That call was followed by many more, along with dozens of proposals from professionals, including consultants, bankers, compensation specialists, and sales motivation experts. Each had a plan or recommendation that should receive my top priority if I wanted to succeed at Gillette.

With all that advice, how do you decide what matters? One of the biggest impediments to success in business—for individuals and companies—is the failure to achieve that understanding.

Whether you're the CEO of a multibillion-dollar company, the brand manager for a struggling product, a director of human resources, or an entrepreneur starting your own business, you're always confronted with an insurmountable amount of information and a number of options, conflicting opinions, and management theories that are as endless as they are confusing.

You're always confronted with an insurmountable amount of information and possible options.

Making these decisions isn't a job for the timid or weak of heart. It takes guts to say these are the things that really matter; I'll pay absolutely no attention to the rest. That's the challenge everyone faces. This book helps you meet that challenge.

$40 BILLION OF LOST VALUE WITH NO END IN SIGHT

For example, I faced no bigger challenge than the decisions we made during my first months at Gillette. Early in 2001, the company had missed its earnings estimates for fifteen straight quarters. Sales and earnings had been flat for the prior four years. Market shares were declining sharply. Advertising spending, the lifeline of consumer products, had been slashed year after year. Overhead costs were high and growing. And competition was intensifying.

Wall Street had lost patience with this chronic underperformance. And Gillette's share price reflected the disappointment. It had fallen from an all-time high of $64.25 in March of 1999 to $24.50 in 2001. That's a 62 percent drop in two years—a loss in market capitalization of close to $40 billion, and there was no end in sight.

So it's no surprise that analysts and investors had plenty of ideas for what had to be done. The problem was that no two suggestions were the same, and many were conflicting. It was up to me to decide which ones really mattered. Or whether it was better to put aside the advice and chart a different course.

MULTIPLE OPTIONS, NO SIMPLE ANSWERS

These wouldn't be simple decisions. And they would make the difference between whether Gillette would survive and prosper, or continue its unrelenting decline. Here are some of the suggestions that were being offered. Many would result in a corporate yard sale.

- **Divest the ailing Duracell business.** This was a $2 billion business that Gillette had spent around $8 billion dollars to purchase just four years before. The post-acquisition performance had been miserable. Duracell had gone from one of the best-performing brands in the consumer products sector to a true basket case. Its market share had slipped by almost 15 percent—from 46 to 40 percent of the alkaline-battery market in the United States. And the competitive pressure was mounting. So on the face of it, selling the Duracell business and cutting any further losses seemed like a pretty good idea.
- **Hold on to the Duracell business,** but slash prices drastically. In other words, we should acknowledge that Gillette's high-priced acquisition of Duracell was a big mistake. Admit that batteries were a commodity business, not an advantaged category. And milk our investment, not try to restore it. Since it's never good to tilt at windmills, this was another seemingly plausible approach.
- **Divest the Braun electric shaver and household appliance business.** Braun represented an early acquisition by Gillette, dating back to 1967. Unfortunately, Braun's performance had been bleaker

than Duracell's for a far longer time. The last time Braun had made an annual budget was such a distant memory that no present senior manager could even remember it. There was no question that Braun's inconsistent performance and costly investments were a major drag on Gillette.

- **Divest the Personal Care business,** which included such brands as Right Guard, Dry Idea, and Soft & Dri antiperspirants and deodorants as well as Gillette Foamy and the Gillette Series shaving preparations. Not only were the market shares for most of these products falling, their profits also were deteriorating, with operating margins that were much lower than competitors'.
- **Strip the company by selling all assets except the highly profitable blade and razor business;** operate Gillette as a pure play in one sector only. The sales would be lower, but the profit margins would be so high that the share price would rocket.
- **Acknowledge that Gillette was yesterday's news and invent a whole new growth strategy.** Enter new product sectors that analysts said were "burgeoning with growth." Multiple acquisitions would redefine Gillette and jump-start the stock performance.
- Or, **acknowledge that Gillette was yesterday's news and throw in the towel.** Call in the investment bankers and work on the best possible "endgame."

These were a broad and opposing group of options, and that wasn't all of them. There were dozens of others, dealing with everything from business and operating strategies to where Gillette's headquarters should be located (it was in the high-rent Prudential Tower in Boston's Back Bay district). I could have filled my days just sorting through the endless opinions that were being offered up on how to manage Gillette. In the end, I worked with my team to set our own course that would restore Gillette to its number one position in the consumer products arena.

DECIDING WHAT REALLY MATTERS

But how do you make such decisions? How do you know what really matters? Is there an approach that can work regardless of the circumstances? Something that can put you on the right course more often than not? There is. It's what I call the *fast-track quick-screen elimination process*. Many times in my career—especially when working through the fog of conflicting opinions—I've found the right direction by answering a few critical questions that allow me to eliminate most, if not all, other options.

Let's go back to the advice on Gillette to see how it works.

Divest Duracell In order to divest Duracell, there had to be someone willing to buy Duracell. So Duracell had to be worth more to someone else than to Gillette. But, there wasn't anyone. The battery category was so irrational and competitive no company that could afford to buy Duracell wanted to get into the fray. And even if they did, Gillette's price-earnings (p/e) ratio, which is the price investors will pay for a stock expressed as a multiple of its net earnings, was far higher than the (p/e) of any possible buyer. So Duracell was worth more to Gillette than anyone else. By utilizing the fast-track quick-screen elimination process, I could eliminate the "sell Duracell" option. No need to give it a second thought.

Quick screen took me to the right answer without having to slog through a swamp of details.

Milk Duracell A second option was slash the prices on Duracell, admit it's an undifferentiated commodity, and milk the business. This time I applied my past experience in the quick-screen process. Was a Duracell battery more or less of a commodity than Kraft Singles—the cheese slices that carried, on average, a 25 percent higher price than private-label products when I managed the Kraft business? (Literally, in blind taste tests, consumers could detect only a slight difference between Kraft and private-label.)

The differences between Duracell batteries and the private-label and price-brand batteries were perceived by consumers to be significant on a number of factors, including reliability and durability. In addition, the performance difference between alkaline Duracell and general-purpose zinc batteries was enormous. So why give up on Duracell, a branded product with great equity and an impeccable twenty-year record of high growth and profitability, simply because it had stumbled for the last three years? Again, the quick screen took us to the right answer without having to slog through a swamp of detail. (Don't get me wrong; we later did an exhaustive study of the battery business. Our new management team had to assess the category's potential and determine the best way to get it. And that required detailed analysis.)

The quick screen told us that Duracell was the leader in the alkaline battery category, which meant it should be *disciplined in how it led* the category and in *how it imposed discipline* when the nonleaders got out of line. Duracell had done neither.

The leader in a consumer products category must invest in marketing to drive growth and increase the consumer equity and preference for the brand. Instead, Duracell had cut its advertising substantially.

A category leader must demonstrate that it won't allow competitors to steal its market share. Duracell allowed repeated theft of market share by relatively minor competitors that emboldened them for future initiatives. Category leaders must avoid creating a frenzy of out-of-control promotional spending in order to enhance short-term results. Duracell had succumbed to a pattern of frequent and heavy promotional activity.

None of these observations required in-depth, protracted analysis. They were fact based and verifiable. You have to know what to look at.

In consumer products, the first place you go—in addition to sales and earnings trends—is market shares. Are they rising or falling? Advertising-to-sales ratios—again, are they up or down? And promotion and trade spending to sales ratios—an upward trend signals trouble.

In other businesses, the key metrics will vary. But they always exist, and they will give you the quick read you need to move forward. Yes, you'll go back and spend time conducting the analysis necessary to execute a plan of action. How much should you invest in marketing? What does marketing-mix modeling tell you about where to invest? How much of a price gap does your brand and market advantage allow? How effective is your sales force in working with your trade customers? What channel of trade is driving growth? Do you have the right trade-channel strategy? There's a lot you'll have to cover. But you can't allow it to bring you to a halt at the outset. You have to go with the quick screen so you can act.

Key metrics will vary, but they always exist.

Let's look at one more option, the real scorched-earth option.

Sell Everything Sell everything except the shaving business and focus on Gillette's strongest and most profitable franchise. With all its assets combined, Gillette was a medium-sized consumer products company. It had $10 billion in sales, compared with $48 billion for Unilever and $70 billion for Nestlé. Strip Gillette down to its blades and razors and you have a $4 billion company. Now, what sort of presence would this stripped-down Gillette command with its principal customer, the $300 billion Wal-Mart? Slim to none. We might just as well hang a for-sale sign on the door.

The quick-screen approach does not eliminate all options. A

variant of the 80/20 rule works here. You almost always can screen out four-fifths of the choices, which means that what matters is the remaining 20 percent. In effect, something that seemed larger than life is now scaled down to manageable proportions. You will find specific steps for applying this approach at the end of the chapter.

Your assessment must be well thought through and fact based.

BENIGN NEGLECT LEADS TO BAD RESULTS

When using the fast-track quick-screen process, it is important to reduce issues to their simplest elements. However, your assessment must be well thought through and fact based. The superficial application of concepts, even of good, well-grounded concepts, will get you in deep trouble.

For example, two of my guiding principles are the importance of alignment and the value of utilizing scale. Those were the precepts that had led the prior Gillette management to place the $800 million Gillette Personal Care business within the Blades & Razors Business Unit (BU). They believed that shaving preparations—such as Gillette Foamy and the Gillette Series—and antiperspirants and deodorants (AP/DEO)—such as Right Guard, Dry Idea, Soft & Dri, and the Gillette Series—should be closely tied with the Gillette-branded blades and razors. The scale of all the products combined would have a big impact on customers, which should translate into a greater in-store presence for the Personal Care products.

Those are good concepts. But applied to the Gillette Personal Care business, they caused problems. Tucked within the Blades & Razors Business Unit, the Personal Care business was managed like a stepchild. There are times when benign neglect is the best course of action for a low-growth, low-return business. However, when the neglect causes self-inflicted wounds, then it's time for a change. And that was the situation when we started at Gillette.

Peter Klein, my longtime associate, first worked on the Gillette Personal Care business in the 1970s. He became part of the new Gillette management team and pointed out that deodorants and antiperspirants required great attention to detail and a constant flow of new fragrances, forms, and other consumer benefits to stay ahead of competition. But as part of the much larger and more profitable Blades & Razors Business Unit, Personal Care became an afterthought. It was a training ground for young managers, and not a place with a lot of institutional knowledge about the ins and outs of toiletries.

Those were the insights we used in the fast-track quick-screen process that resulted in my setting up Personal Care as a separate business unit. Rather than focusing primarily on utilizing scale and limiting the personnel expenses associated with running Personal Care, we paid attention to the vitality of the brands and increased cost control that a dedicated management would bring to these products. Within three years of splitting off the Personal Care division, market shares were rising, profits had returned to competitive levels, and the new-product pipeline was bursting with innovation.

THAT LITTLE RED RAZOR

Another element in the quick-screen process is to weigh your own experience in assessing an option or making a decision. Your assessment must be well thought through and fact based. You cannot rely on your gut alone to arrive at make-or-break decisions. But you cannot permit what are supposed to be facts or solid judgments to overwhelm your experience and common sense. Oftentimes you'll find some facts will turn out to be "old truths" that were never tested or challenged.

One of my favorite old-truth stories at Gillette involves what came to be called "that little red razor." We talk more about this "problem" that was really an opportunity in chapter 12. But the essence of the story involves a strongly held old truth among the marketing and market-research gurus of the Blades & Razors Business Unit. The overall marketing talent in this unit was impressive. Many of the senior managers had been with the company for twenty to even thirty years! These people were in an excellent position to know old truths.

Don't let supposed facts or solid judgments overwhelm your experience and common sense.

In 2001, Gillette introduced a variant on our Mach 3 razor that was designed to increase its appeal and penetration among young shavers. The product was called *Mach3 Cool Blue*. And the name says it all. It was a Mach3 razor with an attractive, vibrant blue handle. Nothing more. No new features. No performance advantages. Just a new blue color. But the color did exactly what it was supposed to do. It boosted our appeal with young males and increased our overall Mach3 razor sales by a remarkable 15 percent.

Now fast-forward about six months to a planning meeting with our Blades & Razors Business Unit. We reviewed a number of new-product options for the future. In the discussion, I suggested that we build on the success of our blue razor by introducing a red razor. Well, based on the reaction of the Blades & Razors marketing people, you would have thought that I had suggested selling dull blades as an innovative breakthrough.

Didn't I know that red was the color of *blood*? That anything suggesting blood would subconsciously tap into shavers' fears of cutting themselves? That a red razor would *not* increase our sales, but rather drive untold millions of our loyal shavers to competitive brands? That was a hard-and-fast old truth. I felt chastised, to say the least, yet not really convinced. Our Blades & Razors marketing people were impressive, just about as sharp as their products. On this one, however, I felt they made a bad call. But we dropped the subject.

Now fast-forward another year to a time when our arch competitor, Schick, has trumped our Mach3 with a four-bladed cartridge called Schick Quattro. Our testing told us that Quattro gave a shave that was far inferior to our Mach3 Turbo. But we needed something to blunt the anticipated $75 million marketing blitz that Schick would use to launch Quattro. Our next new-product breakthrough wouldn't be ready for market for another fifteen months.

The Little Red Razor that Could Reenter the red razor. Not really convinced of the old-truth validity of the cut-and-blood basis for eliminating red as a razor color, I went back to our Blades & Razors Business Unit and asked them to put the testing of a red razor on a fast track.

The results, backed by an excellent marketing program, were staggering. The red razor became our *Mach3 Turbo Champion.* The concept that powered the marketing initiative was racecar-driver champions behind the wheels of *red* supercharged cars. High-powered men in high-performance cars taking on the gutsy challenge of high-speed racing.

The imagery, symbolism, and attributes were an exact fit with the brand concept we wanted for Mach3 Turbo Champion. It became not only the most successful product extension ever introduced at Gillette, it also stopped Quattro dead in its tracks. A year after its introduction, Quattro's share in the United States was 4 percent. Mach3's share stood at 34 percent. And when I met the chairman of Schick's parent company at a business function, he said that he couldn't believe we did all that damage with "that little red razor." So much for the validity of supposedly fact-based old truths.

By doing what matters and using the quick-screen approach, we made decisions and set directions for Gillette that might have taken many months, if not a year, had we moved painstakingly through all the advice that was heaped on us at the outset. Not all of our decisions were right; we made mid-course corrections. But our big decisions were winners. We bet on strong growth for Duracell and over three years, its sales increased, profits trebled, and market shares grew. We focused on Personal Care, and the new business unit was able to drive profit margin from the lowest in its product categories to the highest. And we held on to the Braun business and transformed it from a financial black hole to a high-powered innovator that fueled growth in our Oral Care and Blades & Razors businesses as well as its own.

GET TO HEART OF THE MATTER

I opened this chapter with an observation that success in business boils down to knowing what really matters and then doing it. Regardless of your position in a company or organization, there is always a flood of information and data, and a lot of conflicting ideas and opinions. In the end, how you get to the heart of what matters will define you as a leader. While there are no simple formulas, there are approaches that help facilitate the process. The fast-track quick-screen elimination process is one way to cut through conflicting opinions. It helps find a direction by answering the few critical questions that allow you to eliminate other considerations. It's this type of thinking that we'll be demonstrating and discussing throughout the book.

How you get to the heart of what matters will define you as a leader.

PUTTING THE QUICK-SCREEN PROCESS TO WORK

- Reduce the problem or issue to its simplest elements; strip out extraneous factors. Zero in on the key metrics or levers. In consumer products, for example, look beyond sales and earnings to market shares and marketing and promotion to sales ratios as barometers of health. In other sectors, find comparably important metrics.

- Ask fact-based questions that require you to give fact-based answers. Go beyond generalizations. For example, saying a product has "become a commodity" offers little insight about its growth and profit potential *if* it were well managed. Statements or beliefs that aren't fact based can easily lead you astray.

- Force yourself to give simple, clear answers; complex multifaceted answers probably aren't focused on basic concepts. For example, you don't need the data derived from marketing-mix modeling or a segmentation study to know if you have an advantaged product or service in a growth category. Keep things simple at the outset so you're in a position to act, not to inhibit action.

- Decide whether further immediate analysis is needed. With your best option in hand, would further analysis *now* yield more clarity and a better decision? Or would it just postpone the time for action? I've found that four out of five times, you can screen out the non-starters and also-rans and be confident that you've identified the winning option.

- Conduct the detailed analysis and collect the data necessary to act at the right time. Making an initial decision does not mean there's nothing more to do. There's a right time for getting into the weeds. But don't let the need for future action result in real-time, immediate paralysis.

CHAPTER 2

FOCUSING ON FUNDAMENTALS MATTERS

When you're young and impulsive, everything seems possible. Even doing everything at once doesn't seem daunting. But experience teaches you that nothing gets done when you try to do too much. You either whirl around in circles or slump into a paralysis when facing endless options simultaneously.

While the relevance of this simple observation to the business world seems evident, it is baffling how many intelligent, well-trained, and experienced executives fall into the trap of trying to make themselves and their companies all things to all people. It's especially true of CEOs and CFOs who want to accommodate every wish and whim of analysts and investors—even if what Wall Street wants isn't in the best interests of their companies.

Rather than chase wishes and whims, you must focus on the fundamentals that set the right course, pace, and direction for your business. But how do you know what fundamentals to focus on? Let me use an illustration from my experience to make the point that fundamentals really influence everything, and that, conversely, a failure to focus on them virtually assures problems.

THE MISTAKEN QUEST TO BE NUMBER ONE

We live in a society where every man, woman, and child wants to be number one. Settling for number two is cause for sadness and derision. We all know the expressions: A miss is as good as a mile; there's no prize for second best; winning is everything.

Business people, and especially CEOs, exhibit this trait in spades. "I want my company to be best in class, year in and year out, or there will be hell to pay." It's ironic that setting the objective of being number one year in and year out virtually assures the opposite.

Setting the objective of being number one year in and year out virtually assures the opposite.

Over the years, I had studies performed on the leading corporations in more than a dozen different sectors—sectors ranging from food and personal-care products to durable goods and industrials. While there were some sector-specific variances, one thing was common across all the sectors.

Over a five-year period, in each sector, the best-performing company overall had not scored number one, or even number two, most frequently. It was the company that ranked within the *top third* of the sector *consistently* for the entire five-year period.

Avoid the Yo-Yo Effect That means top-tier consistency is much more important for becoming "best in class" than setting your sights on *always* being number one. While achieving the top spot brings short-term euphoria, the long-term consequence inevitably is a "yo-yo effect." Companies would hit the top for one or two years, and then plummet to the depths for a while—one or two years. Then, they'd jump back to the top, followed by a steep slide, and the cycle continued.

But imagine this scenario. You're in a thirty-company sector. To be best in class, you must perform within the top third for five consecutive years. Your ranking could range from number three to number seven to number four—with a ranking of number one and number nine also thrown in—and you would stand an excellent chance of winning best in class for your sector over the five-year period.

One of my toughest struggles to stay the course on consistent earnings growth occurred when I was heading Kraft. Ironically, it involved the Nabisco company, which emerged from a bruising leveraged buyout; its sights were set on an annual earnings growth rate of 30+ percent so it could start paying off its mountain of high-interest debt that Kohlberg Kravis Roberts (KKR) racked up in making the largest-ever LBO in history.

For two years, Nabisco rode the roller coaster up, which prompted the senior managers at the Philip Morris Companies, the parent company of Kraft, to ask why Kraft couldn't match Nabisco's performance.

If Nabisco could grow by more than 20 percent annually, asked Geoff Bible, Philip Morris's CEO, why was Kraft getting just single-digit increases? Why not accelerate Kraft's earnings so Nabisco wouldn't be the only "darling of the food sector"? Geoff was one of the toughest and brightest bosses I've ever worked for, and he always pushed hard to extract top shareholder value.

It didn't take a lot of research to show that Nabisco was well into the "yo-yo cycle" of unsustainable earnings growth. With its strong market positions—the Nabisco brands represented nine of the top-ten cookies and crackers sold in the United States—it was relatively easy to raise prices significantly without an immediate sales drop-off. These were snack items, indulgence foods, that consumers were willing to pay for. So Nabisco profits soared, and it was number one for two years.

But the price gaps Nabisco had opened between its brands and those of Keebler's little elves, the top competitor, were enormous. While consumers are loyal to such powerful brands as Oreo, Chips Ahoy!, Newtons, and Ritz, they have their limits. With price differences of 30 to 50 percent, and virtually all marketing support withdrawn from its products, Nabisco headed down the roller coaster at an alarming speed.

Nabisco was on its crash-and-burn trajectory when I became the new CEO at the beginning of 1989. As my research predicted, market shares were declining for more than 90 percent of Nabisco's business in the United States, and my new team had to start plotting its turnaround.

Realizing the importance of consistent, measured growth is one example of fundamental analysis. It guides you in knowing what targets to set and goals to achieve. It sets the base upon which virtually everything else is built.

GROWTH AT WHAT RATE?

Let's look at another form of fundamental analysis—identifying the right rate of growth for your business, not just for a year or two, but one that you can sustain for the intermediate and longer terms.

I am not someone who believes in ten-year plans. My strategic plans run a three-year cycle. The real world rarely conforms to planning templates. It's hard to predict the future, and given the tough odds, you must anchor your plans on rock-solid fundamentals, the most important of which is assessing the right rate of revenue growth.

I focus the most attention on assessing the right rate of revenue growth.

Let me make the point using the food sector, where I spent a good part of my career. If the population growth of the United States is 1 percent a year, and inflation is 3 percent a year, and price increases over the past three years have averaged 1 percent, it is safe to assume that even the most innovative and aggressive packaged-food marketer would have a daunting task to sustain revenue growth of more than 5 percent a year. (Despite the epidemic of obesity, Americans aren't really eating more; they are exercising less and expending fewer calories than in the past.)

If It Sounds Too Good to Be True . . . So if a food marketer promises consistent annual revenue growth of 6 to 8 percent, your suspicion antenna should rise to a high level. And if that marketer moves its revenue growth estimate to "consistent high-single-digit or double-digit increases," your antenna should emit an ear-piercing warning signal.

Unfortunately, all too many executives in recent years were willing to make these logic-defying predictions. And all too many Wall Street analysts were not only willing to join in these hyperbolic estimates, they also often went to the next level by saying that while high-single-digit growth would be good, the real leaders would consistently return low-double-digit annual revenue growth!

Let me give you another example of some fundamental research, performed by a leading national consulting company. Similar results have been calculated by other sources. The data show that only 158 companies out of the studied group of 1,056 were able to sustain double-digit earnings growth for a period of 5 years. That number moved down to 5 companies for 10 years and to just 3 for 15 years.

Yet during the tech bubble of the 1990s, mid-to-high-teen growth was considered anemic. Both CEOs and Wall Street analysts were routinely promising annual increases of 30 percent, 40 percent, and even 50 percent indefinitely into the future.

But when Wall Street turns on the very companies it seduced, it's never pretty.

Exuberance Comes Before the Fall While the Gillette executives of the 1990s weren't in the same league as the high-tech touters, they shared some of their exuberance. When Gillette acquired the Duracell battery company in 1997, the company was quoted in the *Wall Street Journal* as saying: "Gillette's profits will rise at least 15 percent this year . . . growth will surpass 18 percent in the years ahead. Gillette expects Duracell to expand profits at close to a 20 percent annual clip in the next few years, compared with an average of 12 percent in the past three years."

How could any consumer product—even an advantaged one like Duracell in the high-growth alkaline battery segment—achieve *sustained, indefinite growth* at such unsustainable levels! As noted, Wall Street often encourages and joins in such folly for a while. But when Wall Street turns on the very companies they seduced, it's never pretty. With Gillette, the honeymoon lasted about two years beyond the time it was evident the company's performance was not keeping up with the promises, and wouldn't in the future.

When the fall came, it was sharp and unrelenting. The Gillette stock, as I said earlier, plunged from a high of $64.25 early in 1999 down to $24.50 in the spring of 2001. That's what our new management team had to deal with when we took over at Gillette.

There was an ongoing and strong downward momentum on the share price. And there was deep skepticism and suspicion about everything we said. All of this was fully justified.

Bloated estimates, broken promises, and a string of bad business practices—these are surefire ways of wiping out a company's credibility and making any turnaround a difficult feat.

No More Estimates! One of the things we had going for us early in 2001 was a then-recent decision of the board of directors to suspend all short-term guidance to analysts and investors. The company could talk about long-term plans, strategies, and direction. But there would be no more annual earnings estimates with quarterly guidance and midquarter updates. I had not yet joined Gillette, but had participated in informal discussions with several board members in which I supported their decision.

Frankly, the Gillette board was both embarrassed and frustrated by the track record of the company's management. For fifteen consecutive quarters, the estimate made by Gillette preceding each quarter was missed by the end of each quarter. These were not Wall Street's estimates, or so-called earnings consensus. These were the company's own estimates. Yet quarter after quarter, not just for one year, but for almost four years, the company's forecasting skills were so bad that Gillette couldn't hit its own projections.

To the Gillette board, these misses suggested a company that had major control and discipline issues. And the board members were definitely not a collection of old cronies of the management. They were among the best-known and brightest investors, financiers, and business people not only in the United States, but in the world.

Informal leader of the board was Warren Buffett, the sage of Omaha, the second-wealthiest person in the world, and a man with an unparalleled reputation and unquestioned integrity. Warren had joined the Gillette board in 1989 at a time when the company had endured, and just barely escaped, several hostile takeover efforts.

HORDES OF BARBARIANS AT THE GATE

Starting in 1986, the Gillette management, headed by CEO Colman Mockler Jr., had to fight off a hostile raid by Ronald Perelman, who was backed by the leader of the junk-bond craze, Drexel Burnham Lambert. Then, early in 1988, a group of financiers, called the Coniston Partners, launched a proxy fight for control of the board.

Gillette won the proxy vote by the narrowest of margins but faced litigation by Coniston, claiming the company's ads during the stock battle deceived and misled shareholders. Ultimately, Gillette agreed to a massive share buyback through which Coniston dropped its litigation. However, as a result, Gillette's debt exceeded its equity.

In the spring of 1989, Warren Buffett placed a call to Gillette. "It was my thought," Warren recalls, "that they might be interested in a big investment in their shares because they had used up all their capital in repurchasing shares." By July, Warren had invested more than $600 million in Gillette and had become a director.

So Warren had a lot riding on Gillette's performance. He was not just a director; he owned nearly 10 percent of Gillette's stock. And Gillette's performance had some influence on how investors perceived the prospects of Berkshire Hathaway, the holding company that was the repository of Warren's wealth and reputation. A $1 drop in Gillette stock meant an unrealized loss of nearly $100 million for Berkshire Hathaway. So between 1999 and 2001, Berkshire had a drop of close to $4 billion in the value of its Gillette stock.

Be Suspicious of Managers Promising to Make Numbers

Warren expressed his concerns about overly aggressive earnings estimates both at Gillette board meetings and in public comments. For example, in 2001, Warren said: "For a major corporation to predict that its per share earnings will grow over the long term at, say, fifteen percent annually, is to court trouble. . . . The problem arising from lofty predictions is that they corrode CEO behavior." And a few years later, he added: "Be suspicious of companies that trumpet earnings projections and growth expectations. Managers that always promise to 'make the numbers' will at some point be tempted to 'make up' the numbers." Warren wasn't suggesting chicanery on the part of the Gillette management, but he was concerned about the corrosive effect that chasing unrealistic earnings estimates would have on the entire fiber of any company.

Second to Warren on the board in reputation and accomplishments was the famed master of the takeover, the private-equity king—Henry Kravis. Henry had a distinction that few directors in any company could claim. There was an entire book and full-length movie, *Barbarians at the Gate,* in which Henry played a leading role. The book and movie chronicled the actions of Henry's firm—Kohlberg Kravis Roberts (KKR)—and a gaggle of Wall Street notables who defined the leveraged buyout era of the 1980s and 1990s. The KKR buyout of RJR Nabisco was the stuff that Wall Street myth was made of.

"Managers that always promise to 'make the numbers' will at some point be tempted to 'make up' the numbers."

Henry had joined the Gillette board in 1996, following the acquisition of Duracell by Gillette from KKR. As part of the deal, KKR received Gillette stock as well as cash, totaling nearly $8 billion, a nice gain for a company that KKR had bought eight years earlier for $1.8 billion.

The acquisition wasn't without some difficulties. Warren Buffett approved of the acquisition, but not of the $30 million in fees sought by KKR, which was acting both as Duracell's owner and investment adviser. In the end, KKR received the fee payment, but Warren abstained. The vote in favor of the Duracell acquisition was unanimous among the directors who voted.

Henry was not only concerned about the Gillette management's blown estimates and poor forecasts, but also about the overall performance of Michael Hawley, the Gillette executive who had succeeded Al Zeien as CEO of the company in 1999. Zeien had an eight-year tenure leading Gillette that was hard to follow.

No less notable than Kravis was Jorge LeMann, a Brazilian financier and businessman, who split his time between São Paolo and Switzerland with regular trips to the United States. Jorge had a string of companies in Brazil ranging from food stores and beverage companies to a railroad and industrial holdings. He merged his South American brewery holdings with Interbrew of Brussels in a complex deal that put Jorge and his partners at the head of what is the world's largest brewery (by volume of beer sold) with holdings all around the world. Jorge was not only a brilliant businessman, he was also well respected for his macroeconomic and financial insights.

While not as well known as the others, Marjorie Yang of Hong Kong was no less formidable. Marjorie had taken over an unknown apparel maker, the Esquel Group in Hong Kong, from her father and made it into one of the largest, upscale shirtmakers in the world. Esquel was a fully integrated company that owned everything from the fields that grew cotton to the mills that made the cloth and the factories that turned out shirts for a number of notable brands and department stores, including Ralph Lauren, Tommy Hilfiger, Nike, and Nordstrom. Marjorie provided a perspective and insight on China and Asia that had assisted Gillette in its development efforts. (By the mid-1990s, when most American companies were just contemplating possible expansion into China, Gillette already had a 90 percent share of the Chinese wet-shaving market. But don't be misled by the share size. The Chinese market was virtually all double-edged blades, which sold for pennies per blade, not the dollars per cartridge that characterize the United States and other developed markets.)

Another director with an outstanding international background was Herbert H. Jacobi, chairman of the supervisory board of HSBC Trinkaus & Burkhardt KGaA, the preeminent German private bank established in 1785. Herb had started his career as an economist with Deutsche Bank. He later joined Chase Manhattan Bank, where he rose to the position of executive vice president of corporate banking. In subsequent positions with HSBC, he served as nonexecutive director of the Midland Bank in London and group general manager of the HSBC Group.

Coming from the health-care sector was Wilbur Gantz, who began with Abbott Laboratories and then joined PathoGenesis, where he established the firm's $110 million European business. He became president and CEO of Hydra Biosciences, which focuses its research on using the body's mature cells to regenerate damaged tissue or muscle.

Dennis Hightower worked for Xerox, McKinsey & Company, General Electric, and executive recruiter Russell Reynolds prior to a long stint with the Walt Disney Company, where he served as president of Television & Telecommunications, then Disney's largest division measured by revenue and operating income. Dennis later became a professor of management at the Harvard Business School, from which he received his MBA.

Michael Gifford had worked for years in food and consumer products before moving to the British entertainment company giant, the Rank Organisation. He had served and retired as its chief executive officer.

Richard R. Pivirotto had been the chairman of Associated Dry Goods and was a director of several financial-services companies.

Carol R. Goldberg, one of Boston's best-known and most powerful women, had been president and chief operating officer of Stop & Shop, the large regional supermarket chain that was founded by her father.

Those were the exceptional external board members whose concerns mounted as Gillette's earning forecasts continued to fall short. The question of whether Gillette should avoid providing any further short-term forecasts was discussed, but tabled, at several board meetings.

After Mike Hawley left as CEO of Gillette and Ed DeGraan was selected as acting CEO in October 2000, the board decided that the time was right to impose the prohibition on any further earnings guidance. Ed DeGraan, who is one of the brightest and most dedicated executives I've ever worked with, saw the wisdom of the move. Life would be difficult enough for him without having the distraction of making forecasts that more likely than not would be a "bad guess."

Wall Street Gets Ugly However, Wall Street was a different matter. To Wall Street analysts, "no guidance" wasn't wisdom; it was a disaster. It's important to recall that back in 2000 virtually every large-cap company routinely gave detailed guidance. And those that didn't had a history of not providing guidance. However, Gillette was attempting to break new ground. Though it had fallen on some tough times, Gillette was still a bellwether company. It was looked to, respected, and often followed whenever it took a significant action.

Cutting off guidance was a significant action. It was one that irritated Wall Street greatly, especially the sell-side analysts who made their money by hawking and critiquing the earnings estimates of the companies they covered. If there were no company-supplied quarterly estimates, the analysts would have to do the work necessary to generate their own forecasts. Good analysts would welcome that freedom to generate estimates without being restricted by a company's own guidance. But the indifferent or poor analysts would see it as more work and higher personal risk.

To Wall Street analysts, "no guidance" wasn't wisdom; it was a disaster.

At any rate, Wall Street got ugly with Gillette when the no-earnings-guidance policy was made in December 2000. And most analysts were certain they could convince me to abandon the policy when my selection as CEO of Gillette was announced in January 2001. Were they ever wrong.

Two of my lifelong mantras are *Underpromise and overdeliver* and *Say what you're going to do, only after you've done it.* Part of my focus-on-the-fundamentals approach to business was to get Wall Street to focus on—and understand the importance of—the same fundamentals.

And my focus was to restore Gillette to robust health by jump-starting its revenue growth. Despite the introduction of Mach3, one of the best new consumer products of the past ten years, and despite having a portfolio full of icon products in advantaged categories, Gillette had gone through several years of no-to-slow revenue growth.

FORECASTING *ONLY* WHAT MATTERS

I knew that if we could reignite the revenue growth, everything else would fall into place. So I put all the best resources available to identify the right revenue-growth target for Gillette. We wanted a tight growth range that would be realistic, but would also be a stretch. A range that would generate earnings to place Gillette within the top third of our peer companies over a five-year period. If we did that, Gillette would be back as the best consumer products company in the world. And that certainly was our goal.

Identifying that range wasn't a task taken lightly. We sought opinions from a number of outside advisers: two of our top consultants, McKinsey and Bain; several of our investment bankers, including UBS, Goldman Sachs, Morgan Stanley, and Lehman Brothers; several boutique consultants; plus the small cadre of executives who were moving to Gillette from Nabisco—my coauthor of this book John Manfredi, our senior vice president for investor relations, communications, and public affairs; our senior vice president for strategy and planning, Peter Klein; and our vice president of financial planning, Joe Schena. In the end, we agreed that 3 to 5 percent annual sales growth was the right range. For the next five years—from 2001 until the consummation of the merger of Gillette into Procter & Gamble—that revenue estimate was the only forecasting we did for Wall Street.

While we didn't give a lot in the way of estimates and forecasts, we provided a great deal of information on how we would manage the company and what would make the difference in the future.

I told Wall Street, as discussed in subsequent chapters, that our approach would be based on simple but powerful concepts. They were the same thoughts I laid out for Warren Buffett when he interviewed me for the Gillette position. I'd done preliminary research on Gillette, knew some of its major issues, but was no expert, which I readily admitted.

When Warren asked what I'd do at Gillette, I told him what I'd done throughout my career with consumer products companies: start with the top of the profit-and-loss statement and focus on accelerating revenue growth. Then go to the middle of the P&L, where you control costs and get savings to invest in good things like research, new-product development, and marketing that supports the brands. The net result is enhancement to the bottom of the P&L—increased earnings. Warren liked what he heard.

We told Wall Street the same thing. Gillette's cost structure would be brought in line with the best in class within our sector. Eliminating unnecessary costs would free up hundreds of millions of dollars. Much of those savings would be invested in marketing and product development, which would accelerate the growth of our icon brands that had been starved for years of adequate support. As costs were being stripped from the company, capabilities would be improved. The net result would be an organization characterized both by superior efficiency and effectiveness.

Month after month, quarter after quarter, we provided Wall Street with details that gave credibility to each of the fundamental concepts that drove our turnaround. Renewed credibility with Wall Street didn't come overnight. It took many quarters to get the focus away from the short term and onto the evolving story of how the company was changing in real and fundamental ways.

It took many quarters to get the focus away from the short term.

SHIFTING THE FOCUS TO FUNDAMENTALS

If you're a CEO . . .

. . . one of the most difficult things for a leader to accomplish is to gain Wall Street's support for a focus-on-the-fundamentals approach to managing a business. With so many forces spotlighting the short term, how do you gain credibility for the importance of fundamentals? I've found several things that work.

- Articulate three to five fundamental concepts that will drive your performance; the fewer the better, but definitely don't exceed five.

- Always focus on these fundamentals; don't feel Wall Street needs a new theme every quarter to stay interested in your stock; be consistent. (I stuck with the same fundamentals for three years at Nabisco and five years at Gillette; the rewards were great.)

- Frequency matters. You won't get your messages through if you have only occasional contacts with Wall Street. You need at least five to seven meetings *every quarter*, preferably with small groups of eight to twelve current or prospective investors and analysts.

- Don't spend your time on quarterly sales-and-earnings conference calls. The time spent preparing for these well-staged events doesn't yield good returns in terms of impact and influence.

- Let your staff handle the quarterly conference calls—your CFO and heads of investor relations and corporate affairs. Devote yourself to one-on-one meetings and small group sessions that give investors and analysts the ability to look you in the eye, assess your character, and gauge your knowledge and conviction as well as truly understand your vision and plans.
- Continually evolve your story about the fundamentals with new details on both execution and impact. The fundamentals won't come to life and be relevant unless they truly drive results.

FOCUS ON THE FUNDAMENTALS

So if you're not the CEO . . .

. . . You're a midlevel leader on your way up. What fundamentals do you focus on?

- Remember to keep things simple. Basic concepts will help you understand your business and will help everyone in your unit share your understanding.

- What concepts are basic to any business at any level? Start with the importance of accelerating revenue growth. Everything flows from the increasing revenues, so determine the key levers to its growth. Is it more research? Increased effort behind new-product development? A heightened marketing and advertising budget? What will give you the best bang for your investment?

- Identify where you can eliminate the unnecessary costs and get the savings necessary to invest in driving revenue growth. What part of the middle of your P&L will yield the biggest savings?

Benchmark your overhead costs against other units or your competitors. Study your purchasing efficiency. And remember that cost savings aren't a onetime effort; they must become part of your unit's operating style—an ongoing quest for continuous improvement.

- Let your unit know what the savings are for—investment and growth. People are willing to make cuts and sacrifice if the objective is positive and constructive.

- Avoid "yo-yo" growth. Anyone can achieve a onetime score—a big gain that brings high praise. But roller-coaster growth will hurt you and your unit. Businesses want managers who are predictable in their ability to deliver sustained growth.

- Regardless of the pressure, resist the temptation to overpromise. Spend the time necessary to understand exactly what your unit can deliver over time and on a sustained basis. If your bosses don't agree, you have a problem, and your future might be better elsewhere.

CHAPTER 3

INTELLECTUAL INTEGRITY MATTERS

Coaches and fans of the Boston Red Sox dealt with the disruptions and sometimes chaos that their star slugger Manny Ramirez created for the team with a shrug of the shoulders and the brief comment "That's just Manny being Manny." The reality was that despite his pivotal role in winning critical games with a single swing of his bat, Manny was more trouble than he was worth. After several years of denial, the team's brass faced reality and, even though he is still in his prime, they started talking with other teams and trying, unsuccessfully, to trade him.

At their Boston headquarters, the senior managers of Gillette also spent several years caught in a failure to confront reality. When market shares slumped on system blades and razors—the crown jewel of the Gillette business—managers would shrug and say, "It doesn't really matter; our share of market is more than seventy percent."

When Duracell lost 15 percent of its market share and more

than half of its profitability, that was "just a transitional situation that would reverse itself in time."

When Wall Street observers said Gillette seemed to be overloading retailers with a lot of product that consumers weren't buying, Gillette responded that "an overloaded customer is a motivated customer" who'd find ways to sell more product.

Gillette was suffering from a serious lack of intellectual integrity.

Integrity, of course, means adhering to a code of behavior for ethics and fairness. In business, intellectual integrity means all this and more. It is the ability to hold up a mirror to your organization—whether that's just a few people in a small office or thousands of workers in hundreds of global locations—and the willingness to view the reflection with total honesty.

The often-told story of the frog and the boiling water makes the point that it's easy to lose objectivity and perspective when you get immersed in the culture of an organization. The story goes like this: If you put a frog into boiling water, it jumps out. If you put a frog into cool water and slowly raise the temperature, the frog gets cooked before it knows what's happening. Unfortunately, in many companies, intellectual integrity can go from clear and objective to tarnished and biased through a similar process.

Usually, in your first day on a new job, you spot a number of things that don't make sense; some seem inefficient and ill-conceived, and still others are just plain wrong. But it's day one, so you decide to hold your tongue. You don't want to seem like a know-it-all. You make a mental note, but decide to wait before saying anything.

Two weeks later, you're still making mental notes about things that don't seem quite right. But you're also having second thoughts. Some of those "wrong things" seem perfectly fine within this new environment. Your peers are good people, and they're OK with this stuff. Maybe you were being too harsh?

No, more than likely, you're in a pot that's been slowly heating and is about to boil.

AVOID THE SLOWLY COOKED FROG DILEMMA

One way to avoid the slowly cooked frog dilemma and limit the risk of a biased perspective is by doing advance work before taking any new job. For most people, the first one hundred days are the most important time in a new assignment. Conventional wisdom holds that whether you're moving into the CEO position or starting an entry-level marketing job, your future prospects will be defined by your initial efforts. No question about it. A strong and certain start is important.

But for me, the time that really matters is the work I do before the clock starts ticking on the first one hundred days. In other words, what matters is gaining a good understanding of what lies ahead—the problems, the opportunities, the possible approaches and likely obstacles—before I even set foot in the office. The reason relates directly to *intellectual integrity* and the need for a clear focus on reality. And there is no time that intellectual integrity is more important and more challenged than at critical moments such as turnarounds.

The time that really matters is the work I do before the clock starts ticking on the first one hundred days.

For a CEO, turnarounds usually mean taking a multibillion-dollar enterprise from disaster to star performer. But turnarounds also occur on a smaller scale and crises occur regularly—a new brand manager who has to improve the performance of a product that's lost its luster; a human resources manager who has to bring order and sense to a company's chaotic process of compensation and promotion; or a financial manager who must move his function from control and audit to proactive business partner.

Turning around business situations is something that I've confronted throughout my career. Initially, I resented being given the tough and intractable assignments. *Why me,* I would ask? *Why can't I get a business that already has momentum? Something I can build and grow!* But over time, I realized two things. Nothing in business moves inexorably in just one upward direction. And proving your mettle in challenging business situations—in a turnaround situation—not only enhances your business reputation, it also gives you the type of experience you need to move to the top. Importantly, success in business demands that you comprehend and confront the reality of your business situation regardless of your position. Without a full and honest assessment, your basis for action is flawed from the start and future actions will suffer.

WHEN YOU HAVE A LEMON

Early in my career, I was promoted to product manager for Country Time Lemonade, a new beverage mix that was about to be introduced by the General Foods Corporation. The company had been a longtime leader in the beverage-mix sector with our Kool-Aid brand. It's a huge product with more than $300 million in sales. By the 1970s, Kool-Aid had been around for more than thirty years and held a dominant market-share position of more than 75 percent.

It would have been easy to assume that the accumulated knowledge and shared opinion of the beverage group was accurate. Everyone believed that powdered beverages were a mature, slow-growth business of uninteresting products. So the best course of action wasn't to hope for miracles. It was to accept a future of ongoing tepid growth, and milk the business.

But even as a young manager, I was wary of accepting the assumptions of others. If our team studied, probed, prodded, and identified the right consumers to target and understood all the dynamics of the market, we believed that we could uncover a different reality. Using old and new research, we looked at the entire beverage market through the eyes of the consumer, not the General Foods marketers, to find out what we could bring to the world of powdered-beverage mixes. If the research showed the answer was nothing, we'd accept it.

But we found there was a lot. For example, even though parents bought Kool-Aid for their kids, about 60 percent of the consumption was by adults. So there was an adult acceptance for powdered drinks. Our studies showed that adults wanted the taste of real lemonade, and they were not getting it from any powdered drink. They also were not getting the taste they wanted from homemade lemonade, which, it turned out, few people knew how to make correctly. So Country Time was conceived and positioned as a convenient form of lemonade with a good-old-fashioned lemonade taste.

The reality that we uncovered turned out to be big. It was the difference between Country Time being a nice, routine extension of Kool-Aid versus the Country Time brand being a $100 million stand-alone franchise with one of the highest profit margins of all beverage mixes. Country Time, with multiple line extensions, turned around the growth momentum of beverage mixes and is still a robust business thirty years later.

A few years after we introduced Country Time, we further fueled the powdered-beverage turnaround with Crystal Light drink mixes. These took powdered beverages to a new level of adult usage, driven by the first commercial application of the low-calorie aspartame sweetener, NutraSweet.

The point is the importance of searching for the true reality regardless of your situation or position. It was important in the Country Time and Crystal Light situations in assessing the range of opportunity and growth. It's even more important in the situation where a brand, or a company, is locked in a downward spiral and the mandate is *Turn it around*.

AN ELEGANTLY SIMPLE WINNER

That was the mandate later in my career at Oscar Mayer. The processed-meat business was characterized by low growth and a reliance on commodity meat products. All previous efforts to increase margins and accelerate revenues had fallen flat. The investment analysts and industry experts knew processed meat was an out-of-favor category that was bucking the consumer trends of health and well-being. But the Oscar Mayer management wouldn't accept that reality. They were convinced that sliced ham and bologna could still generate high growth.

As the new guy on the Oscar Mayer team, I felt the Wall Street analysis made sense to me. But I also was convinced there should be another way to revitalize the business. And there was. We created a new platform that transcended cold cuts. It was Lunchables—a high-growth vehicle that, some twenty-five years later, is still being extended into new flavors, varieties, and formats. Today, the Lunchables line generates well over a half billion dollars in sales.

Lunchables is one of those products that makes you say, "Aha, that's a winner. Why didn't I think of it sooner?" The concept behind it is elegantly simple. What's better? Trying to counter a lifestyle trend by selling more packages of sliced bologna and hot dogs at low-margin prices? Or selling value-added, on-trend, convenient luncheon kits, complete with a ready-made sandwich plus dessert, at a higher margin? Parents hated the early morning routine of preparing lunches for school when they were rushed and torn in a thousand different directions. And there was nothing more deflating to parents than kids coming home saying they hated their lunch. Kids loved Lunchables, and our marketing positioned them as saving parents from the heartache of struggling to make what often would be a rejected lunch—great convenience with no bitter aftermath.

OUTSIDE FACTORS

Someone once said that the secret to happiness is the ability to look reality in the eye and deny it. That may work in melodramas and novels. But if you're trying to turn around a business or accelerate growth, it is the most destructive thing you can do. The best way to focus on reality is to view the situation from the outside.

My move into the top position at Gillette provides an excellent case in point. In the winter of 2000, I was overseeing the final phase of the sale of the Nabisco Company to the Philip Morris Companies. My three years as CEO of Nabisco had been among the most intense and successful in my career. My senior team and I took a once-great company that was on the brink of self-destruction and restored it to the top tier in the food industry.

The best way to focus on reality is to view the situation from the outside.

Confronting a Larger Reality Our turnaround efforts were often confounded and complicated by several factors that went well beyond the marketing of cookies, crackers, and an array of the best and most recognizable brands in snacking and condiments. Increasing the sales, market shares, and profitability of Oreo, Chips Ahoy!, Ritz, Planter's nuts, Life Savers confections, A.1. Steak Sauce, and Grey Poupon mustard was relatively straightforward. As it turned out, we hit all of our targets early on and with such regularity that Wall Street applauded.

The factors beyond Nabisco's control were not just large; they proved to be overwhelming. When I joined Nabisco, it was publicly traded, listed on the New York Stock Exchange. However, its majority owner, with an 85 percent controlling interest, was the RJ Reynolds Holding Company, whose other principle assets were the RJ Reynolds tobacco companies in the United States and around the world—the makers of the Camel, Winston, and Salem brands of cigarettes.

While my job was to restore the company to the top position in snack foods, there also was a larger reality. The ultimate fate of the company was tied to the broader, tobacco arena, and especially to the politics and litigation issues that engulfed tobacco.

We would focus on making Nabisco the best company in the food sector, which we did. External factors such as the climate of tobacco litigation and the ability of Wall Street raiders to mount successful takeover attacks would determine whether Nabisco would survive, grow, and prosper as a stand-alone company, or if it would be acquired and absorbed into another company.

As it turned out, corporate raider Carl Icahn, who at one time controlled TWA airlines, launched multiple attacks to seize control of Nabisco on the cheap. Icahn built his career by taking stakes in corporations and then trying to shake up the managements that run them, force a bust up, or take them over himself. Steve Goldstone, CEO of RJR Nabisco, and his team, parried each of Icahn's thrusts. Steve had been a senior partner at the prestigious corporate law firm of Davis Polk & Wardwell. Over the years, he had served as a trusted adviser and outside counsel to the CEOs who ran RJR Nabisco. Some of the best managers in business had tried unsuccessfully to unlock the value contained in the powerful assets controlled by RJR Nabisco. They included Lou Gerstner, who left to run IBM, and Mike Harper, fabled former CEO of ConAgra, who had one of the best records of performance in the food industry.

Steve Goldstone came in as CEO on the assumption that a lawyer would be better qualified to deal with the politicians in Washington and at the state level, as well as with the investment bankers and deal makers, who would help sever the food business from the liabilities attached to the cigarette business.

It worked. Steve not only conceived and helped fashion the tobacco settlement with the federal government and state attorneys general, he also worked through the legal entanglements that finally established RJR Tobacco and Nabisco as independent entities.

With the separation successfully accomplished, the corporate raiders descended and it was only a matter of time before Nabisco was acquired. While the sale of Nabisco to the Philip

Morris Companies was not the outcome we had sought, it was the best alternative possible to Carl Icahn.

It gave excellent value to our shareholders, many of whom had suffered through years of an ever-declining stock price. It placed Nabisco into the food group of Philip Morris—Kraft Foods. And having spent more than fifteen years at Kraft, three of those leading the company, I knew that would give Nabisco's people and brands the best prospects for development and growth.

Plus, I was comfortable with the prospect of my own retirement. My thirty-year career of brand building had culminated with the turnaround success at Nabisco, which was lauded by Wall Street and the news media alike. My personal finances were well beyond my needs, and my two passions of fishing and golf had been on hold for all too long.

MEETING WARREN BUFFETT FOR THE FIRST TIME

So I did not react with great interest or enthusiasm when Tom Neff, head of the topflight executive recruiting firm of Spencer Stuart, called to feel me out about taking on the CEO position at Gillette. Yet I could not just shut the door on one of the top positions in consumer products in the world. Within consumer products companies, there were Gillette, Coca-Cola, Philip Morris (now Altria), Procter & Gamble, and all the rest.

I met with Warren Buffett and the other members of Gillette's search committee, but not before doing a week of research and having discussions with several sources to gain some perspective on Gillette. I definitely was no guru on the company, but my initial assessments won over Warren, who as noted earlier, owned close to 10 percent of Gillette's stock. Years later, Warren would tell *Fortune* magazine that I was a "rarity" because I gave him "absolutely no baloney." That's high praise coming from someone who epitomizes the direct, straightforward style.

Three weeks later, Warren announced to the company and outside world that I would become Gillette's CEO. That was in December, but my actual start time was weeks later in February. There were several reasons for the timing, but importantly, the interlude gave me the opportunity to expand on research already started.

Those next weeks were possibly more exhausting than any that have followed in my years at Gillette. I assembled several longtime associates and valued advisers—investment bankers, consultants, ad-agency executives, market-research specialists, and others. We gathered all the publicly available information on Gillette, on the product categories in which it competed, and on its competitors. I also spent hours on the phone talking with my friends and contacts in the trade. These were the key customers whom I had dealt with throughout my career, and they were the same people who constituted Gillette's core accounts.

POWERFUL BRANDS; CRIPPLING PROBLEMS

Utilizing the information gathered through this process, we developed a detailed situation assessment and an outline of our key focus areas and priorities. While the assessment was necessarily incomplete since it contained no inside information about the company, in hindsight, we correctly captured about 90 percent of the issues and key elements of our subsequent turnaround plan.

Midway through the process, we realized that although my start date was in February, we would have to write the chairman's letter for Gillette's 2000 annual report in time for its early January press run.

The letter captured a lot of our thinking. It started by noting that while my detailed review of Gillette had just begun, I wanted to share my initial views, underscoring the obvious strengths of the company. There are few companies with more powerful global brands than Gillette, and there are even fewer companies that had so successfully used innovation to increase the market strength and consumer appeal of their brands.

And I also laid out the issues. Innovation is important, but only when it drives real increases in shareholder value by improving sales, market share, and earnings. The cost of research and development and the cost of resources invested to bring new products to market must have positive returns, yet for Gillette, those returns had softened in recent years. While market share for blades had improved since 1997, they were flat to down for our other core categories of batteries and oral care.

There were problems on capital spending. It had stepped up significantly starting in 1997 and was well above other leading consumer products companies. Gillette's return on invested capital, after dropping for several years, was just back to its 1997 level, while the performance of peer companies had been improving over the same period of time. And Gillette's sales had been flat.

If those were the only issues, Gillette's situation would have been serious. But there were more.

Despite several new-product launches, Gillette's advertising-to-sales ratio had declined dramatically to a point where its advertising spending was one of the lowest in the peer group of consumer products companies.

Gillette's operating and cash cycles—the cycles that measure both the effectiveness and efficiency of such elements as inventories and accounts receivable—had slipped considerably over the past several years and differed materially from competitors. Reported selling, general, and administrative spending had increased since 1997, and sales per employee were far below the industry leaders.

My conclusion was direct, simple, and specific: "Improving

each of the areas that I've outlined will be my focus and the entire Gillette organization's focus for the future. Each area will be analyzed and assessed; detailed strategies and action plans will be developed; then, we will move forward aggressively. And I assure you that results will follow."

The letter also noted that we would free up funds to invest in driving the growth of Gillette's brands. And these additional resources would be used for other strategic options to accelerate growth—exploring acquisitions and alliances; extending and strengthening our global penetration; and expanding into high-growth, complementary product categories. There were enormous opportunities to pursue.

After more than five years, the completion of one strategic growth-plan cycle and the start of a second, those focus areas and strategic directions were still driving the company when we announced our merger with Procter & Gamble in 2005.

The work done before starting on my first one hundred days is what really mattered. It laid the foundation for everything that followed. As a point of contrast, compare my initial assessments and that reality with views presented by my senior managers at a meeting held on my first day at Gillette.

The Total Equals Less than the Sum of the Parts Based on everything I had seen, read, and heard, two things were crystal clear: Gillette's overhead costs and capital spending were far too high, and its sales and earnings expectations were totally unrealistic. No consumer products company can consistently achieve double-digit sales growth and earnings growth of 15 to 18 percent year after year. Yet those were the targets that Gillette had set and missed for the last fifteen quarters.

But when I asked my direct reports about costs, their responses reflected a denial of reality. Each one acknowledged that overall company costs were high, but their individual units were tight and lean. In their minds, the sum of all the parts somehow was lower than the actual total. More on this in the next chapter.

Their reaction on earnings targets was even more baffling. Without fear of any penalty, I asked the operating managers to give a revised and realistic target for their earnings—a number they were confident they could hit. To a person, on the first go-round, they held to their unreachable targets. To put this in perspective, those targets turned out to be on average 30 percent higher than the actual numbers for the year.

When I asked each of my direct reports about costs, their responses reflected a denial of reality.

This is by no means a blanket condemnation of that senior management team, since many stayed with me for the five years of the turnaround. Rather, it underscores the difficulty of confronting reality and the importance of an unbiased preassessment.

Accepting a Painful Truth Refusal to accept reality happens all the time across all kinds of business. It was the case at both Nabisco and Gillette, but definitely is not limited to them. The reasons for denial vary. Sometimes it's the belief within an organization that its senior management doesn't want to hear the truth. Or if confronted with reality, senior people will not accept a tough or risky solution to the problem.

Mark Leckie, who headed the Gillette businesses after the merger with Procter & Gamble, tells of the difficulty he encountered when he told his leaders at Kraft that their Post cereal business was losing share to private-label brands.

Mark worked for me at both Gillette and Kraft. He is a talented manager with keen insights and great tenacity. At times, Mark reported directly to me, as he did when he ran the salad-dressing unit at Kraft. More recently, I brought him in to help turn around the Duracell business that so many of the analysts wanted us to jettison.

When he was in charge of Post, Mark reported to the heads of Kraft's U.S. operations. Nonetheless, I kept a close watch on Mark because he had great potential.

Mark realized that not only was Post in a declining and vulnerable position, but that the entire U.S. ready-to-eat cereal sector also was continuously driven by short-term objectives and was acting in a way that would severely damage Kraft's future sales-growth and earnings prospects. Throughout the 1980s and early 1990s, the cereal companies—led by the dominant players, Kellogg and General Mills—would take an average of two price increases annually, each about 4 to 5 percent, and then spend back between one-half to two-thirds of the revenue increase. Part of the funds went into increased advertising and about 60 to 70 percent went into promotions, especially buy-one-get-one-free offers.

The shelf price for a large box of cereal was close to $5 in 1995. But there was hardly a week that went by when Kellogg, General Mills, and even Post weren't making buy-one-get-one-free deals.

This "price-up" and "deal-back" business model worked for Kellogg and General Mills because of their scale. Kellogg had about a 35 percent share of market; General Mills had about 23 percent. With only a 15 percent share, Post's marketing dollars had a tough time penetrating. Profits were squeezed, and from 1995 through early 1996, Post lost over $100 million of retail sales.

Incremental Changes Won't Work As Mark looked at the overall market, he knew that incremental changes wouldn't fix this mess. A radical solution was necessary—one that would provide long-term benefit for Post and the entire cereal sector. The solution had to break the cycle of ever-higher shelf prices, followed by product giveaways that tended to erode the power of the brands and the loyalty of the consumers.

The plan that Mark and his team generated was indeed radical, and it potentially was risky and costly. In fact, if it didn't work, it could mean that Mark's next assignment would be developing an exit strategy out of the cereal business for Kraft.

In brief, Mark and his team proposed taking down the price of cereals from around $5 a box to an everyday low price of $2.99; eliminating all the product giveaways; and cutting both the frequency and depth of promotions. Mark anticipated relatively infrequent promotions that would take the price down to $2.49 a box—slightly more in promotion-sensitive markets.

If the plan worked, Post's gains in market share and its reductions in marketing dollars would more than offset the revenue loss coming from the price cut. If the gains didn't come, Post would implode.

Importantly, the strategy would level the playing field by moving consumer focus back to brand equity, advertising, and new products, where Post was strong; it would move focus away from expensive promotions, where Kellogg's and General Mills' scale gave them the advantage.

Confronting Market Reality In Mark's view, the plan had risk, but there was no alternative. The senior management of Kraft saw the plan's risk, but didn't share Mark's view of the cereal-market reality. So every two to three weeks for a period of nine months, Mark and his team traveled from the Westchester, New York–based operations of Post cereals to the Northfield, Illinois, headquarters of Kraft to present and represent their plan. As Mark recalls, "We would literally go out every three weeks and give all the reasons why it needed to be done; how we would execute it; how we thought we could ensure that we could pull it off, in excruciating detail."

The story does have a happy ending. I was having informal conversations with Mark and his team in New York, where I also was located, so I knew their thinking and the level of detail that had gone into their analysis. And I also thought Mark had confronted the reality posed by conditions in the cereal market. At the end of nine months of meetings, I invited myself to yet another meeting. By the end of that session, we all agreed that Mark's team should have the go-ahead to implement their price-reduction plan, which they did in the spring of 1996.

To say that it was successful would be an understatement. Post's market share went up nearly 20 percent, from 15 to close to 18 percent. The business was stabilized. Profits grew after one year of investment. And the business model for the cereal sector was changed, with both Kellogg and General Mills also eventually moving to everyday pricing.

Many companies are culturally and organizationally hardwired in a way that makes it difficult to say, "This isn't working. We have to start again." That's exactly what happened when the dot-coms were kept on life support long after their business model had flatlined.

FLAWED DECISIONS, NOT WORLD-CLASS BLUNDERS

Most companies get into trouble not because they make world-class blunders, but due to a succession of well-intentioned yet flawed decisions that build on one another, until a much larger problem is created that is extremely difficult to unravel. Some years ago, when Roger Deromedi took over as the sole chief executive officer of Kraft, he faced a significant challenge. The cost of cheese, which is Kraft's most important commodity, soared to historic highs. Roger confronted $300 million in commodity costs that he knew couldn't be passed through as higher prices to consumers.

What should he do? He could have burnished his reputation with Wall Street by slashing his marketing budget and perhaps even stinted a little on the quality of Kraft cheese. The short-term impact would be solid earnings that analysts and investors would love. But longer term, that flawed decision would have set in motion an erosion of brand equity and loss of consumer preference that would have been difficult to reverse. Instead, Roger did the right thing. He called down his earnings, sustained his marketing, and looked for some productivity savings that could help out in the longer term.

Most companies get into trouble not because they make world-class blunders, but due to a succession of well-intentioned yet flawed decisions that build on one another.

To sum up on intellectual integrity, it's easy to lose the ability to view your reality with total honesty. You can give yourself a head start on getting things right by doing some homework before you take on a new assignment. While midcourse corrections will be necessary, many of your earliest assessments and plans will prove to be valid.

INTELLECTUAL INTEGRITY: IT'S MORE THAN LOOKING INWARD

Intellectual integrity involves much more than applying personal values to making business decisions. That's important, but just doing the right thing isn't enough when you're trying to understand the issues, challenges, and opportunities in a company. You must go outside yourself and outside the business for input. Here's how to do it.

- Cast your net as broadly as possible. When you're assessing your business, compile a list of constituents, critics, and observers. Make it as comprehensive as possible; you can cull it later, if necessary.

- Always include customers. In the consumer products sector, that would be the retail chains, mass merchants, and other stores that sell the company's products. You can gain tremendous insights by tapping into the day-to-day knowledge that customers have about the company.

- Suppliers can tell you more about a company than just whether they pay their bills on time. Suppliers of services, such as ad agencies, can tell you about the company's management style, marketing savvy, understanding of consumers, new-product-development skills, and much more. Suppliers of goods know whether the company leverages its scale, has clear lines of responsibility, is skilled in forecasting, and has efficient logistics.

- The information available about any public company is enormous. There are not only quarterly sales-and-earnings statements, annual shareholder reports, and proxy statements; encyclopedic information is easily accessible on EDGAR, the online electronic repository of the Securities and Exchange Commission, which has all the filings required by law.

- Most large companies are covered by investment analysts who spend their lives studying and reporting on a small group of companies. They have specific knowledge about companies, how well they compare to peers, and how well regarded they are by Wall Street and other key stakeholders.

- Consultants, without giving away confidential information, can provide great insights about companies, ranging from their culture and attitudes to their management process and strategic-thinking prowess.

CHAPTER 4

ENTHUSIASM MATTERS

Everyone in business wants enthusiastic people who have a fire in the belly and can drive change. All too often, however, the leader's role in instilling enthusiasm is underestimated. The common notion of a leader, especially a buttoned-down and old-fashioned leader, is someone who's remote and doesn't spend a lot of time stoking the energy and conviction of the organization.

But true leaders must fill that role. You have to break through the complacency and instill confidence. You must be visible and passionate in making the case that the business must grow and change. You have to give members of the organization an understanding of what has to be done and then create the belief and conviction that they have all the tools necessary to be successful.

And infusing enthusiasm isn't about being a hail-fellow-well-met or a garrulous extrovert who fills every silence with a "let's go, team" platitude. Enthusiasm is much more. It's the force of personality and ideas that can infuse an entire organization with a sense of purpose and mission. So enthusiasm is big. Yet it also works on a one-on-one basis in ways that are small, but meaningful. In short, enthusiasm has many meanings and manifests itself in a number of ways.

Enthusiasm also has to be sustained over time. It's not something that you put on just for the closing remarks at a national sales meeting.

Enthusiasm also has to be sustained over time. It's not something that you put on just for the closing remarks at a national sales meeting. It must be there every day in each contact that you have inside and outside your organization. In a large organization, it also means having broad and regular contacts by visiting the troops, group by group by group.

Enthusiasm is involved in everything you do, from the fundamentals of running a business to the interpersonal relationships that shape the character of your management team and the external perceptions of your accomplishments.

LEARNING TO EMBRACE ZERO OVERHEAD GROWTH

Let's start by looking at enthusiasm through an unusual lens, the big challenge of cost reduction. One of the things I am known for in each company I've worked—General Foods, Kraft, Nabisco, and Gillette—is my unrelenting efforts to remove unnecessary costs. If a company's cost structure is bloated and high versus its competitors', winning is virtually impossible. If you remove unnecessary costs and use those funds to invest in new products, increase marketing, and improve capabilities, winning is within your grasp.

But eliminating costs, which invariably means lowering headcount both through attrition and by cutting people, isn't something any organization wants to embrace. At best, it will be viewed as a onetime trauma that has to be endured. You'll never encounter an organization that wants cost cutting as its long-term mantra. Yet short-term or onetime cost cutting inflicts a lot of pain without yielding any lasting results. To be successful, cost cutting must become a way of life.

As difficult as it is to imagine, generating enthusiasm for cost cutting and creating a real belief of its importance throughout the organization were primary missions for me. It was not a one-shot deal, but an everyday full-court press, as was the case especially at Gillette.

Eliminating costs, which invariably means lowering headcount . . . isn't something any organization wants to embrace.

At the end of my first year, our Corporate Affairs group tallied the number of my formal meetings and communiqués with the organization and then compared them with those of the two prior Gillette CEOs. My total contacts were three times more than my predecessors.

Of those contacts, more than half were largely or completely focused on the need to eliminate unnecessary costs, and virtually every speech, presentation, roundtable, town hall, chairman's letter, and video or audio communiqué referenced costs. In order to have impact, all vehicles and media must be used.

As a former marketing man, I also knew you need something memorable to gain saliency. Something the organization would hear once and remember forever. And that's how ZOG—Zero Overhead Growth—was born. Chapter 12 will look at some of its applications. Here we'll look at the process that took the organization from denial that excess costs were an issue to acceptance of ZOG, and its next-phase relative, NOG, or Negative Overhead Growth, as a way of life at Gillette.

My pre-start-up homework provided the evidence that Gillette's costs were far higher than those of competitors such as Colgate, Kimberly-Clark, Clorox, and Procter & Gamble. The absolute numbers were bad, and the trends all were accelerating. Gillette's costs were increasing while every other company in the competitive group was eliminating costs and driving their totals down.

Moving from Denial to Acceptance I raised the issue at my day one meeting with the senior executives of Gillette. These were the top dozen people responsible for all of Gillette's business—both staff and line, domestic and international. Without exception, they were all long-tenured executives whose service with the company had lasted from twenty years to more than thirty years. They had taken Gillette to its heights in years gone by, and then saw the company's market capitalization cut in half over the prior three years.

I raised the issue of excess costs for a variety of reasons.

First and foremost, it was a major issue. No question about it.

Second, the best way to break through complacency is to raise an important issue early, at the first chance possible in this case, and then repeat it endlessly.

Third, it was necessary for the Gillette management to work through the denial phase of the process before they could move on to the resistance phase and, ultimately, to the acceptance and action phases.

My experience at Nabisco told me exactly what the reaction would be, and I wasn't disappointed. I finished my discussion about Gillette's cost structure, noting how much higher Gillette's costs were than all peers, especially versus the best-in-class peer, and how low employee productivity was. Then I asked for a show of hands. *How many of you believe that Gillette's costs are too high?*

Every hand shot up. No surprise here; the logic was incontrovertible. Then I asked for another show of hands. *How many of you think that the costs for your unit or function are too high?* Not a single hand was raised. Again, not a surprise. Denial is invariably the reaction of a management in trouble.

Denial is invariably the reaction of a management in trouble.

I then invited each member of the group to meet with me individually at the end of the session to give their perspectives on the issue of excess costs. Again, no surprise. Every executive came to my office and said the same thing: "My unit is lean and mean, but we have a real problem with XXX." The only thing that varied was the XXX factor—the part of the company that was the real problem. For marketing execs, it was the operations group; for finance, it was marketing; for information technology, it was finance; and so on.

Everyone Is to Blame, No One Is Accountable Everyone else was to blame, and no one was accountable. Clearly, if we were to make progress, denial had to yield to acceptance. But that was not going to happen without a process and without my assurance that we would succeed.

The group had to know that I had done similar exercises, large and small, hundreds of times in my career, so I knew what lay ahead. There were no possible permutations that could throw us off course. We could deal with all aberrations. If Gillette followed the tried-and-true ZOG process, we would be lowest in costs within our peer group in five years. I would stake my reputation on the outcome.

When Ed DeGraan, the acting CEO before my arrival, thought back on ZOG and the cost-reduction initiatives, he felt that two of the key differentiators of our approach were conviction and commitment. Most cost-reduction efforts are flavor-of-the-month programs that ebb and fade. Ours was a long-term strategic platform. We focused not just on the here and now; we looked out three to five years. We were saying that *ongoing cost reductions* would be the major source for *ongoing funding of programs* to turn the company around—increased investment in marketing, upgrading of our capabilities, accelerating new-product-development initiatives, and more.

As with any strategic platform, Gillette needed fully worked out action plans. "We didn't simply throw out a concept or edict; we really worked it through," Ed said. "We developed our plans, and then shared those plans so everyone knew what was happening."

I worked with every member of my operating committee to orchestrate our efforts. In the end, all my direct reports had living documents with detailed operational plans that were cascaded throughout the entire organization.

ZOG BECOMES A WAY OF LIFE

Enthusiasm means that people must believe they have all the tools necessary for change and that using them fully will assure success. The seeds for implanting that belief started on day one at Gillette. The efforts continued nonstop for the next five years.

With my group, we had to deal with the denial of each of my executives that they were part of the problem. Rather than looking only at the macro numbers for Gillette, we had to see that the problem was widespread throughout the company, not restricted to a few functions, businesses, or even geographies. So I asked each of my direct reports to do three things.

First, perform a self-assessment of their unit: How did the management team of the unit feel it was meeting its role within the company? Would it rate its capabilities as best in class, medium, or poor? Would it rate its costs as lowest, medium, or high? Would it rate its headcount as lowest, medium, or high?

Second, have the rest of the organization assess their unit on the same criteria of how well they were performing: quality of their capabilities and people; efficiency and costs of their unit.

Third, benchmark their unit against the best-in-class competitive companies. If this part of the exercise was too complex or difficult to do on their own, they could utilize one of the outside consultants on retainer who had vast experience in conducting these assessments.

With ZOG launched among the executive group, it also was time to launch the company-wide understanding of the initiative. On March 28, 2001, slightly more than a month after I started at Gillette, everyone in the company received my announcement that would make ZOG a part of their lexicon and way of life for the next five years.

My letter dealt with the effort head-on: "Gillette's general and administrative spending has increased significantly since 1997 . . . and our sales per employee are now far below the industry leaders . . .

"As part of our overall efforts to enhance Gillette's growth, we are initiating a new program that will limit increase of our future expenses. Called Zero Overhead Growth, or ZOG, this effort will be an important element in assuring Gillette's competitive edge in the future."

ZOG did not "involve any pre-set reduction levels." However, I expected many units to exceed ZOG and achieve Negative Overhead Growth, which would actually reduce costs from the previous year's level.

In Cost Cutting, Everyone Means Everyone I then went on to make two points that are essential to gain acceptance for a job-reduction and cost-cutting effort.

First, everyone would be affected. There would be absolutely no exceptions unless otherwise noted. For Gillette, there was one: the domestic sales unit, which had just gone through a major reorganization and downsizing and was our first line of contact with our trade customers.

Second, everyone means everyone. There would be no favored functions or people. Everyone must and would ZOG. In fact, I told my longtime colleague John Manfredi that I wanted him to be the ZOG poster child. I wanted his units of Investor Relations, Communications, Public Affairs, Issues Management, Community Affairs, and Corporate Philanthropy to lead the way on headcount and cost reductions. John did not disappoint. Over the next three years, he reduced headcount by 60 percent and total budget by 50 percent, while also increasing both the quality and quantity of the work. He was definitely a trendsetter for the company.

Making the Case for Major Surgery Within four months, the results of our three-pronged cost-and-capabilities assessment were in, and they took us all aback on several counts. I knew from the total numbers that there would be some significant cost gaps versus our peers in parts of the Gillette organization. However, I had no idea how widespread it would be. Virtually every unit within the company was at a cost disadvantage to our competitors. In several of our largest and most important areas—such as finance, human resources, and information technology—the gaps were the largest. They ranged as high as 30 to 40 percent. More than a few nips and tucks were needed to fix these issues; this called for major surgery.

While all the managers were in denial about their costs, it was surprising how off base they also were on their overall assessments of their units versus those of the rest of the company. If 30 to 40 percent wasn't atypical for cost *overages,* 30 to 40 percent also wasn't atypical for capability *underages*. Each senior manager was convinced he or she had world-class people providing world-class services with finely honed efficiency and effectiveness. Again, in virtually every case, the assessment varied sharply from the reality as observed by the rest of the organization.

As a case in point, the executive who headed our information-technology function claimed that his unit was not just good, or very good, it was "the best IT department in the world." In his judgment, IT implemented world-class applications and systems "well ahead of schedule and well below budget." When the external benchmarks and internal ratings came back, IT turned out to be Gillette's least reliable, least effective, and most costly staff function. Its management was considered nonresponsive to business needs; implementation timetables were honored in the breach; deadlines were almost never met; and budgets seemed to serve an X-factor purpose, as in the "actual costs will be 3X the initial budget."

Finally, although the consultants were used mainly to supply data and validate comparisons, they provided an overall assessment that assured me and each of our managers that we had a significant and widespread issue to deal with.

With these data and materials, the initial phase of the acceptance process could begin. My role was to convene a meeting of the top two hundred leaders of the company to review the results, the implications, and specific action plans, and then to proselytize throughout the company and around the world. Over the next six months, I conducted meetings with each of our major business units in the United States—Blades & Razors, Oral Care, Duracell, and Personal Care—plus our Braun business unit in Kronberg, Germany, our European commercial and functional units in London, and our Asian business and functional leaders in Singapore. In addition, I met individually with each of the key functional units—Operations, Finance, Human Resources, Information Technology, and Purchasing.

I also introduced and narrated a video—distributed

worldwide—that was both a how-to video on implementing ZOG and a reprise of early ZOG wins to inspire confidence. The closest analogy for the early months of ZOG at Gillette would be a politician running a campaign to capture his party's presidential nomination. It was intense and nonstop—for me and the entire organization.

Cost Reduction—Not a Single Project When eating lunch in the Gillette cafeteria, employees would pass by and say, "We're ZOGing." The pros and cons about ZOGing were talked about on the Internet message boards. Each one of our weekly executive meetings had at least one report and several references to ZOG activities. ZOG was ubiquitous at Gillette. It was clear that my message that ZOG was everyone's responsibility was getting through when several executive administrative assistants formed a group to explore what they could do to assist in the process.

Did it work? You bet it did. We'll cover details of the projects and accomplishments in chapter 10. The overall achievement can be summarized by saying that at the end of five years, we had eliminated about $800 million of unnecessary costs and overhead as a percentage of sales dropped from 31 percent to 23 percent.

Cost reduction was not a single project, but a comprehensive organizational initiative. We introduced a company-wide Gillette Strategic Sourcing Initiative, or SSI, less than a month after launching ZOG. I explained to the organization on April 9, 2001, that SSI would "identify savings opportunities around the world that exist in all of our external spending for goods and services . . . Where we now have many individual units purchasing the same items—whether it's plastic for packaging or rubber bands for office use—SSI will enable us to gain benefits of scale in filling our needs as one through centralized sourcing."

I went on to assure people in the organization that "I know from past experience that the aggressive application of strategic sourcing and the latest approaches in e-procurement can yield substantial savings in a compressed time period." Then I detailed our goals: ". . . We are targeting annualized savings this year of approximately $100 million. And we believe incremental savings of $200 million annually are possible in the next year or two." Those are sizable savings, to say the least, on what were purchases of $3.5 to $4 billion annually for Gillette. We not only met these targets; we surpassed them. SSI continues as an active process within Gillette and is now moving throughout Procter & Gamble. Enthusiasm on a grand scale makes all the difference.

Cost reduction was not a single project, but a comprehensive organizational initiative.

BASEMENT MEETINGS TO BOOST MORALE

Sometimes enthusiasm is a form of moral reinforcement that works on a one-to-one basis. How do you let someone know how important his assignment is? How much you value his contribution? How much his success and the organization's are linked? One of the best ways is to use your own time off to work with people in a nonoffice environment. That usually means on weekends and holidays.

Over the years, I have spent countless Saturdays and Sundays working with members of my management teams on everything from mapping out business plans to figuring out how we would deal with an unanticipated crisis.

Bob Eckert, the successful CEO of Mattel, remembers our weekend meetings when he was general manager of the Kraft Cheese Division as "having absolutely no distractions and the ability to totally focus." We would sit in my basement with no phone calls, no secretaries, and no interruptions, totally immersed in the issue of the day.

Dave Rickard, who is now CFO of CVS, the nation's largest retail drug chain, recalls a calamitous time for the Kraft Cheese business that also called for weekend meetings to "keep us all on our game."

Shortly after I took over as president of Kraft USA, the federal program of price supports for milk prices, which had been in effect since World War II, virtually ended. The changes put the commodity milk business into uncharted waters and created a great deal of volatility. Kraft Cheese, which constituted over half the earnings of Kraft USA, went from a sleepy, easy-to-forecast and -manage business to a high-risk, speculative venture.

Dave, who was our vice president of finance, was in the thick of everything that was happening. All of the business systems, which were set up for a stable price environment, had to change. Dave notes that our buyers of milk had as their principle skill the ability to make reasonably intelligent estimates about what federal policy makers would do relative to the price of cheese. "Would they lower it an eighth of a cent a pound? Or would it be a quarter of a cent? All of a sudden," Dave says, "that skill was useless," and they had to make economic judgments about supply and demand. Milk prices back then were acting like oil prices today.

Buying Cheese in Green Bay "Those big price changes meant we had to change a lot of things. For example, we had to change our terms of sale to the grocery trade. It used to be that we'd announce a price increase that would be effective a month later. Prior to the effective date, the trade would buy as much Kraft cheese as it wanted. And that was fine with us when the change in costs was an eighth of a cent. But when the change was, say, fifty cents, that became a disaster. So we had to change that. The trade didn't like it, but we had no choice. We also had to change our marketing approach, our couponing, our advertising. In fact, more was changing than staying the same."

As a result, a lot also was changing for Dave. Even though he is one of the most intense, driven, and brightest financial people I've ever worked with, those were extraordinary and trying times. We had to change the way we bought cheese, and for a while Dave took on the responsibility for cheese buying. Off he would go to the Green Bay, Wisconsin, exchange and trade for Kraft's cheese needs—not quite a part of the financial vice president's job description.

So every Sunday morning for a period of months, Dave and I would get together in the basement of my house. He'd review what had happened in the week past and what was coming in the week ahead. I'd do the same, and then we'd agree on what had to be done.

Dave recalls that he would get his marching orders. "I could then go out and execute with full confidence, consistent with Jim's needs, as well as the health of the business. It was a good, healthy, supportive relationship that was especially important during a time that was just crazy." Periods of intense activity and rapid change can sap a lot of energy. That's why finding ways to stoke the energy is so important.

HOW ARE YOU DOING?

Enthusiasm is what you need for big changes like tamping down overhead growth. A different type of enthusiasm enables you to motivate and reinforce your managers for special projects and extraordinary events when a market goes into turmoil, as was the case with Kraft. Still another application of enthusiasm works on a day-to-day, almost hour-to-hour basis.

When he was mayor of New York, Ed Koch used to wander the streets of the city asking people on the street, "How am I doing?" At Kraft, Nabisco, and Gillette, I used to wander the halls asking people, "How are you doing?" But I wasn't asking it in a general way. I would ask about a specific assignment, task, project, or program that the individual was working on.

Part of the inquiry was based on genuine curiosity about what was happening and part was a prod to make sure that something was happening. However, the chief reason was to reassure and bolster people. Let them know what I expected and that I needed them to act.

Often when a CEO gives someone an assignment, the parting words are to give a due date—when the assignment must be completed. And that's the last time the CEO is heard from until the assignment comes due. The drill with me is different. While deadlines are important, so, too, is contact between the start of an assignment and its finish. It's not unusual for me to call someone two or three times a month with an observation, a new thought about the project, a recommendation for a possible direction to pursue, or a how-are-you-doing conversation.

This contact serves a purpose on a variety of levels. It definitely keeps the project on track. If you know the boss is going to be asking for updates, you are going to be focused on making progress. But it also yields better results. As new information comes in and insights are refined, midcourse corrections are sometimes necessary. And if you're plugged in along the way, you can assist in making those decisions.

GENERATING THE EXCITEMENT OF A BILLY GRAHAM CRUSADE

Does enthusiasm matter when you're dealing with the outside world, especially with the investors and Wall Street analysts? Let me answer that by stepping back a little.

Moving up in the organization at General Foods and then Kraft, I was surprised at how little time and effort went into major presentations, especially to outside constituents such as shareholders at annual meetings, or presentations to analysts and investors at major Wall Street conferences, or questions and answers for use at company press conferences.

These were singularly important events that would influence perceptions about the company for the long term, not just a day, week, month, or quarter. Yet more often than not, the company CEO or president would take a script prepared by a corporate PR department, give it a peremptory reading, and then stumble through it with a monotone delivery at the event. There was no sense that the company was excited about its prospects, committed to its messages, or eager to implement its plans. Excitement and enthusiasm were totally absent. Why? Why wouldn't a company want to approach any important external audience with all of the excitement of Billy Graham on a crusade?

Why wouldn't a company want to approach any important external audience with all of the excitement of Billy Graham on a crusade?

The answer is simple. Most CEOs, presidents, CFOs, and other corporate executives are not only untrained in public speaking, they often tend to think enthusiasm, excitement, and vigor are unbecoming. They believe their presentations should be serious and emotionless. But without enthusiasm converting analysts and investors into believers, it's virtually impossible to achieve.

Throughout my career, I have considered both the content and the quality of my presentations—both external and internal—among my most important responsibilities, especially as a CEO. That explains why my coauthor John Manfredi has been with me throughout my career and why he had such an elevated role at both Nabisco and Gillette as a confidant and adviser, as well as communications guru.

For both the food and consumer products business, the

Consumer Analysts Group of New York (CAGNY) held the most important investor and analyst conference of the year with more than a thousand top professionals from around the world in attendance. For me, preparation for my presentation at the conference was almost a yearlong undertaking. I would start right after completing one year's presentation by talking with my staff and looking for compelling themes that would accurately differentiate my company—Nabisco and then Gillette—from all others in my sector.

Sixty Revisions and Counting I wouldn't limit myself to company people. I'd reach out for the advice of investment bankers. My career-long relationship with Blair Effron of UBS and Jack Levy of Goldman Sachs always gave me two excellent sources for advice and insights.

My relationships with a number of analysts—such as John McMillan of Prudential, Nomi Ghez, formerly of Goldman Sachs, Ann Gillin Leferer of Lehman Brothers, and Andrew Shore of Deutsche Bank—also allowed me to talk with them on a personal basis to find out what concerned them most about my company and where they wanted to see more action or explanation. The list of contacts was extensive.

Six months before CAGNY, I wanted a full outline of my presentation—not just a few bullet points, but a fact-based, data-rich outline that would enable me to know whether we could proceed, or had to go back and start from scratch.

If I gave the go-ahead, the real work would start. We would agree upon a detailed timetable for drafts of scripts and visuals. Then we also would agree on key milestones in terms of when we would invite feedback from key internal units—the business units, finance, planning, and others. Once those were finished, we would focus on external feedback—from bankers, consultants, and others.

Finally, it would be time for *my* hard work. I would get

actively involved in what had passed the screens of many others both inside and outside the company. Now we had to make sure the script captured my thoughts and beliefs for what the company was and where it was headed.

John Manfredi and his staff would say this was the most dreaded period of all. As one of John's lieutenants, Eric Kraus, then vice president of communications, tells it: "Whenever Jim Kilts said the script was 'ninety-five percent there,' you knew you were in trouble. He would come back the next day and ask for revisions on ninety-five percent of the copy."

Eric may have exaggerated. But we usually went through fifty to sixty revisions before we wound up with what John would call a "final script." Then my heavy lifting would begin. While speech training doesn't rank on a level with physical torture in terms of pain and suffering, it certainly exacts a toll—especially on your psyche and identity.

While John was an able trainer, he knew that even our long relationship couldn't withstand the type of taunts, slings, and arrows that a skilled trainer must use to get the most out of a presenter. Our trainer was one of the best and most renowned in the business—a well-grounded, former midwesterner, Virgil Scudder.

I've worked with Virgil for more than twenty years, so I know what to expect. But knowing what to expect and then having it hit are different. One is mental; the other is actual, and usually emotional. When Virgil says, "Jim, is that important?" after I've just talked about Gillette becoming "the best consumer products company in the world," I know that my delivery was flat and lacking something—no, lacking everything. I have spent as much as two to three days with Virgil, going through my speech as many as twenty times, in whole or in part. And realize that the speech runs about forty to fifty minutes.

The hours spent on going over a speech obviously is time not spent doing something else. However, if you were to ask me now, my only regret about communications is that I didn't spend even more time thinking about what should be said and working on how to say it with enthusiasm, conviction, and impact. It really does matter.

In summary, enthusiasm often is misunderstood and underestimated. It's not backslapping and reciting clichés in a loud voice. It's not something that's confined to sales meetings. It is something that's complex and relevant to both big company issues and one-on-one personal relationships. It matters internally and externally. And it is important for the present and for the long term.

DOS AND DON'TS OF ENTHUSIASM

- *Don't* view enthusiasm as a onetime event; a call-to-action speech at a sales meeting has value, but it's not enthusiasm.

- *Do* think of enthusiasm as a nonstop activity, assuring people throughout your organization that they have all the talent, tools, and capabilities necessary to succeed.

- *Don't* think that people will be turned off by overcommunicating.

- *Do* talk often, and do it with consistency and confidence.

- *Don't* worry about repetition causing listener fatigue or indifference; people will be more concerned if they think you're changing course or altering your prior messages.

- *Do* communicate a sense of urgency and need for action.

- *Don't* assume that a "stay-the-course" message can energize people; a call to maintain the status quo is not a motivator.

- *Do* make your expectations and accountability clear. People must understand the specifics of what you want and how you'll judge them.

- *Don't* assume that scapegoating and witch-hunting will produce positive results. An environment of fear and apprehension cripples creativity and stifles initiative.

CHAPTER 5

ACTION MATTERS

It's like a nightmare, a recurring dream that never ends. You're in a meeting where options are painstakingly discussed and analyzed. The group is close to making a decision when someone diverts discussion onto a tangential issue. As the session continues, consensus slips away. You don't know why it's so hard to get resolution, but it is. The meeting ends with agreement only to meet again. Action is deferred.

Good information, full discussion of options, and adequate time for analysis—all are essential. But knowing when to either move forward or pull the plug and get on with action is the key. In business, you'll never have all the information you want when you want it. That was the case when I joined Gillette and faced many conflicting options. Worse than making a wrong decision would have been to go into a prolonged quiet period and take no action.

Imagine the chaos if I had told the organization and Wall Street, *We'll be exploring options for the next few quarters to decide if we'll divest Duracell, eliminate the Braun appliance business, sell Personal Care, or take some or none of these actions.*

The stock would gyrate like a whirling dervish, rising and dipping on an endless flow of rumors and speculation. People inside the company who felt at risk would flee. Others would seek a low profile by limiting their action. The company would be paralyzed by indecision. It would be a mess.

Even if you don't have complete information, you have to decide on an approach and then work it hard. You have to set a direction that makes the most sense, based on the best information you have.

While you're filling in the missing blanks with one hand, you have to show forward movement with the other. Some things can be postponed until you have more information; others need action immediately.

Some things can be postponed until you have more information; others need action immediately.

That's the point I made when I got together with the interns and graduate students who worked during the summer months at Kraft, Nabisco, and Gillette. A large portion of my remarks would focus on the importance of action. I would say that I liked people who deliver results. They are people who walk the walk and give you what they promise when they promise it. They are much more comfortable being a doer than being a bystander. And in my view, it's doers who make the world go round.

I LIKE SNAKE KILLERS!

Being a doer, especially at a high level in a company, is tough. It takes dedication and persistence. If top jobs were easy, anybody could do them. In the business world, products fail, factories break down, people disappoint you; it's all part of the territory. You have to keep finding a way to get things done regardless of what's thrown in front of you. You've got to come up with solutions. You've got to act.

The story I would tell to make the point, quite possibly apocryphal, involved H. Ross Perot when he was on the board of directors of General Motors. Perot was constantly frustrated by endless, circular discussions and the lack of action that he felt characterized GM's approach to decision making. "Where I come from," Perot told the GM board, "if you see a snake, you kill it. Here you appoint a committee on snakes that goes out and hires a consultant on snakes." I told the students that Perot's approach also was mine. I like snake killers!

The main driver of my career and success always has been getting things done. That doesn't mean forget the planning, the analysis, and the testing. Anyone who goes through the graduate business program at the University of Chicago comes away with an indelible imprint regarding the importance of planning, quantitative analysis, detailed and systematic assessments, and extremely rigorous testing. The Graduate School of Business is like two years of intensive boot camp.

Despite my ardor and belief in the importance of planning and study, nothing irritates me more than their misuse. Nothing is more troubling than seeing valuable time, resources, and energy being dithered away on poorly constructed or poorly led efforts that never should have been started, or definitely should have ended long ago.

Let me give you an example from Gillette. As I attempted to identify some of the root factors that were inflating Gillette's costs, one apparent problem was the proliferation of products or stock-keeping units (SKUs, for short).

Unlike Kraft, the Gillette business is streamlined. Kraft participates in dozens of different product categories such as coffee, dry and bottled beverages, cheese and other dairy products, ready-to-eat cereals, snack foods, confections, processed meats, frozen foods, and more. Plus, there are few global brands or universal tastes in the food sector. With the exception of Philadelphia-brand cream cheese, Kraft had no brand that was the same for a product in every country around the world. In the United States, Kraft's number one coffee is Maxwell House; in Germany, it is Jacobs; in Sweden, it is Gevalia; and in France, it is Carte Noir. And so it goes, all over the globe.

Nothing is more troubling than seeing valuable time, resources, and energy being dithered away on poorly constructed or poorly led efforts.

Gillette had just five core global businesses—Gillette blades and razors; Oral-B toothbrushes; Duracell batteries; Braun electric shavers; and Gillette shave preparations. (Gillette's other personal-care products—antiperspirants and deodorants such as Right Guard and Dry Idea—were sold almost exclusively in the United States and the United Kingdom.) And each of these businesses had global brands that account for 80 percent or more of the total sales of their categories. Mach3 was the number one razor and shaving cartridge in the United States, the United Kingdom, Germany, France, and Sweden. In fact, it was number one throughout all of North America, Europe, and most other parts of the world.

And the Mach3 that sells in the United States is the same as the Mach3 sold everyplace else in the world. There are virtually no adaptations or local variations by geography. Actually, all Mach3 products were made, and still are, in just two manufacturing centers—one in Boston and the other in Berlin.

PROBLEMS PROLIFERATE EVEN FASTER THAN PRODUCTS

The power generated by this global uniformity and presence should have been enormous across the board—not only in manufacturing and operations, but also in purchasing, marketing, sales, and every element of the value chain.

Yet the key metrics showed just the opposite. Gillette wasn't best in class in terms of the amount of inventory we had on hand; we were one of the worst in our competitive group. Gillette wasn't top of the heap in terms of meeting our customers' deadlines with fast and accurate product shipments; we had customers threatening "to punish" the company if we didn't get better. And when it came to SKUs, it was the same story.

A company with only five core product areas and many strong global brands had more than twenty thousand SKUs, which kept ratcheting up year after year after year. Unfortunately, the problems associated with the growth of SKUs proliferate even more quickly than the actual number of SKUs. More SKUs mean higher inventories and greater complexity in the systems needed to track and identify each product, and in the pricing data that have to be reconciled for each unit, and on and on.

And as the numbers grow, the attention paid to the problem tends to diminish. Why should anyone spend time figuring out what to do with one SKU that represents twenty cases of, say, a three-year-old Gillette Mach3 packed with a sample size of Gillette Foamy when he or she knew that another one hundred SKUs would be added in the next few months?

Using the Fast-Track Quick-Screen Process As noted in chapter 1, I often use my *fast-track quick-screen elimination process* to deal with important issues. That's what I used to cut through the SKU morass at Gillette—in just one day.

On the face of it, this approach might seem to violate all the precepts taught by the GSB at the University of Chicago. It doesn't. It actually gives you the ability to do lengthy, exhaustive studies when and where they will add real value. Excessive SKUs is not one of those instances.

When I asked our top executives about the SKU issue at an off-site meeting, the reaction was prolonged silence as people looked from one person to another, in effect saying, "I don't want to be the one to talk about this ugly quagmire." Finally, Mike Cowhig, head of global distribution for Gillette and a veteran of more than twenty-five years, spoke up.

Mike explained that the previous CEO had asked a management team to study the SKU issue and that's exactly what they'd done for the past eighteen months. Mike said he headed up the SKU Reduction Committee, which consisted of more than a dozen top managers, who had countless meetings at which they discussed criteria for cutting SKUs and developed action plans for implementing the reductions. But each time they got close to acting, someone, somewhere, in the organization, would object.

Eliminate an SKU special pack of Mach3 with Duracell batteries and Customer X will reduce our total shelf space.

Eliminate the special three-pack of Gillette Series shave cream and we'll miss our budget for the quarter.

Each time they got close to acting, someone, somewhere, in the organization, would object.

In the face of this pushback, Mike said that the committee would pull back.

Breaking the Log Jam At the end of his saga, I asked Mike how many SKUs had actually been eliminated during the eighteen-month process. I knew the number would be low, but was totally nonplussed to learn it was *zero.*

It's rare that I lose my cool, but I came close because my next words were "The SKU Reduction Committee has a choice; either you identify a fifty percent reduction in SKUs that will be implemented over the next three months and give them to me by the end of the week, or I'll do it for you."

The committee came through and actually exceeded the targets. Within nine months, Gillette's SKUs went from more than twenty thousand down to seven thousand—a two-thirds drop in units that represented less than 2 percent of our total sales. I should also note that over the next five years Mike Cowhig had a number of promotions, rising to president of our Global Technical & Manufacturing organization.

KNOWING WHEN TO ACT

So how do you know it's time to act? Action must always be a top priority because one of the biggest issues at large corporations—in fact, at organizations of any size—is their proclivity for inaction.

Taking action involves taking risks and the courage to take on criticism. For people working in companies, there's an inertia that usually rewards inaction. Unless strong forces and a firm direction encourage and require action, organizations gravitate toward inaction.

Let's look at four times when you must act: to overcome a state of ongoing, protracted analysis; to break through inertia; to secure a first-to-market advantage; and to invest in building brand equity.

First, it's time to act when assessments are dead-ended and discussions have become circular, as with the SKU reductions.

Second, it's time to act when the lack of action is perpetuating a corrosive status quo. That may seem self-evident. But all too often, those people who have created the status quo are unwilling to take the action necessary to change it.

At Nabisco, the company had a number of problems. Capital spending was excessive; overheads were out of control; marketing investment had fallen; new-product development had virtually dried up; and market shares were way down.

But the biggest immediate problem was a sales force in deep trouble because of a flawed restructuring that was more than two years old. The company's sales and delivery system, which had been a unique competitive advantage for Nabisco in the cookie and cracker sector, had turned into its Achilles' heel. When competitors wanted to convince trade customers to take action against Nabisco, all they had to do was mention its sales organization.

After the news media reported my election as CEO of Nabisco, I received calls from dozens of my friends who were customers of both Kraft and Nabisco. These were senior people of the top supermarket chains, convenience stores, and mass merchandisers from around the country. Their message was so consistent, it seemed scripted. The first part of the conversation would be congratulatory, and the next part would be a warning: *Glad you're back, Jim. Nabisco is a great company; but if you don't fix up that mess of a sales organization fast, we're going to start delisting your products.*

NABISCO TAKES CAREFUL AIM . . . AND SHOOTS ITSELF RIGHT IN THE FOOT

Following the fabled leveraged buyout of RJR Nabisco in 1989, Nabisco had several years of record earnings growth. A 40 percent rate of earnings growth was required to pay down the high level of debt taken on by Kohlberg Kravis Roberts to do the deal. In the process, Nabisco worked itself into a vicious Circle of Doom that we'll be talking about in chapter 10.

As it attempted to sustain an inflated rate of earnings growth, the Nabisco management sought areas where large chunks of cost could be extracted and dropped to the bottom line. Unfortunately, the sales organization became their prime target. Two years before I arrived, Nabisco loaded up, took careful aim, and shot itself right in the foot by reorganizing the sales force.

Nabisco's sales and distribution system had been the envy of the food sector. Unlike Kraft and most other food manufacturers, Nabisco used a direct store delivery system. With the exception of Coca-Cola and PepsiCo, others use a warehouse or wholesaler system. Products go from the food processor's plant to a customer's warehouse, where they are stored for a while before they're combined with other products for delivery by the customer to their retail stores. At the store, the product often went into a back room until a clerk placed it onto the shelves.

Trailing Sales Reps as They Chat with Store Managers With Nabisco, cookies and crackers went from the bakeries directly to the customer's stores, where they were packed onto the shelves by Nabisco people. There were no intermediaries and no delays.

Nabisco salespeople had unique relationships and stature. Other companies' sales reps weren't even allowed into retail stores. Nabisco people had the run of the stores and were in them every day. They had a precise knowledge of the store's consumers and their shopping preferences. The sales force consisted of thousands of category-savvy people with years of experience and strong personal connections with virtually every supermarket manager in the country.

When these reps entered a store, they had carte blanche to set up the shelves in the biscuit aisles, put up front-of-store and end-aisle displays, and ask for a special favor if they needed something to make their targets. When most companies introduce new products, they plan on retail distribution that builds over months as products move from plants to warehouses, and sometimes even to a wholesaler's warehouse, and then to a customer's warehouse and finally to a retail store's back room. Nabisco was able to achieve 90 percent retail distribution within two weeks. The marketers at Nabisco knew with certainty the precise time that introductory advertising could begin without the risk of consumers searching in vain for products when they went to the stores.

Direct store delivery had great benefits, but it also was a costly system. The fleet of Nabisco trucks needed to make store deliveries was costly to buy, run, and maintain; the time needed to pack product onto stores shelves was lengthy; and the salaries of the long-tenured sales people who were at the core of the system's great knowledge and relationships were high.

So Nabisco brought in expert consultants. People with stop-watches trailed sales reps as they chatted with store managers, packed Nabisco product onto shelves, and built displays. Lo and behold, back came the recommendations.

Since fleet costs were high, the number of trucks was cut; since gas and maintenance costs were high, the number of deliveries was reduced; and since long-term salespeople were highly paid, they were terminated. In their place, Nabisco hired novices—often recent college or high school graduates. And the starting salaries were so low that turnover in the sales organization reached fast-food-restaurant levels.

Tinkering Around the Edges, as Customer Outrage Mounted

With a constant flow of new, unknowledgeable, inexperienced Nabisco salespeople passing through their stores, customers complained. Not only had their longtime associates and friends been fired, they were winding up with too much product that consumers didn't want and bare shelves in place of products that they did want.

When I arrived, as noted, the reorganized sales group had been in effect for almost two years. During that time, sales were stagnant and market shares were sliding across the board. Customer outrage was growing. Many of the fired salespeople had taken positions with our competitors and were making further inroads into our business.

Yet bad as things were, the incumbent Nabisco Biscuit management was convinced the situation would be righted with some tinkering around the edges. Perhaps a small increase to the Spartan starting salary would cut employee turnover.

Maybe a few more managers could provide closer supervision to the neophyte sales reps. Maybe fewer new products would lessen the workload. On and on it went.

Yet what the management's position and attitude really amounted to was inaction. They had worked so hard on the reorganization and counted so heavily on the savings that they truly believed the status quo was best, and, ultimately, everything would right *itself.*

Price of Action Is Not Cheap Needless to say, I did not share their delusion. The incumbent management had to go. We assembled a new team, headed by Rick Lenny (who is now the CEO of Hershey, which he has energized and transformed), whom I had worked with for years at Kraft. He had broad experience that included both sales and general management and his previous position was heading North American operations for Pillsbury. Rick was a perfect match for the position and challenge and set to work immediately developing a major change for the sales organization. We would have to blow up the redesigned sales force and start over again.

Our new plans called for a structure that restored the best of the old system; incorporated some streamlining from the reorganized structure; and, importantly, instilled the morale and swagger that had characterized the old sales group.

However, the price of action is neither easy nor cheap. I still had to go to the Nabisco board of directors and tell them that the prior restructuring, which had been presented to them as a state-of-the-art organization structure, had to be scrapped. And that the new organization would cost $100 million more. Even though I was new and untried as CEO, the board swallowed hard and voted in favor of the new plan.

There is an important addendum to wrap up this story. Rick Lenny moved quickly and attacked the problem with a massive reorganization that restored the one-on-one relationship between the stores and sales reps. Despite a yearlong change that put 70 percent of the Nabisco sales force in new positions and brought two thousand new people into the five-thousand-person sales group, results came immediately. Sales, which had been down for each quarter of the preceding year and a half, started growing again. Within a year, the Nabisco sales force was back to its glory days as one of the most powerful selling organizations in the sector.

ONE + ONE = GROWTH

I faced another challenge where action had to overcome organizational inertia in my efforts to integrate the Kraft and General Foods businesses into one entity. These were two multibillion-dollar companies that had been purchased at different times by Philip Morris and had been operated separately. The companies had a lot in common, and a lot that also kept them apart. The result was two companies with great brands and potential, but with combined operating margins of 8.6 percent. By successfully integrating them, restoring growth, improving their portfolio and realizing synergies and savings, the operating margin increased by nearly 40 percent to 12 percent.

SEIZING THE FIRST-TO-MARKET ADVANTAGE

A third instance when action should trump all other considerations is when speed is a critical issue. There are times when every *t* should be crossed, every *i* dotted, and every step of corporate process should be followed scrupulously. All testing should be done; all plans should be carefully drawn and vetted; and all contingencies should be contemplated before action is taken. That's especially true when large capital expenditures are involved—for example, when a new product is being launched that requires a new manufacturing facility or equipment, which could be a total loss if the product bombs.

However, if speed to market is a key factor that would influence the product's likelihood of success, then some planning and process may have to be sacrificed. It happened to me at Kraft when we were working on a major new product in the frozen-pizza sector.

If speed to market is a key factor that would influence the product's likelihood of success, then some planning and process may have to be sacrificed.

I was heading Kraft North America when we acquired Tombstone, a regional pizza company based in Wisconsin, which we planned to take national. Within a year, we had rolled Tombstone out across the country and had a frozen-pizza business of about $440 million, more than a quarter of the $1.6 billion overall frozen-pizza market.

However, our goal was to double sales within five years, so we knew there was a tall mountain to climb. Running the pizza-marketing team at the time was Betsy Holden, a young manager whom I knew at General Foods and felt was destined for great things. (Betsy marched quickly through the ranks at Kraft, and a few years after I left the company, she was named co-chief executive.)

Betsy realized that the best way to achieve our aggressive target was to expand the competitive frame of reference for our pizza business. The frozen-pizza business was less than $2 billion; but the carryout/home-delivery pizza business was nearly $15 billion.

As Betsy recalls: "We understood how the market segmented. The consumers liked frozen pizza, but they thought the crust tasted like cardboard. The gold standard was home-delivery pizza. And fortunately, we had some new dough technology that we could leverage to give us a product that would be superior frozen pizza. We had a self-rising dough that was never baked until the consumer put it in her oven. It tasted like fresh-cooked dough. If we could position this pizza against home-delivery pizza, the prize would be very large."

Delivering at Warp Speed Betsy's group had a good understanding of the market. They knew it was a brand-structured market, so creating a new brand was better than attempting to leverage the Tombstone brand. Consumers liked Tombstone, but they considered it the "best *frozen* pizza." Our new brand—DiGiorno—with our fresh-baked crust was positioned against home-delivery pizza, and consumers put it even with, or even above, carryout/home-delivery pizza, which was unimaginable.

However, performing all of the testing normally required prior to committing the sizable capital expenditure needed for DiGiorno would create a problem. If DiGiorno was going to be ready for the heavy pizza-consumption season, it would have to be commercialized in less than six months. Yet additional test marketing would take more than three months. If DiGiorno's launch were delayed by a year, there was a good possibility that one or more of our competitors would acquire the same fresh-dough technology.

To me, the decision was simple. We had to accept the risk and get to market as soon as possible. We weren't reckless. We had a plan B on how to use the equipment if DiGiorno fizzled. However, we moved with warp speed and got DiGiorno to market in less than half a year.

The rest, as they say, is history. DiGiorno was named the most successful new product of 1996. Our market share grew by more than 30 percent in a year, and we hit the billion-dollar mark a year ahead of our plan.

Being first to market with an innovative product doesn't necessarily assure success, but it's always an incredible advantage. Many books have been written on the importance of speed to market and first to market. While some of them are breathless and overstated, all of them underscore the importance of taking action, of getting on with the initiative and avoiding analysis paralysis and other common corporate syndromes.

INVESTING IN BRANDS, *NOT JUST* SPENDING MARKETING DOLLARS

The fourth instance where taking action is the clear mandate is when the action backs a basic principle or strategy. I consider myself a brand man, having spent my entire career building existing brands and developing new ones. So one of my basic beliefs is the importance of investing in brands. But those investments, which involve big dollars, should be made on the basis of detailed analytics and sophisticated marketing intelligence.

During my tenure at Kraft, we developed something called IMI—Integrated Marketing Intelligence—which gave us state-of-the-art insights into our brands, their categories, and consumer dynamics; how responsive they were to different forms of advertising and promotion; how much spending was optimal; and much more that will be explored later. When we spent marketing dollars at Kraft, we were truly *investing* in brand building.

At both Nabisco and Gillette, little marketing intelligence was in place. While Kraft was at a graduate level in IMI, Nabisco and Gillette were at an entry IMI-101 level. But despite the absence of solid data, we had to act. Investing in the brands was an imperative, even though we did not have everything we needed.

Feeding the Little Bears At Nabisco, for example, the marketing funds were decimated in order to inflate the bottom line following its leveraged buy-out (LBO) and initial public offering (IPO). Nabisco's advertising and consumer spending was cut almost in half, from 8.2 percent of sales in 1987 to 4.5 percent in 1997. So virtually all of Nabisco's iconic brands were starved for support. We immediately started to restore marketing spending while at the same time improving our IMI capabilities.

For example, you may remember a little cookie called Teddy Grahams. They came out in the late 1980s and their sales shot up to $150 million in only eighteen months. But then Nabisco let the little bears fend for themselves, and by 1998, their sales had fallen to $25 million. Bringing back Teddy Grahams required going back to the basics of marketing—sharpening the packaging graphics, refocusing on the youngsters who loved them, adding some new varieties, and backing it all with some of the best-scoring advertising ever in the biscuit category. The result? Teddy Grahams sales for the year jumped to $100 million.

And we saw similar results across the entire biscuit portfolio. Oreo was the crown jewel—an eighty-five-year-old icon brand with sales of half a billion dollars at the time—but it wasn't growing. So we pulled out all the stops. We launched heavy advertising and one high-visibility promotion after another. There was something going on with Oreo every month of the year. In the first quarter of 1999, we had a great promotion that you may even recall—"Don't Eat the Winning Oreo." We backed it with great advertising, and sales increased more than 9 percent.

With rejuvenated marketing, the sales of our Newtons franchise went from a decline of 10 percent to a plus 4 percent, and Cheese Nips had growth of 28 percent.

Moving Market-Share Increases from 10/90 to 90/10 In fact, our biscuit market share increased across the overall cookie and cracker portfolio for twelve consecutive periods. Remarkably, the growth started the first month after we initiated our marketing rejuvenation efforts. It continued virtually uninterrupted, reversing the steep market-share decline that had spanned the preceding three years.

At the start of 1998, sales from 90 percent of the company's products in the United States had *declining* market shares. A year later, 90 percent of Nabisco's sales came from products that had *growing* market share and *growing* consumer takeaway. Taking action paid off.

As we'll cover in chapter 8 in discussing the leadership process, actions and achievements are the basis for my approach to business. Tireless effort is great, but if it doesn't yield something, it can't be rewarded. All too many organizations get in trouble because they reward people for how hard they try rather than for the actions they take and achievements they score. Without a sharp and unrelenting focus on action, little will get done.

All too many organizations get in trouble because they reward people for how hard they try rather than for the actions they take and achievements they score.

To sum up, having all the information you need exactly when you need it would greatly simplify business decision making and reduce the mistakes. But business always involves trade-offs. Often it's a wait-or-act decision. And in those instances, you must act rather than risk protracted analysis and circular discussion. You must act to break through a crippling status quo environment. You must act where speed to market is critical. And you always must act to invest in brands.

THE TIME FOR ACTION IS NOW!

Everything seems to be on track. Sales are increasing; profits are growing; market shares are moving up. Can you assume no further action is necessary? Probably not.

- Cruise control is never the right rate of speed to keep pace with competition that is getting faster and better every day.

- Daily sales reports are essential. Knowing what's happening in real time lets you take the small corrective actions necessary to avoid big problems.

- Weekly staff meetings are a great way to stoke action and assure accountability.

- Insist on reports from your top people about what happened in the prior seven days and what will be done differently in the coming seven days to address any shortfalls. (And there *always* are shortfalls.)

- Circulate investment analyst reports on your key competitors and ask your business units how they plan to address new initiatives. Even if the competitive actions were anticipated, your plans should get another look.

CHAPTER 6

UNDERSTANDING THE RIGHT THINGS MATTERS

Sometimes it is tough to know what matters. Even the old-school approach can fall short when it comes to *really understanding* what matters. But the great leaders get it right more often than not, and they know how to frame what matters in a way that clarifies issues for their people.

When Jack Welch took over as CEO of General Electric, he had to bring order, discipline, and a sense of urgency to the large, cumbersome industrial conglomerate that was GE. And he had to identify what was really important for success. While a number of approaches might get at parts of what he had to achieve, Welch wanted a single overarching framework—an encompassing concept to guide the company's progress. The elegantly simple concept that he developed became the company's long-term mantra.

GE only would be in businesses where it was—or could become—a clear leader. It would be or become number one or number two, or get out.

This umbrella concept provided a clear understanding of what would matter as Jack Welch re-created GE as an enterprise that would be highly valued by all constituents—including investors, customers, and employees. It's a concept that guided the actions of Welch as CEO, each of his business heads, and all other managers as they decided on objectives and plans.

In following Welch as CEO, Jeff Immelt found that he needed a new framework for the work ahead. Even though Welch had a long run as one of the most successful CEO's of the twentieth century, Immelt saw that the focus of GE's global research was too diffused by working on more than two thousand projects. Immelt acted quickly to identify just three areas that GE would lead and "own"—nanotechnology, molecular medicine and renewable energy, and energy efficiency and environmental technology. He cut the number of projects from two thousand to eighty.

When A. G. Lafley took over as CEO of Procter & Gamble, he had to find ways to increase the company's sluggish growth. As he looked at Procter & Gamble's prized research-and-development capability, he saw part of the problem. While his people were good inventors, they weren't the best in a number of areas; many inventions *outside* the company could be commercialized into new-product successes.

The solution: *the connect-and-develop concept*. Lafley said that P&G would connect and develop with external innovators and move its partnered projects from 10 percent of its overall product development activity to 50 percent. Within five years, P&G had moved the needle from 10 percent to 40 percent . . . and was well on its way to 50 percent.

My overarching framework is centered on the consumer and customer. Early in my Kraft experience, I created a concept that's been central to my management philosophy for three decades. I call it Total Brand Value, and it has served as the vision statement for each of the companies I headed.

Total Brand Value means that a company must innovate to

Total Brand Value means that a company must innovate to deliver consumer value and customer leadership faster, better, and more completely than the competition.

deliver consumer value and customer leadership faster, better, and more completely than the competition. That's a simple statement, but it is all encompassing, covering all aspects of business and everyone in the organization.

TOTAL BRAND VALUE—TRANSLATING INSIGHTS INTO WINNING PRODUCTS

For people in research and development, it means they must listen carefully to consumers and translate the insights gained into winning products and packaging.

In the operations areas of purchasing, manufacturing, and distribution, people will add value by efficiently procuring raw materials, by manufacturing high-quality products at the lowest costs, and by distributing them to trade customers when and where they want them.

For marketing people, it means understanding the consumer better than competitors, making sure that the prices reflect the value of the products, and then creating the best advertising and promotions to communicate the benefits and superiority of the products to consumers.

Salespeople have to help trade customers understand why the company's products are superior, how the company's expertise in its product categories is unmatched, and how the company's products and strategy will build profitable volume.

In the area of trade and customer service, value is added by providing customers with actionable information and by anticipating and being responsive to customer and consumer needs.

And finally, in the staff areas of finance, human resources, public relations, information technology, and the like, the job is to bring great expertise and professional knowledge to internal customers that will create partnerships and facilitate the building of Total Brand Value.

Total Brand Value provides an all-important point of connection for creating plans and programs.

When a company achieves each element of the vision by innovating to give consumers products they value, and providing customers with excellent service and profitable growth, it will beat back any and all competitors and become a winner.

As we'll see in chapter 8, strategies and growth plans are a direct outgrowth of achieving the Total Brand Value vision. In fact, I always use Total Brand Value to frame the big picture. It enables me to know what's important and what's not. If taking an action doesn't promote Total Brand Value, then it receives a much lower priority.

You need an overarching concept to frame and filter issues regardless of your industry. Total Brand Value works within consumer products, and its key elements of achieving results that are better, faster, and more complete than competitors' results also apply broadly across many business sectors.

Better and Faster Total Brand Value is the first filter that I use in considering any action or proposal. There are many things that are nice to do. There are lots of engaging and interesting ways to occupy your time. But they must help your business achieve something better, faster, and more completely than your competition, or you should think twice about taking them on.

Total Brand Value is the first filter that I use in considering any action or proposal.

And Total Brand Value works regardless of size or importance. It will work on assessing a new product introduction as well as it will on a mega-merger or acquisition. For example, when we were considering the launch of DiGiorno pizza at Kraft, we knew that we had a better product. The self-rising crust was fresh cooked by the consumer and compared favorably with the gold standard of home-delivery pizza. It satisfied the "innovative" and "faster" elements of the vision. DiGiorno could be first to market with a new and notable difference. And DiGiorno provided a completely positive experience through its attractive packaging, great value for price, and ease of preparation. So making the go or no-go decision was relatively easy, as was the decision to forgo some of the usual test marketing in favor of a first-to-market advantage. Total Brand Value gave us the assurance that the likelihood of success was greater than the risk of failure.

So Total Brand Value has great and wide usefulness. It's an old-school, fundamental concept. Yet all too often even large, sophisticated organizations fail to grasp the importance of basic, fundamental concepts.

The basic primer on marketing says that for a product to be successful you must understand the overall market, the products you are competing against, the consumer dynamics of the product category, how the consumer views your brand, and the value they attach to it. But ignoring even this most basic of basic precepts is often the rule, not the exception, at many companies.

Ignoring Consumers; Writing Off Battery Toothbrushes At Gillette in 2001, for example, our Oral-B brand was the global leader in the toothbrush business. In the United States, Oral-B had a commanding market-share lead in the manual-toothbrush business, at 1.2 times larger than its nearest competitor. In Europe, Oral-B Braun was virtually unopposed in the power-toothbrush market. Braun's knowledge of small electric motors provided Oral-B with a great technological advantage. Braun drew upon its vast experience with electric shavers and a complete range of small appliances to create exceptionally durable and efficacious power for the Braun/Oral-B electric rechargeable toothbrushes. Oral-B's sister company was Duracell, the largest alkaline-battery company in the world.

So in the 1990s, when a small start-up company scored some excellent results selling Dr. John's SpinBrush, an inexpensive battery-powered toothbrush, you would expect Oral-B to act. And, in a way, it did. It looked at the slim profit possible on a low-margin, gimmicky brush priced at $5 versus the very attractive gains coming with the high-margin, top-of-the-line, $100-plus Oral-B rechargeables and decided not to enter the battery market.

The consumer received virtually no attention. So far as Oral-B was concerned, if the consumer wanted a toothbrush in the $3 to $6 bracket, they should purchase the Oral-B manual. If they wanted a power brush, they should spring for the premium-quality, $100 Oral-B rechargeable electric toothbrush.

It turned out that the consumer had a different thought. Spending a few bucks to try a power brush was appealing; spending a hundred dollars was a nonstarter.

Competitors Rush In Within a few years, battery-toothbrush sales went from zero to $500 million. All the other players in the manual toothbrush market saw the battery segment as an easy way to steal market share from Oral-B manuals. In short order, Colgate, Procter & Gamble, Johnson & Johnson, and several other smaller companies had battery entries.

As the battery market surged, Oral-B's manual share eroded. The battery market appeared so attractive that Procter & Gamble, which had tried and failed for years to make inroads in the manual market, agreed to pay a staggering sum of almost $500 million for SpinBrush. (In the interest of full disclosure, P&G had to divest SpinBrush as part of the terms stipulated by the Federal Trade Commission to acquire the Gillette Company and our Oral-B franchise.)

All of Oral-B's competitors looked upon the battery segment

as providing the possibility for a paradigm shift. Toothbrush consumers tended to be brand loyal for life. As with blades and razors, consumers would trade up to better-performing products within a brand; it was difficult to switch them to another brand, even with claims of comparative superiority. The battery-brush phenomenon broke the model because Oral-B had nothing consumers could move up to. The likelihood existed that the Colgate and Crest battery-toothbrush users would shift their lifetime brand loyalty. (After the acquisition, P&G quickly changed Dr. West to the Crest brand to fully exploit this opportunity.)

STACKING THE ODDS *AGAINST* SUCCESS

Although it was last to enter, Oral-B did move into the battery market and within eighteen months held clear leadership in the segment. However, as I probed with the Oral-B people about what they would do with their new battery-brush users, I learned that they had not performed a segmentation study of the toothbrush market.

In other words, despite all the turmoil in the toothbrush market, we had never brought together people from our marketing area, research and development, advertising agency, and outside specialist marketing firms to find out which consumers used what products, how they used them, and why.

We didn't know why consumers chose manual, battery, or rechargeable power brushes; what they wanted from them; and how much they were willing to pay.

We didn't know if a battery-brush user would trade up to rechargeable power or would trade up within the battery category only to a better-performing product.

We knew that a segment of consumers brushed their teeth in the morning, during the day, and at night. But we didn't know how significant the differences were in what they needed from a brush in each of those uses. Clearly, without a segmentation study, we were stacking the odds against our own success.

Space-Age Technology The point is that these omissions aren't atypical. There were big gaps even within the Blades & Razors unit, which was the heart and soul of the Gillette Company and one of the most advanced and sophisticated organizations in all of consumer products.

The more I got to know about Gillette's shaving business during my first year at the company, the more impressed I became. A friend of mine, who headed up manufacturing for a large industrial company, had told me years before I joined Gillette that his tour of the Gillette manufacturing center in Boston left him astonished.

What he had seen on a site in South Boston was a state-of-the-science blade and razor plant that he said was NASA-like in all aspects. Mach3 cartridges with three blades of imported stainless steel—stropped to an edge fifty times sharper than a surgical scalpel—were assembled with nine other parts into a plastic cartridge at a rate of six hundred units per minute. The allowable-defect tolerance was zero since any defect, even a microscopically pitted blade edge, would likely have painful and bloody consequences for the unfortunate shaver who purchased the faulty cartridge. The heavy use of robotics and customized Gillette-built manufacturing equipment assured the precision and reliability of the process and products.

Delivering on Promise of Superior Products Gillette's manufacturing skill was more than matched by its research-and-development capabilities. More than 270 researchers—160 of whom had PhD's in chemistry, metallurgy, physics, mathematics, and engineering—devoted their professional lives to understanding every aspect of the science and art of shaving and the process and equipment needed for high-speed manufacturing.

The depth of knowledge is incomparable. For example, the

Mach3 Turbo shaving system is protected by thirty-five patents. These patents represent unique features that only Gillette could use. No competitive product could even attempt to imitate them because when they did, we would immediately bring legal action to stop them.

Gillette's newest shaving system, Gillette Fusion and Fusion Power, set a new high for patents—seventy. It's no wonder, then, that Gillette's new products have such high acceptance with consumers. They truly deliver on their promise of product superiority, innovation, and the highest performance.

Knowledge—Beyond Encyclopedic Yet technical innovation is only one part of the story. The Gillette development process involves contacts with more than one hundred thousand shavers annually to gain insight on every aspect of shaving—the preshave, actual shave, and postshave experiences; the physical, emotional, social, and psychological aspects of shaving; the differences in how a twenty-year-old shaves and thinks of shaving versus a thirty-, forty-, or fifty-year-old.

The understanding is beyond encyclopedic. It comes as close to all knowing, or omniscient, as any mortal undertaking can be. Most companies have a decent understanding of how consumers interact with and use their products; Gillette takes that to the outer limit.

Before coming to Gillette, I assumed that it took somewhere between twenty-five to fifty strokes for me to shave my face with my Gillette razor. Gillette researchers know that on average it takes more than 130 strokes. Since beard hair is as tough as copper wire, they know that the best way to enhance the closeness and comfort of a shave is to soak the face with warm (not hot or cold) water for three minutes, which reduces the force required to cut the beard hair by 70 percent. But they also know that three out of four men don't wash their faces at all.

Since a man's facial hair is 50 to 60 percent larger in diameter and more irregularly shaped than women's hair, which is primarily oval shaped, the recommended preshave soaking time for women is two minutes.

Men shave an area of 48 square inches; women shave an area of 412 square inches—9 times larger. But, on average, a man's beard has the same number of hairs as a woman's legs and underarms combined.

The number of hairs on a man's face? That would be between seven thousand and fifteen thousand, which are genetically determined; few grow after birth. The rate of growth of a whisker? One-quarter of an inch a month.

How much facial hair will the average man grow in a lifetime? Try 26.5 feet. And how much time will he spend removing it? About 780 hours (32.5 days).

How do the sexes differ in their view of shaving? Men view shaving as a skill; women see it as a chore.

Losing Sight of Disposables With all of this knowledge and insight, I was puzzled and, quite frankly, bothered by what had happened to Gillette's market share in the disposable segment of the razor market. Traditionally, disposables were the low-end, low-price segment of the wet-shaving market. As with the total market, Gillette held the largest share, reaching well into the 80 percent range during the 1980s and early 1990s.

However, from 1995 to 2000, Gillette's share of the global disposable market dropped sharply. This decline coincided with a period of solid innovation by Gillette's chief competitor in the disposable sector, the Schick-Wilkinson company. During that period, Schick introduced several new products that culminated with the Xtreme3—a three-bladed disposable that offered a reasonably good shave at a price of $1.35 per unit. Importantly, it gave a far better shave than any Gillette disposable.

The reason for the performance gap resulted from thinking that was similar to the Oral-B management's thinking about battery-powered toothbrushes. If men want a disposable razor, they should buy Gillette's Good News disposable that sells for fifty cents per unit, they thought. If men want a quality shave, they should buy a quality shaving system such as Gillette's two-bladed Sensor Excel or the then-top-of-the-line, three-bladed Mach3, which cost from $5.48 to $6.58 for the razors to $1.15 to $1.62 for the cartridges.

THE GREAT RAZOR WAR

For the Gillette Blades & Razors Business Unit, there was a long history that reinforced this thinking. Back in the 1970s, when the French-based société BIC company introduced the first disposable razor, the Gillette management of the time engaged in a protracted and heated debate about "plastic" (disposable razors) versus "steel" (system shavers). The plastic faction said Gillette should accept the inevitability of a future in which low-priced, plastic disposables became the shave of preference for men around the world. Attempting to fight against this inexorable shift to plastic would result in disaster and ruin for the company. Gillette should ride the wave and shift its efforts to plastic.

On the other side, the steel-shaving-system proponents cried heresy and treachery. Steel systems were not only Gillette's tradition and legacy; they also represented the future. Gillette must devote itself to innovation and the highest-quality shaving systems that would offer such superior performance consumers would never abandon them. Plastic disposables should continue only as an afterthought for Gillette.

When the dust settled, the steel side won; the plastic advocates were vanquished, and Gillette went on to innovate with some of the best and most successful brands in all of consumer products—the Sensor and Sensor Excel in the 1980s, and the Mach3 and Mach3 Turbo in the 1990s and early 2000s.

Shifting Consumer Loyalties So when the disposable question arose again in the mid-1990s, the Blades & Razors managers went back to their battle stations. Unfortunately, they made their decision without fully taking into account either the consumers or the changing financial dynamics of disposable razors.

While system shavers were still the gold standard of wet shaving, a segment of shavers was committed to disposable razors. They would never convert to systems, but they would trade up to better-performing products within disposables. If Gillette didn't innovate and provide those disposable trade-ups, then we would be encouraging consumers to shift their loyalties to new products from Schick and BIC, which also was upgrading within disposables.

Another troublesome aspect about the disposable resurgence was the number of first-time shavers being lured into the segment. In the past, Gillette's brands, marketing, and heritage had attracted virtually all new shavers in their teens and early twenties to Sensor and Mach3. Now, with its youth-oriented advertising, featuring the tennis champion Andre Agassi in his prime, who used the Xtreme3 to shave both his head and face, Schick was making some modest inroads.

Disposable Margins—Robust and Growing Compounding the entire issue was the fact that the new higher-priced, premium disposable razors were highly profitable. No, they didn't have the near pharmaceutical-like margins of system razors and cartridges, but they were far better than the anemic disposable margins of the 1970s and 1980s, and even far better than most other consumer products, including batteries, toothbrushes, shaving preparations, and antiperspirants.

While the disposable issue was a nuisance in the United States, it was a more significant business consideration in other parts of the world. The split of system shavers versus disposable shavers was 80-20 in the United States. In Latin

America, for example, the numbers were reversed. Disposables were by far the dominant market; systems were a niche segment.

Waiting for Consumers to Come Around Yet in Central and South America, where Gillette's market shares of disposables went as high as the 90 percent level, there had been no new products or innovation from the company within the segment for decades. The same short-handled, blue plastic razors that Gillette sold in the 1970s and 1980s were still being sold in the 1990s. Meanwhile, both Schick and BIC were bringing to market sleek, long-stemmed disposables with ergonomically designed, elastomeric handles; they had new stand-out packaging; they went from one blade to two blades and then to three blades.

Gillette's response was to introduce our new system shavers that were both priced too high for the market and also weren't something shavers were even willing to consider. And at the root of this situation was the strongly held belief that Gillette was a "steel-shaving-system" company. Systems offered both the best shave and the best profit. Ultimately, all consumers would come around.

Gillette Comes Around: Learning to Walk and Chew Gum at the Same Time The senior managers of the Blades & Razors Business Unit were shocked when they heard that in my former positions at Kraft and Nabisco, a market-share loss of one-quarter of a point was grounds for a full-fledged inquisition. A market-share loss of the size sustained by Gillette disposable razors would have made the Valentine's Day Massacre look bloodless.

The market-share loss had to stop. Gillette had to regain momentum in the disposable market. Gillette would continue to innovate and drive shavers toward systems in the overall market. But we also would innovate and trade up consumers within the disposable segment. Disposables were Gillette's second-most profitable product, and it would become even more so in the future. I summed it up by saying we would just have to learn how to walk and chew gum at the same time.

It took awhile, but Gillette did reverse the disposable market-share decline and started on the road to regain primacy. As it turned out, some of our best disposable innovations made use of manufacturing assets that had been idled by innovations in our systems business. Our Sensor3 disposable utilized plants and equipment that had been mothballed when Mach3 was introduced and attracted Xtreme3 users to the new franchise. So our new disposable strategy gave us a double win.

ONE-SIZE-FITS-ALL THINKING—DANGER AHEAD

While remembering that old-school basics matter, here's another equally important precept: Avoid assuming that one size fits all. In other words, pay attention to the old-school principle that says: Don't superimpose a successful formula from one area onto another and automatically assume you'll get similar results.

And a related precept: Applying old solutions to new issues can be risky.

Avoid assuming that one size fits all. In other words, pay attention to the old-school principle that says: Don't superimpose a successful formula from one area onto another.

At Gillette, the attempt to use the successful trade-up model that worked so well with both blades and razors and toothbrushes yielded nightmarish consequences when it was applied to batteries. We'll go into more detail about the battery debacle in chapter 11, but a few highlights here will point out the danger of one-size-fits-all thinking.

When Gillette acquired Duracell in 1996, the alkaline-battery category, which Duracell had pioneered and led for more than thirty years, was one of the best categories in all of consumer products. Not only had it enjoyed consistent growth; its rate of growth at about 5 to 8 percent annually was well above the average branded consumer products' growth of 2 to 4 percent.

Unlike most other categories, alkaline batteries were a branded category with a low level of private-label penetration and very high consumer brand loyalty. Consumers trusted and valued the Duracell brand and were willing to pay the right premium for it.

So when Gillette acquired it, the management assumed that Duracell was ideally suited to be transformed to the blade-and-razor trade-up model. It was a powerful brand that was premium priced with great brand loyalty and only nominal private-label competition. Why not move consumers away from the Duracell CopperTop battery, the mainstay of the Duracell business for more than a decade, and trade them up to a new and improved product, Duracell Ultra, which would be priced one-third higher than CopperTop.

Trading Up to Premium—Unrelenting Declines Consistent with the blade-and-razor model, all advertising and promotion for CopperTop would be terminated; advertising would focus exclusively on Duracell Ultra. Shelf space and in-store displays also would shift away from CopperTop in favor of Ultra.

The result was an unrelenting decline in Duracell as the sales of CopperTop dropped markedly and sales of Ultra grew moderately. When I joined Gillette, the battery meltdown had been going on for three years and there was no end in sight. The whole mess came as a big surprise to me, because I knew the Duracell business well from my time at Kraft.

Duracell had become part of the company as a result of the short-lived merger of Dart Industries and Kraft. (Not long after the merger was entered into, both companies mutually decided to dissolve the union and go their separate ways.) As head of the strategy-and-development function, it was my responsibility to divest the Duracell business, which wasn't considered a strategic fit for the new Dart-Kraft entity.

My due diligence prior to offering Duracell for sale showed a track record of growth, organizational strength, and category advantage that was impressive. Duracell seemed to have prospects for a long vista of above-average growth due to the proliferation of electronic devices that devoured batteries.

It was with mixed feelings that we sold the business to Kohlberg Kravis Roberts in 1988 for $1.8 billion. And it was with great delight that I had anticipated my reunion with the Duracell business.

Consumers Balk—Batteries Aren't Blades and Razors So how did a powerful brand in an advantaged category fall on such tough times? It was by assuming that one size would fit all; by imposing the trade-up strategy on a product that was different from blades and razors, despite the superficial similarities.

The consumers' interaction with a shaving system is greater than with virtually any other product. Every day, shavers swipe supersharp blades of steel across their faces and throats, and they assess the product performance immediately. If they try a new improved shaving cartridge, they know immediately whether there is good value for the higher price.

With a battery, there is no immediacy; the time factor is protracted and the ability to assess value is more limited. An improved battery goes into a flashlight, TV remote changer, pager, or some other electronic device. It is weeks or months before the batteries must be changed, which is far too long for consumers to know that the new and improved battery lasted 17 percent longer.

The price premium for Duracell Ultra versus other branded

batteries soared to 40 percent, and versus low-end and private-label products the price gap was more than 50 percent. Consumers balked, and the decline ensued.

As with the incumbent management at the Nabisco Biscuit unit, Duracell's senior leaders were convinced that the trade-up strategy was sound and marketplace success was just around the corner. At that point, I reached out for Mark Leckie, who would be ideal for the job. With his experience turning around Post cereals, Mark would know how to look at price, value, positioning, and all the many elements that could restore Duracell to a position of category leadership and growth. As we'll see in chapter 11, that's exactly what he did.

BEWARE OF OLD SOLUTIONS FOR NEW ISSUES

Some solutions seem like a perfect fit for a problem, but turn out to be an old solution for a new issue. Enough of the old elements are present to give the appearance that a tried-and-true approach should apply. But the results prove otherwise. This was the case with Gillette's initial experience with body sprays for men.

The company had long been a leader in the men's anti-perspirants and deodorants (AP/DEO) category with the Right Guard and Gillette Series brands. Nobody knew more about men than Gillette, and in the United States that aura extended beyond shaving to personal care.

Well into the 1990s, Gillette maintained a strong lead in the men's segment of the AP/DEO category. The category was far from vibrant. Gillette's profit margins eroded and sales were stagnant. However, Gillette managed to hold its market share in the annual slugfest with world-class competitors that included Unilever, Procter & Gamble, and Colgate.

Starting in the late 1990s, the dynamics of the segment

began to change. P&G pumped in high levels of development and marketing spending into the once-moribund Old Spice franchise, which it had acquired in the 1990s. The brand started to get traction and take share from Right Guard.

Teed Up for Failure Despite heavy promotional and advertising spending by all the players in the segment, sales remained sluggish until Unilever introduced its Axe body spray to the U.S. market. While not actually an antiperspirant or deodorant, Axe had been wildly successful in England, where, branded as Lynx, it had debuted a few years earlier. Its U.S. launch followed a similar trajectory—an immediate, blockbuster success. Our Right Guard people knew they had to answer with a similar product. They were confident that even though we weren't first to market, the Right Guard and Gillette brands on body sprays would win the day against Axe, a new brand with no established equity.

Within six months, Right Guard Xtreme body spray in three different scents, which outscored Axe in testing, were ready for market with an ad campaign that had runaway testing scores. Gillette's sales group did an excellent job of selling the new products to customers and securing both shelf placement and incremental displays.

Based on the old formula, everything was teed up for success: powerful brand, attractive product offering, excellent product distribution, high-scoring advertising copy. But the product sales languished, and within eighteen months, Right Guard Xtreme was withdrawn from the market.

What went wrong? Old formula; new issue.

Leaving Old Formulas and Fathers' Brand Behind The demographics for body sprays were teenagers and men in their early twenties. The reason: They used body spray as a sex lure, namely, to attract girls with a fragrance that they thought acted like an aphrodisiac. Concern about underarm sweating was the furthest thing from their minds, and so was Right Guard, "their fathers' antiperspirant." Rather than reassure the target audience about the efficacy of the body spray, the Right Guard brand turned them away.

How do you get young men to try your new product? You'd better put more emphasis on word of mouth, buzz marketing, the Internet, and special events . . . not just thirty-second TV commercials.

A year after we withdrew our Right Guard Xtreme body spray, we came back with TAG Body Spray for Men. Not only was there no mention of Right Guard or Gillette Series in any of the marketing, the agate type on the product package didn't identify Gillette as the manufacturer; instead, it cited a newly created subsidiary, TAG Fragrance Company.

TAG employed a wide variety of New Age media vehicles, including print ads in magazines like *Cargo, Wired, Maxim, HM, Fader,* and *Stuff,* and the ads clearly showed how far the TAG positioning moved from the traditional AP/DEO ads of "stay dry longer."

Within a year of its launch, TAG had taken the number two position in the body-spray market. It was behind Axe, which continued to invest heavily in its brand. But it moved well ahead of Procter & Gamble, whose efforts were stuck back in time. As Gillette had done initially, P&G used the Old Spice brand to launch its body-spray entry. Unlike Gillette, it stayed with the dated brand despite its limited success.

Understanding what matters will always be challenging. It takes a lifetime of experience to master all the skills needed.

In summary, understanding what matters will always be challenging. It takes a lifetime of experience to master all the skills needed. But a few simple precepts can provide a lot of help along the way.

UNLOCKING THE CHALLENGE—UNDERSTANDING WHAT REALLY MATTERS

Here are a few dos and don'ts that will help in your lifelong quest to understand what really matters.

- First, regardless of your field, adopt a straightforward vision of what you want to do . . . and how you want to do it. Make it actionable and easy to understand. For consumer products, the concept of building Total Brand Value worked for me over a period of more than twenty years at three of the best companies in the field.

- Second, don't get caught up in the fad theory of the day. Stay focused on the fundamentals and apply them rigorously and across the board. They may seem trite and trivial; they usually turn out to be profoundly important.

- Third, avoid a one-size-fits-all approach to problem solving. Templates work within limits; they do not travel widely with the same effect. Study each situation carefully and make sure the solution custom-fits the problem.

- And fourth, just because something worked in the past does not mean it will work in the future. Things change, nowadays, very quickly and fundamentally. So beware that superficial similarities aren't hiding some deep differences.

SECTION II

LEADERSHIP MATTERS

CHAPTER 7

THE RIGHT TEAM MATTERS

"*We're all going to get fired. Wiped out. Kilts says he'll give us all a chance. But we're history.*"

Those weren't the words Peggy Guillet expected to hear from her husband, Ned, as he returned home from my two-day off-site meeting, the first one for the Gillette management team.

Ned wasn't a direct report. He was the number two person in human resources. He came to the meeting because he was working on a special project. So he had a good chance to observe and think about what he was seeing. As a star football player at Boston College who also played some pro ball, Ned's mind turned to sports analogies. He told Peggy that Gillette had become a "losing team" and Kilts was the newly hired "head coach." New head coaches don't keep any of the former head coach's staff of assistants, and Gillette was "so dysfunctional in terms of how misaligned" the Operating Committee (Gillette's executive committee) was that Kilts might get rid of the entire team. They were such a "bunch of losers" that things couldn't get any worse if Kilts were to take out everyone and put his own people in their places.

WHY IS EVERYONE AN OVERACHIEVER?

It had been a tough initial session, but it was important to let my direct reports know how we would work and what I expected of them. Even though it was clear that there had been an absence of good leadership and a loss of discipline, I never considered doing anything other than what I said in my day one communiqué to the organization. There were no preconceptions of who should go or stay, or how many new people should be brought in. Everyone would be judged based on whether they could perform by meeting or beating the objectives that were agreed upon.

I would judge everyone based on whether they could perform by meeting or beating the objectives that were agreed upon.

Ned's doubts were based on more than just the off-site. They also went back to a meeting with him within a few days of my arrival. Bob DiCenso, our senior vice president of administration and human resources, who was Ned's boss, asked him to do an overview presentation on how Gillette was organized and the performance management system.

As Ned began it, I asked how many categories there were. Ned said there were five—*Does Not Meet Expectations, Needs Improvement*, *Meets Expectations, Exceeds Expectations,* and *Outstanding*. I said that sounded good, and asked for the rating of the leadership group on the 1 to 5 scale. What percentage were in each of the categories? Ned said he would guess about 65 percent of the organization were *Exceeds Expectations* and above. I said that's where most companies are, and Ned nodded.

Then I said I wanted to ask just two more questions; Ned said sure, fire away. First, 65 percent of our top people are scoring Exceeds Expectations and above, so what were the business results last year that yielded those ratings? I could see unease cross Ned's face as he realized that he was about to slide down a slippery slope. Gillette had *zero* sales growth and *zero* profit growth, Ned said.

Here's my final question: What was everybody so highly effective at? Ned looked like he wanted to die, but he came out with a totally honest and accurate answer: *effort*.

That's right, I said, you rewarded effort, which was great. But effort that does not turn into results is not good job performance. I then explained my beliefs on rating and rewarding performance.

Effort is the price of admission. Everyone has to work hard, usually very hard. But if effort doesn't turn into results, something is wrong. Perhaps with the objectives or targets that were set. Or with the actions being pursued. Or maybe with the person involved. Whatever it is, effort without results indicates a *problem* that must be addressed. It does not mean *highly effective performance* that should be rewarded.

Moving to a Performance Culture Following that awkward and shaky start, Ned remained on the team and became one of our strongest managers. In fact, within a matter of months, Ned's boss, Bob DiCenso, who had been with Gillette for more than twenty years, retired. Bob, a veteran of the finance group, held key roles as Gillette went through both its good times and then its challenges. He had worked closely with Colman Mockler and the executive team who fought off the Perelman attacks and the proxy battle launched by the Coniston Partners. It was Bob who found Colman Mockler laid out in the hallway near Bob's office not that long after Gillette's narrow victory over the Coniston group. Colman had suffered a massive, fatal heart attack.

Bob, who was in his mid-sixties, thought I needed someone who could work with me throughout the turnaround. I promoted Ned to head the human resources function and told him that his mandate was to help me transform Gillette to a performance culture. We wanted to move from an effort-based to a performance-based rewards system.

In the process, we would reorient the thinking of the company. Managers would think realistically, know their businesses better than anyone else inside or outside the company, and then set targets they were certain they could meet. Those targets would be a stretch, but realizable. And when they were met, the performance rating would be *Meets,* a 3 rating. However, those managers were going to be playing on a winning team, one that aspired to become the best in the world, so the bonus payout for an *Effective* rating of 3 should far exceed even an *Outstanding* rating of 5 with the former Gillette, where targets were missed, resulting in the board holding back much of the bonus pool.

I wanted managers to think realistically, know their businesses better than anyone else, and then set targets they were certain they could meet.

Both Ned and I realized that change would be difficult. Ned said he had received Exceeds Expectations and Outstanding ratings for years. If he were reduced to a Meets, a 3, he'd think of himself as a C-rated, average manager; not a high potential superstar. And Ned was not the exception.

As we checked back on the performance rating of three thousand global managers for the year 2000, 59 percent had been rated Exceeds and 4 percent Outstanding. Only 34 percent received a Meets rating and 3 percent a Needs Improvement or *Inadequate* rating. Doing something that would be viewed as tantamount to a major downgrading by two thousand managers would be a risky, but necessary, undertaking.

"Only My Mother Could Really Think I Was Exceptional" We wanted to make sure we were sending out the right message that would have a positive impact. We wanted managers to look upon an Effective rating as an A, not a C. In other words, you, the manager, set your targets. If you hit your targets, and you do so in a quality way, you get 100, an A. That's a Meets Expectations rating. If you exceed your targets by 10 percent, you would get an A+—an Exceeds Expectations rating. And if you beat your targets by even more, you would get an A++—an Outstanding rating.

"I think that deep down, most of us realized that we weren't *outstanding,*" Ned recalls. "We were working exceptionally hard, putting in long hours and a lot of effort, but the results weren't there. So, only my mother could really think I was exceptional. You can't think of yourself as exceptional if your business is in deep trouble."

So as we started on the turnaround journey to take Gillette back to its top-tier ranking in the consumer sector, we also started on our cultural transformation to make Gillette a performance-based company. Let me fast-forward, for a moment, so you can get a sense for how dramatic a change we were able to implement.

From 1999 to 2000, Gillette's sales growth was zero; profit growth was zero; and earnings per share were up 4 percent. Yet two-thirds of the managers (three thousand around the world) were rated Exceeds Expectations and Outstanding. Gillette's growth for 2004 versus 2003 was up 13 percent for sales; 23 percent for profit; and 25 percent for earnings per share. And the rating of the three thousand global managers reflected our new culture—nearly three-quarters (74 percent) received a Meets Expectations rating; 19 percent an Exceeds Expectations; 4 percent an Outstanding rating. The balance (3 percent) received a Needs Improvement rating.

Motivating Outstanding Performers In addition to creating a culture change, the recalibrated ratings also served as an added motivator for truly outstanding performers. Few things are more demotivating than receiving the same rating that two-thirds of the organization gets despite achieving walk-on-water results.

Few things are more demotivating than receiving the same rating that two-thirds of the organization gets despite achieving walk-on-water results.

An Outstanding rating in a performance-based culture carries the distinction and benefits that it should. As we had promised, rewards increased dramatically as the performance-driven culture took hold. Managers who needed an Outstanding rating to be able to get even a token bonus when Gillette was missing many of its targets and growing earnings per share by 4 percent were receiving awards that far exceeded their expectations at the start of the process.

And the satisfaction went well beyond financial rewards. As we had at Nabisco, we brought in the Gallup Organization to conduct an attitude survey of managers throughout the organization. I've used a number of different questionnaires and surveys over the years. Most of them, whether internally developed or supplied by an outside service, suffer from the same problem—they are far too long, detailed, and complex. It often takes a half hour or more to fill in, which limits the number of respondents who participate. The data that come from these behemoths tend to be just that—exhaustive sheets of data that are hard to interpret and even harder to act on.

The Gallup survey consists of just twelve questions that are answered on a 1 to 5 scale. Completion time is a few minutes, and the insights that Gallup provides are excellent. Gallup has a data bank of responses from hundreds of thousands of employees who have participated in these surveys over the years. Gallup has correlated results with the subsequent trajectories of the companies, both those that have succeeded and those that have flopped. So you have an excellent understanding not only of what the responses mean, but also of what they foretell for your organization's future performance.

TAKING ACTION TO CHANGE ATTITUDES

Not surprisingly, the results of our first Gallup attitude survey, which was given early in 2002, placed Gillette at the forty-fourth percentile of all companies that had participated in the survey in terms of employee engagement. The turnaround was starting, and so, too, was the elimination of unnecessary costs, which included eliminating the jobs of thousands of people who were filling positions that were not adding value. In other words, it was a time of transition, anxiety, uncertainty, and distress for those workers who had been or were about to be terminated.

The Gallup results were actionable, and we took actions all across the organization. We formed more than fifty teams throughout the company in our business units, commercial operations groups, and functional units to analyze the results, agree upon the top three priority issues, and then develop and implement action plans to address them. Our Gallup survey follow-through became a priority for every one of my direct reports. This was not an HR problem or program; this was a company-wide issue, and everyone was responsible and accountable for their portion of it.

The next year, when we decided to resurvey the organization, Gallup said their data showed that if we had been highly successful in our follow-through efforts, we would increase our ranking from the forty-fourth percentile to around the fiftieth percentile. With all that was going on at Gillette, we were concerned that we might fall short. Therefore, we were pleasantly surprised when the 2003 results showed a 34 percent increase, more than double the Gallup projection, which placed us at the fifty-ninth percentile. Employee engagement and satisfaction definitely were increasing.

GROWING MANAGERS TO FULLEST DIMENSIONS

Our efforts to develop our managers also were increasing. One of the most important responsibilities of a leader is to create the right environment and then give the employees development opportunities that enable them to realize their full potential. I like to use an analogy that I heard some years ago of the Japanese carp, known as the koi, to make the point.

One of the most important responsibilities of a leader is to create the right environment and then give the employees development opportunities that enable them to realize their full potential.

The fascinating thing about the koi is that if you keep it in a small fish bowl, it will grow to be only about two or three inches long. Place the koi in a larger tank or small pond and it will reach six to ten inches. Put it in a large pond, and it may get as long as a foot and a half. However, if you put it in a huge lake where it can really stretch out, it has the potential to reach sizes up to three feet.

People, like the koi, will grow to the dimensions of their boundaries. Fortunately, unlike koi, we have the advantage of helping our people select their boundaries. And it is the leader's job to set the kind of boundaries that allow people to reach their full potential.

Headhunters in Pursuit Over time, our people started to receive the attention of other companies and executive recruiters that I had said would accompany a successful turnaround. When we got into the third and fourth year of the turnaround, rarely did a week go by that one of our top managers wasn't approached by another company. Fortunately, we learned of most of these offers from people who turned them down. We had little involuntary turnover as we moved into our ascent back to the top.

Another indication of the attractiveness and quality of our managerial ranks is evident in what has happened in the aftermath of the merger with Procter & Gamble. I had thirteen direct reports who made up the Gillette Operating Committee. In the staff areas, our chief financial officer, Chuck Cramb, was named CFO of Avon cosmetics. Our chief information officer, Kathy Lane, became CIO at the U.S. operations of National Grid in the United Kingdom; Ned Guillet, our head of HR, remained in that position and was wooed by P&G to stay on; our head of planning and development, Peter Klein, has resumed his consulting practice; and my coauthor John Manfredi has his own consultancy in addition to his writing career. On the line side, three of our executives assumed top-level positions with P&G, which is viewed as a rarity in a company that traditionally has a strong promote-from-within policy: Bruce Cleverly, who headed our Oral-B Global Business Unit, headed the entire P&G oral care business, which includes Crest-brand toothpaste, mouthwash, and whiteners, as well as the Oral-B toothbrush business. Ed Shirley, who had headed Gillette's International Commercial Operations, became president of sales for P&G North America. That gave Ed responsibility for the most advanced and sophisticated selling organization in all of consumer products, which sells more than $34 billion of products annually. Joe Dooley, who had headed our Commercial Operations group for North America, was promoted to head the Duracell business. As I have mentioned, Mark Leckie became head of all the Gillette businesses; Mary Ann Pesce, who led our Personal Care BU, became president of New Business Development, Deodorants/Male Personal Care, and Personal Cleansing for P&G; Joe Scalzo, who had headed our supply-chain operations as well as serving as group head for Personal Care, was recruited to become president and CEO of WhiteWave Foods, the leading maker of soy and organic milk, based in Broomfield, Colorado; and Mike Cowhig moved up to assume Ed DeGraan's responsibilities as head of research, development, manufacturing, purchasing, the supply chain, and engineering. Peter Hoffman continued to run the all-important Blades & Razors BU until his retirement at the end of 2006.

If you drop down a level, the moves are similar. A number of senior managers either moved up within the Gillette business unit or P&G, or continued in their positions; another segment moved on to better positions with other companies; and some retired.

The results remind me of both Nabisco and Kraft. At Nabisco, the head of our two business units—Rick Lenny and Doug Conant—each became CEOs of major food companies. Rick went to Hershey and Doug to Campbell Soup. Beth Culligan, head of our international operations, became president of A&P (the Great Atlantic & Pacific Tea Company). Our CFO, Jim Healey, started a public accounting firm. Our number two finance executive, Bob Schiffner, went to Campbell as CFO along with Doug Conant. Dave West, our vice president of planning, went to Hershey as head of sales and later became CFO and then COO of the company under Rick Lenny. John Manfredi, Peter Klein, and Joe Schena came with me to Gillette. And at the midlevels, there also were many success stories.

Executives with Remarkable Upward Movement The upward movement of executives who have left Kraft is perhaps the most remarkable. Rick Lenny and Doug Conant should probably be double-counted, as graduating from both Nabisco and Kraft to become CEOs. And there are several others: Bob Eckert moved on to become CEO of Mattel; Alan Lacey went on to become CEO of Sears; Bob Morrison headed Quaker Oats and, following its acquisition, became vice chairman of PepsiCo; Dick Bailey became COO of Dean Foods; Luc Vandevelde became chairman of Marks & Spencer; Ann Fudge headed up Young & Rubicam; Irene Rosenfeld initially moved to run Frito-Lay for PepsiCo and then returned to become CEO of Kraft; and Dave Rickard is CFO for CVS, having also served as CFO of Diageo and RJR Nabisco after leaving Kraft. Both Betsy Holden and Roger Deromedi worked with me for years and years at Kraft; they became co-CEOs when I left. Roger then became sole CEO. Both are former CEOs at this writing, but my guess is not for long.

DEVELOPING MANAGEMENT BENCH STRENGTH

What's the reason for the depth of top-quality managers who reached such heights both within the companies and elsewhere? One effort to explain the phenomenon was done by Bain & Company, whose research noted that while other companies' development efforts are carefully controlled and isolated from the daily work of the organization, our efforts complemented our business model. They took place on the job and were important to the job.

At Kraft, as promising managers advance, they moved through a series of challenges that enabled them to learn the company's principles, processes, and values. The development process can be viewed as a "leadership corridor" that runs through the business.

Cost Reduction as Part of Strategic Process Early in development years, the manager gets bottom-line responsibility and learns the bedrock concept that cost reduction is not a one-off reactive program. It is an ongoing strategic process to free up cash and other resources that strengthen brands. In other words, cost cutting helps fuel brand building.

The development at this stage also focuses on providing exposure and understanding to the supply side of the business. It often involves dealings with commodity markets, manufacturing, and cash management. We saw in chapter 4 that Bob Eckert, Dave Rickard, and Roger Deromedi all had a "baptism of fire" in dealing with the National Cheese Exchange during some rough times for Kraft's cheese business.

This phase also underscores the importance of encouraging young managers to approach senior managers for direction and assistance, even if that means bypassing some levels within the bureaucracy. It's important that the full talents and experience of the organization participate in important decisions.

Learning the Advantages of "Loose-Tight Management"
The second part of the corridor training is characterized by "loose-tight management." In other words, you agree upon precise financial targets and objectives and demand their delivery. But you allow great flexibility and freedom in how managers execute to achieve their results. You encourage them to create strategies that will make possible reaching much higher goals in the future. In this phase, the young managers also learn about working within the matrix, especially how to gain support from those functions that must be influenced, but not controlled, through a direct-line reporting relationship.

Matrixed organizations can and should be powerful. However, they do present pitfalls. First, you have to be clear on responsibilities and accountabilities across the matrix. Otherwise, lots of important things will fall between the cracks, and lots of finger-pointing will follow. (At Gillette, we brought in the McKinsey consultants twice to work with our business units and commercial operations groups to clarify roles and responsibilities. The first effort produced agreement on the broad areas; the second effort went after unaddressed smaller, detailed areas.) Second, managers early in their careers must go through a learning curve on how to get the most from the matrix. Some never get it; they want to mandate everything. Others become true masters of the matrix. They learn how to enlist people and functions that have no direct reporting relationships to become part of their extended team. They are able to motivate people to act, even though they have no direct power over their compensation or career development.

Placing Company Interest Over Personal Gain The final portion of corridor development teaches the importance of placing the company ahead of individual self-interest. Organizational interests should always take precedence over the individual. The Bain research says that "leadership development at Kraft is not remotely like the kind of succession planning that hinges on identifying 'leadership personalities' and nurturing those charismatic individuals as they rise through the ranks. Self-promoters aren't encouraged to join the company in the first place, and no one in the company's recent history has been hand-picked to be the next anything. [Former Kraft CEO Mike] Miles calls it 'a lack of hubris. People at Kraft are confident, but they are not so sure of themselves that it builds self-centeredness.' The senior people at Kraft must do more than just meet their own targets; they must support each of the other team members and the overall corporate efforts."

The final portion of corridor development teaches the importance of placing the company ahead of individual self-interest.

While the genesis of the "corridor training" goes back to Mike Miles, its development continued throughout my years as head of Kraft USA and Kraft Worldwide, and I've applied the conceptual framework and many of the tactical elements at Nabisco and Gillette. Having the right development program in place helps assure that you will have the bench strength and depth necessary to handle succession throughout your organization, most importantly, at the top.

On-the-Job Development Training Some companies rely on what Bain calls "the carefully controlled hothouse training that is separate from the business operations" or a "series of topical courses" or "intensive study of case materials on organizational dilemmas." All the approaches have value. However, utilizing a development path that relies most heavily on on-the-job experiences has worked best for me. The difficulty with isolated courses that are separate from the business is the challenge the participant faces in attempting to integrate the learning into the day-to-day.

It doesn't do a lot of good to expose a few people to a special course or program, regardless of its merits, if the concepts and materials are foreign to the rest of the management group and organization. In my early days at General Foods, I can remember going to off-campus management-training programs that would have me incredibly excited and eager to get back to the shop to tell everyone about the great knowledge and insights I had learned. And I also recall the incredible deflation I felt when the only reaction back at the office was a quizzical look or a shrug. If one person attempts to introduce a concept that is new or foreign to a company, the likely reaction will be *That's interesting, but it's not the way we do things here.*

TRAINING PROGRAM TO SHAPE CULTURE

At Kraft, Nabisco, and Gillette, we had at least one training course that ultimately would be taken by all managers. The purpose of the program was to teach how to strategically analyze an issue. Called STAR—Strategic Thinking and Results—it provided a detailed, six-phase approach and a complete language that described each step. The program was taught by John Furcon of the Buck Company.

With all of our managers taking the program, we had a common system with a universal, uniform language that could be used throughout the company all around the world. We had the same starting point whenever we came together for a discussion and didn't have to spend a half hour defining terms or agreeing on a process. Training and development programs help shape the culture and attitudes of a business. However, the starting point for any such effort must go back even further. It must start with the people you bring in as members of your team.

But how do you select people who should be on your team of senior managers? What do you look for? What shuts someone out?

As Mike Miles said, we did not have "heir apparents" at Kraft. We did not have charismatic leader types who sped through the organization to a preordained position. And self-promoters were not well tolerated. If anything, the organization quickly coalesced against anyone with a "look-at-me" attitude.

NEVER HIRE JERKS

Mike also had one tenet that we all agreed upon. "There is one thing I look for that I can define. I look for somebody who might turn out to be a jerk. We had a rule at Kraft that we were *not* going to hire any self-centered jerks."

Mike believes that there are enough smart people in the world so "you could pass up the smart jerks and wait for a smart, nice person to come through the door. If you did that you would have a society or culture . . . where people enjoyed their cohorts, [and] where they looked forward to coming to work every day."

Warren Buffett has expressed a similar sentiment, especially when he is considering the possible acquisition of a company. Regardless of how strong the financials and business model look, Warren says he won't proceed with a deal unless he likes the people, respects them, and would enjoy working with them. Like Mike, Warren believes that life is too short to spend it working with people you really don't like.

I totally agree, and not only because a bad actor would be a personal turn-off. He or she also would do damage within the organization. And the higher the person rose, and the larger the circle of responsibility and influence, the greater and graver the damage would be.

Weeding Out Bad Actors One of the practices that I instituted at Kraft, and again at Nabisco and Gillette, was the use of 360-degree interviews for our top senior managers. We worked with Tom Sapporito, Nancy Picard, and their company, RHR International in Philadelphia, to conduct the interviews, evaluate the responses, and work with each of the managers. At both Nabisco and Gillette, there were a number of managers who should have been blocked at the door. They might have been able to meet their targets and knew how to manage up, but the feedback that came from peers, subordinates, and external contacts highlighted some real issues and problems. In some instances, one-on-one sessions with Tom, Nancy, or one of their associates could turn a situation around. In others, it confirmed that we had bad actors who had to go.

Often, these were self-absorbed people who wanted to run a fiefdom in which their word was unquestioned. They were self-promoters who had no interest in developing their people or working for corporate goals. Meeting individual targets and achieving personal self-fulfillment defined their efforts.

Self-promoters . . . had no interest in developing their people. . . . Meeting individual targets and achieving personal self-fulfillment defined their efforts.

Another of Mike's techniques for weeding out candidates was to try to talk the job seeker out of the job. "I would pose challenges in the starkest terms I could think up. If at the end of my horror stories, the candidates still wanted the job, and they still sounded confident about their ability to take it on and do it well, and if they had the credentials and so on, and if they weren't jerks, I was generally comfortable." Mike's track record on choosing the right people wasn't perfect, but it was superb. Better than anyone else I know.

CHOOSING THE TEAM

There are several things that I look for when choosing people for my team. Brains and the capacity for hard work are givens, which is not to say that they are always or even regularly present in a manager. But you must have a certain amount of intellectual wattage and a decent-sized battery to function at the higher levels of responsibility in a major corporation. If they are missing, there is no need for any further consideration. People who aren't highly intelligent and don't have a high energy level just cannot be serious contenders for top-level positions.

At the start of this book, we explored four attributes that I look for in those people I want to work with—intellectual integrity, enthusiasm, action orientation, and an understanding of business and people. Let's look now at some elements of those attributes through a slightly different prism and, in some instances, under different headings. The exploration will give an added dimension to this most important of all roles that a leader must address—selecting and developing people.

We'll look at five critical areas:

- Intellectual integrity
- Results
- The ability to make decisions
- Leadership
- The ability to think conceptually

Intellectual integrity is the ability to hold up a mirror to your organization and the willingness to view the reflection with total honesty. Importantly, you must have that willingness to confront reality all the time—every day of the week, every week of the month, every month of the quarter, every quarter of the year, year after year. Yet there is a strong tendency in some people and organizations to put off coming to grips with bad news. Make sure you are the opposite.

There is a strong tendency in some people and organizations to put off coming to grips with bad news.

Late one evening shortly after coming to Gillette, I stopped by the office of our planning head, Joe Schena, and told him the information I wanted him to gather for me. At the top of the list was a daily sales report so I could track day by day how sales were going versus plan and year-ago, and what was needed to make the target for the week, month, and quarter. Joe, who had been with me at Nabisco, knew exactly what I wanted and my preferred format. When I checked back with

Joe the next day, he gave me the unsettling news. There were no daily sales reports; there were no weekly sales reports; the best that could be done on a worldwide basis was monthly! The desire to confront reality had a much lower importance and sense of urgency at the old Gillette.

That failure to come to grips with reality can be a career-limiting flaw. I tend to cut people a lot of slack, especially when I am getting to know them. By and large, I did just that. But both Ned and Joe said that things got tense with a few of the people who were, to use Ned's term, "smoking their own exhaust."

Whenever someone came to a meeting and said, "We're wonderful; my business did these great things," they were in trouble. I am looking for someone who sees reality, not a self-promoter who wants you to believe they can do no wrong. If a leader comes in and all he or she wants to do is tell me about the good things they have done, I would think to myself, *You are so enamored with what you have achieved that you are not thinking about what else you have to do.* I'm looking for someone who will give me a full view: *We've accomplished these neat things; we have more work to do over here.*

I look for managers who know the real score and can be transparent about it. The only way you can build a trusting relationship is if someone will share their issues as well as their wins. If somebody knows that there is trouble ahead, they must share that knowledge. If the word on the street is that a competitor is about to launch a new product that will leave us one generation behind, I want to know firsthand, not read about it in a trade publication. As I said during my opening off-site with people reporting to me, I don't like surprises. I do everything that I can to earn people's respect. I want my people to reciprocate. Managers should never hide things or manipulate data.

I don't want managers to hide things or manipulate data.

One of the reasons I value Mark Leckie so highly is his transparency on issues. Mark might be enjoying great success in the United States, but right after his report on domestic operations, he would warn about impending competitive difficulties in Europe. Or a new product upgrade on its way in Brazil. He always had a long worry list that he shared fully with me and all members on his team.

The other aspect of integrity relates to the more popular usage of the word—honor, ethics, and good practice. They are givens for me. I believe in honesty and openness in financial reporting. I will not allow cutting corners, shading the truth, playing fast and loose with rules and regulations, or overlooking infractions by others. None of these can be practiced or tolerated. It's remarkable how much you can learn about someone's ethical beliefs if you listen carefully during the interview process. People who like to cut corners and shade the truth often can't resist crowing about it. They're not going to be on my team.

Looking for People Who Walk the Walk The second important trait is results. You can spot the people who know the importance of results, because of the results in their track records. To use the colloquial, they walk the walk and they deliver what they promise when they promised it. People like this, at heart, are simply great competitors. They hate to lose. They understand that the winner is the one who gets results first and fastest. So by definition they are much more comfortable being a doer than being a watcher.

The results-oriented person also focuses on solutions. Mike Miles likes to say that often a good strategy is nothing more than outstanding execution. "It's rare that you have some blinding strategic insight or some incredible piece of technological advancement that gives you a 'sustainable competitive advantage.' It comes from outexecuting the other guy." It comes from a results-oriented person who focuses on solutions. It comes from analyzing what works and why, so you can derive solid fact-based solutions.

I have definite opinions about almost everything, but always yield to the facts. At Gillette, Ed DeGraan says, the environment became "very driven by the facts. Many times in dealing with decisions about the value chain, where Jim had great experience, he would come into a meeting with a strong opinion. However, he would always defer to the set of facts in front of him. And when all was said and done, he also would acknowledge that we were better off not following his gut instinct."

I especially like battle-tested managers. People who have had an easy road through their career and never ran into a tough business situation can be unreliable and unpredictable. If you observe someone when they are going through a difficult business situation, you learn a lot. You know if they can keep their composure, think clearly, and deliver the facts, honestly and with transparency, regardless of how bad the news.

People who have had an easy road through their career and never ran into a tough business situation can be unreliable and unpredictable.

The third trait is the ability to make decisions. There are a couple of pieces to this one. First comes the process part of decision making, the ability to drill down quickly to find the facts that are important to the decision, the ability to look at things quantitatively, and the discipline to proceed in a systematic way, even if others are urging you to turn right or left, or maybe stop altogether. And there's one thing you can count on—there will always be those voices.

The second piece in decision making is risk. You have to be able to step up to the possibility that in spite of your best efforts, your decision may be wrong, and then go ahead and make it anyway.

Finally, the best people just have a feel for business. They do the analysis, but they don't lose touch with something inside that says, "I don't care what the numbers seem to say, something just isn't right here."

Call it street smarts, common sense, or wisdom. It is real, it is important, and it does matter.

Identifying What Leadership Is The fourth quality is leadership, which is like what jazz great Louis Armstrong said when someone asked him to define jazz: "If you gotta ask, you ain't never gonna know." So I won't try to wrap leadership up in some kind of neat definition.

But you can identify a leader by some telltale traits.

First, he or she sees a target, and then organizes people and resources to hit it. You have to be able to give dimension to a project and create excitement, just as President John F. Kennedy did when he said we would walk on the moon, or when Herb Kelleher, the legendary CEO of Southwest, created a highly profitable airline in an industry where bankruptcy was the norm by unswerving adherence to being "THE low-cost" carrier, or even as all the young founders of Internet companies did in convincing Wall Street that their fledgling companies were worth more than their well-established competitors, even though they had yet to turn a profit.

Another key aspect of leadership is the ability to communicate. For many people, it's a real weakness. In writing, in meetings, and in large presentations and small ones, communication skills are critical.

You must gain commitment and make people believers in your causes. There are few great things that can be accomplished alone. You need a team, and the team must want the prize as badly as you do.

Great Leaders Must Be Team Players The team aspect of leadership cannot be overstated. The team must be committed to the leader, but even more important, the leader must be committed to the team and to goals that go beyond your own self-interest. You must believe in and be committed to the corporate objectives, to organizational goals, and you must give them a top priority.

The team must be committed to the leader, but even more important, the leader must be committed to the team.

Most companies today are matrixed organizations and require leaders who will support one another regardless of the reporting relationships. Unless leaders help others achieve their goals and objectives, the company will never be successful, and obviously the leader's individual accomplishments will be meaningless.

Leadership requires maturity and self-confidence in order to deal with the criticism that accompanies it. Good leaders know how to listen to the criticism that is helpful, ignore the criticism that is not, and be able to tell the difference between the two.

Companies and People Fail When Static A good leader also recognizes that people, just like organizations, fail when they are static. When you have the "burning platform" of a company in trouble, a company deep in the Circle of Doom, you have something that everyone can rally around and the leader can use to accomplish the turnaround.

Attempting to sustain the momentum, avoiding the slide back into the Circle of Doom, is even more challenging. And that's why you must build and institutionalize an attitude of continuous dissatisfaction. The status quo never is good enough. The quest for something better must be constant. It is one of the tenets of Total Innovation. All my leaders must be committed to constructive dissatisfaction and continuous improvement.

Finally, I look for leaders who know how to delegate. They know how to divvy up the work, and they also know when to take action if it looks like things are heading south. They understand "loose-tight management"—the benefits of rigorous accountability and challenging financial goals along with the flexibility to grow and innovate in achieving those objectives.

Conceptual Thinkers Spend Their Lives Learning Trait number five is conceptual thinking. Conceptual thinkers are people who can put pieces together and turn those pieces into the right answers. There are people who can see both the forest and the trees. They are able to look at a problem and view it from all angles, turn it over and inside out, and then analyze and frame it in a way that allows them and their team to take the right course of action.

Skilled conceptual thinkers are dedicated to a lifetime of learning, so they are relatively easy to spot. They are the people who learn something from everything they do. They even learn more from what didn't work than from what did. And they load all that knowledge into their personal data banks in order to evolve their own principles of action. Those principles become the game plans they follow to get them through tough situations. It is one of the reasons that I like battle-tested managers.

Conceptual thinkers are people who can put pieces together and turn those pieces into the right answers.

These are the qualities I value and look for in anyone who will be part of the team. But I do not believe in mass firings in order to put new people in place. You have to see if and how people perform. Those who meet the performance hurdles probably will be kept, but they may not be in the right position.

TWO-THIRDS OF TOP ONE HUNDRED POSITIONS

Fast-forward about a year after I joined Gillette, and the managers in sixty-six of the top one hundred positions were either outside hires who were new to the company, or Gillette people who were new to their positions. And the split was roughly fifty-fifty for outside hires versus internal promotions.

Even though we had no wholesale eliminations, the net effect was a lot of change. We wanted to energize and cross-pollinate the Gillette culture with ideas, attitudes, and beliefs from other companies. So we recruited people who had worked at General Electric, Coca-Cola, Tropicana, Procter & Gamble, PepsiCo, and several others.

Gillette had been virtually a 100 percent promote-from-within company. Our new target for the first five years would be 60 percent internal promotions to 40 percent outside hires. Over time, we would move to a 70-30 mix, but I never wanted to revert to a total promote-from-within practice. Even Procter & Gamble, which had been the staunchest proponent of the all-internal-promotions approach, has moved away from it. As a result of their prior acquisitions of Clairol, Iams pet foods, Wella beauty products, and now Gillette, Procter & Gamble estimates that about 30 percent of their promotions will no longer be long-tenured P&G veterans. They will be "virtual outsiders," managers who come to P&G via new acquisitions.

That blend of outside thinking came together nicely with the internal Gillette encyclopedic knowledge of the core categories and values-driven commitment to highest product quality and continuous innovation. The inside-outside mix provided some constructive tension, a sense of continuous dissatisfaction. But it never resulted in polarization, fractionation, or a setting up of enemy camps. The total company values and our objective of becoming the world's best consumer products company cemented the group around a common purpose.

CHOOSING THE RIGHT PEOPLE DEFINES GREAT LEADERS

Putting together a team is part adherence to a set of traits and qualities that are time-proven to predict success and others that are sure to ultimately result in trouble. However, it also relies on gut instinct and chemistry. It is an extension of what Warren Buffett and Mike Miles have said. You want to work with people who you will enjoy working with, and that part of the process is art and personal, not scientific or book-learned. Making the right choices is ultimately a big part of what defines a great leader.

You want to work with people who you will enjoy working with, and that part of the process is art and personal, not scientific or book-learned.

CHOOSING YOUR TEAM

People are the make-or-break factor in business. With the right people, almost anything is possible. With the wrong team, failure awaits. So take your time, but move decisively in making people decisions.

- Identify the skills, capabilities, and attributes you need *in total* for your business. Be rigorous and specific in making your list since it will guide all your decisions. Different businesses require different skills.

- Decide what skills, capabilities, and attributes are needed for each key position. The best and brightest "square peg" will never be a star performer in a "round hole."

- Make sure the sum of the skills, capabilities, and attributes in your key positions cover *all* your important needs.

- Never hire a self-centered jerk—even a smart one. There are too many good smart people to settle for smug self-promoters.

- Performance matters: Give people a chance. If you're a new boss, see how existing people perform before making a decision.

- Intelligence and energy: Eliminate those who fall short in these areas; they are essential characteristics for any top manager.

- Action orientation: Choose people who confront reality and focus on solutions.

- Good decision-making skills: Select thinkers who are both quantitative and qualitative, and proceed systematically.

- Leadership skills: Look for someone who is a good communicator, motivator, and organizer and cares about team success as well as personal gain.

- Enthusiasm matters: Hire leaders who will be positive, uplifting, and decisive—especially in bad times when morale sags, the will to win wanes, and focus gets diffused.

CHAPTER 8

LEADERSHIP PROCESS MATTERS

How important is the actual process of leading and managing a company? Does it really matter? If you put together the right team of talented, motivated, energetic people, do you need to worry about anything else?

Let me answer those questions with a survey finding that shocked me. One of the biggest issues the Gallup Organization finds through attitude surveys conducted around the world is that companies with the lowest scores have legions of employees who don't even know their basic job responsibilities. In other words, they don't know why they come to work every day.

Good process fills that void. It not only lets people know the basics of the tasks and activities they're supposed to do, it also provides an understanding of how individual roles and responsibilities mesh with the broader objectives of a unit, division, and, ultimately, the entire company. So yes, it really does matter.

Great leadership is important, and individual leaders can make significant personal contributions to a company's overall performance. But without a well-defined, well-understood, and rigorously adhered to process for leading and managing a company, nothing can happen.

PROCESS IS CRITICAL TO PERFORMANCE

A company must function like the finely tuned engine of a racecar. It must not only have all of the right components—injectors, valves, pistons, and the like—but each element also must be properly connected with all the others, and the timing and movement of all components must be absolutely in sync. Even the slightest miss in timing will result in poor performance.

Racecar crews are obsessive about getting the just right connections, interactions, and timing of all the engine parts. In business, little time and less-than-adequate attention are focused on aligning all the elements of the business organization. All too often, the attention goes to the glamorous parts of running a business: hiring marquee-name executives to fill high-level positions; acquiring trendy businesses and brands; making headlines with promises of great things to come.

The efforts seem to flag when it comes to the disciplined work of establishing a process that provides an understanding, direction, and detailed timeline and action plan for getting the most out of all assets and all people in the organization.

Leaders tend to assume that the process should be left to the human resource specialists and consultants; they feel that CEOs and senior executives should devote themselves to strategic visions and the big picture. Nothing will get a company into trouble faster than a poorly conceived leadership process, or one that's observed more in the breach than in actuality. For example, most companies say they manage by objectives. But those objectives often are unquantified platitudes and aspirations, not measurable, actionable targets.

Most companies say all managers receive annual performance assessments; yet many managers complain about both the frequency and quality of appraisals. The reviews aren't timely and they are often vague and subjective. The employee's objective was to research and write a report on widgets. Since the supervisor never commented on it, the employee assumed he had satisfied the objective. Only at the performance review did the supervisor express dissatisfaction with the content, depth, and analysis contained in the report. Disconnects of this type are all too common.

My leadership process is founded on my fundamental business beliefs and philosophy and is an outgrowth of how I deal with people and how I want them to deal with me. My management philosophy rests on the concept of building Total Brand Value, the cornerstone of my business thinking for more than twenty years, which calls for continuously innovating to deliver customer value faster, better, and more completely than the competition. In other words, a company must have competitively advantaged products and cost structures.

Each Element Matters Building Total Brand Value is the vision; the way to achieve that vision is with a strategic plan for growth. Together the vision and strategic growth plan are the initial building blocks of the process.

The strategic plan then drives the annual operating plan, which in turn drives quarterly priorities. Performance, which is measured against the strategic and annual operating plans as well as quarterly priorities, provides the basis for rewards and recognition. In combination, they make up the process framework.

Each element is critical. Nothing is included because it

should be there, or *may* be useful in the future. At some companies, strategic plans are produced mainly to satisfy boards of directors: to assure them that management has a plan for the future. As a result, the strat plans tend to be prepared, presented, and then filed until the next board presentation, at which time the plan has to be revised drastically because none of the targets has been met.

Adding the A's to Strat Plans If strategic plans do not provide clear and explicit direction that help create a "one-company" understanding of how to reach the company's goal, they should not be undertaken. If managers are not held accountable for meeting strategic-plan milestones, then they are a waste of energy. Strategic plans must have the two A's attached to them; they must be *actionable,* and they must require individual *accountability.*

Those two A's make the strategic-planning process both more difficult and meaningful to everyone involved in it. When a manager knows that the size of his or her bonus is riding on how realistic and actionable each strategy and initiative in the plan is, it tends to greatly focus everyone's attention.

Strategic plans must have the two A's attached to them; they must be *actionable,* and they must require individual *accountability.*

My managers know how critical each element of the leadership process is to the performance of a business, but there is usually resistance to doing the work necessary to put the structure in place. Or rather, resistance to the timely implementation.

My initial days at Nabisco and Gillette were tough and intense. Both companies were hemorrhaging badly and required a lot of immediate emergency action just to stop the bleeding. In that type of environment, when all hands must be on deck and at battle stations, it is difficult for people to grasp the urgency about putting together a strategic three-year growth plan. Their reaction is, *how can you bail water from a listing boat, fire the cannons, and plot a course for the future all at once?*

With No Destination, Any Direction Will Do The resistance at Gillette was especially strong because the company had discontinued its corporate strategic planning some years before I arrived. Despite the huge size of its administrative staff, Gillette did not have a corporate planning department! Gillette's strategy pretty much followed the aphorism "If you have no destination, any direction will take you there."

However, our team pushed ahead with the process, and within nine months we had a strategic plan for Gillette that gave us the direction we needed to achieve our turnaround. Those were nine very busy months, and the strat plan was one of several important priorities. In addition to working on strategic direction, we also stopped most of Gillette's market-share losses; we started to rein in runaway costs and began to regain control of the business process. We also studied and analyzed each of the company's businesses in depth and assembled the new management team.

In introducing our new strategic plan to a group of the company's two hundred senior managers late in 2001, I noted the criticism of one well-regarded analyst who had said: "Confronted by insurmountable opportunities, great brands . . . great technologies and a great heritage, Gillette never manages to put it all together." The only way to silence that type of criticism, I said, is through solid, consistent performance. Our new strategic plan would provide us not just with a general direction, but also with specific actions that would be carefully planned and closely measured.

MARKET-SHARE SHIFT—FROM TWO-THIRDS DECLINING . . . TO TWO-THIRDS GROWING

While we won't go through each of the five strategies in our plan, I do want to give some texture so you can see that despite the three-year time horizon of the plan, each of the strategies came with several initiatives that provide specifics on how the strategy would be acted on.

Our first strategy was to build our core product categories—blades and razors, batteries, toothbrushes, personal-care products (mainly antiperspirants and shaving preparations), and electric shavers and small appliances.

As market leaders, we had to grow our own sales and sales of the entire category. Yet when I started, Gillette was losing market share in businesses that represented 64 percent of sales. The strategic plan's path to growth was to reverse that trend. We would maintain and grow share across more than 65 percent of our business in 2002 and beyond. By consistently growing market share in two-thirds of your business, you become a successful consumer products company.

There were specific initiatives to back this strategy.

First, we would continue to focus on the highly profitable premium segments in our categories, but we would no longer allow competitors to gobble up our market share in the mid-tier. In Blades & Razors, as noted, we had done a great job with our premium Mach3 and Venus systems. Now we would also focus on mid-tier shaving systems for developing markets and disposable razors in all geographies.

Duracell—No More Product Giveaways Second, we would improve "consumer defined price/value, especially in Duracell." There could be no doubt in the minds of Mark Leckie and Duracell's other new leaders that their future with Gillette was highly dependent on not a quick fix for the battery issues, but a root-cause cure that addressed the consumer's price/value perceptions about the Duracell brand. By the time the strategic plan was finalized, the Duracell team had already taken the message to heart, and a number of plans were coming into focus.

Duracell would relaunch the mid-tier Duracell Copper & Black battery under the CopperTop name with new advertising. The packaging would be redesigned to reinforce the CopperTop imagery. More facings would be added at retail through a reshelving of the entire Duracell line. Pricing would be lowered and simplified to address consumer resistance to the large price gap with competition. Importantly, the level of advertising support to rebuild Duracell's brand equity would be increased, while spending on product giveaways and other wild promotional activities would be virtually eliminated. This advertising increase was not limited to Duracell.

New Mantra: Build Equity . . . Not Overhead Our third initiative said we would *broadly* increase our advertising levels and improve the quality and effectiveness of our consumer and customer marketing investments. The need for increased ad spending was real. From 1995 to 2000, Gillette's funding of advertising as a percentage of sales went from 8.6 percent to 7.1 percent. In a $10 billion business, that was a decline of $150 million. The advertising investment was reduced in each of the core businesses. In Blades & Razors, it dropped 1.5 percentage points. The decline came despite the launch of the Mach3 shaving system, which normally would have been backed with higher levels of advertising. In batteries, it went from 4.4 percent of sales to 3.9 percent, and all advertising for Copper & Black was eliminated. In Oral Care, ad spending was cut by nearly one percentage point over the five years.

When it came to marketing discipline, Gillette had significant voids to fill. We conducted minimal tests on our advertising spending levels throughout the world and had little empirical modeling to help us find the optimal marketing mix for our spending. We needed to better understand the overall effectiveness of our marketing investment. We needed to know a lot more about how much marketing money we should spend. In short, we needed a rigorous process of gathering marketing intelligence to measure the effectiveness of our marketing spending, optimize our spending levels, and establish common evaluation methods.

The second plank in our strat plan dealt with the broad topic of reducing costs and driving the productivity of all assets without compromising quality. Once again, the initiatives that framed this strategy were very specific.

- Implement the Strategic Sourcing Initiative (SSI), which the strat plan estimated would yield savings over three years of $250 million through centralized purchasing that fully utilized Gillette's scale and the most up-to-date techniques, including electronic auctions.

- Rationalize SKUs, a process explained in chapter 5, which was mired in indecision and was costing Gillette untold amounts by adding both complexity and inefficiency to our supply chain.

- Focus capital investment on productivity to reduce product costs. While Gillette's overall rate of capital spending had climbed to an unsustainable level, not enough of the spending was invested in projects that would reduce the costs of producing our products. Far too much of it was being invested in what I liked to call the "Cadillac option." Whenever making a decision about which option to choose—whether for a new plant to manufacture products or additional capacity for an existing product—Gillette would never go with the low-cost "Chevrolet option"; it always had to be the top-of-the-line Cadillac option. This type of thinking derives from the fact that people were not being held properly accountable for the money they spent and returns they should get. Our specific initiative was to make sure that we allocated enough of our total capital-expenditure budget for productivity-improvement programs. As a rule of thumb in the consumer products sector, I like to devote 40 percent of my capex budget to productivity; 25 percent for maintenance; and 35 percent for new products or expanded manufacturing.

- Reduce key administrative functions to benchmark levels. This was a major initiative that would take years to implement fully since Gillette's staffing and costs were so far out of line with peers. The result of detailed benchmarking showed that some large functions, such as finance, were more than 40 percent higher than peers!

- Establish Zero Overhead Growth (ZOG) and Negative Overhead Growth (NOG) as operating principles versus benchmarks. Again, with Gillette's costs being so much higher than benchmarks and with the rate of growth in recent years tracking at 15 percent annually, putting a lid on increases was essential. We targeted zero as a minimum acceptable level, and I knew from past experience that we would get "negative growth"—a reduction—in many areas. Once you get started on a best-practice initiative, it takes on a life of its own. As Martha Stewart would say, "It's a good thing."

We targeted zero [overhead growth] as a minimum acceptable level, and I knew from past experience that we would get "negative growth"—a reduction—in many areas.

- Improve working capital. We will give details on this in chapter 10. For now, let's say that shining a bright light on practices that have become a part of the culture and fabric of a company can yield great results. And this area of improving working capital had one of the most dramatic transformations of all.

Competitive Imperative—Be Sure You Know Who's Gaining on You The first pass at a strategic plan is always tough, especially when, as with Gillette, so little from the past could be relied on and so much time had passed with no planning. The value of strategic planning is that it compels you to look both internally and externally. Internally, you must assess your strengths and weaknesses and identify your unique competitive advantages. Externally, you must look both for opportunities where new products or services could thrive and threats that could change the dynamics of your market or signal the likelihood of new competitive challenges.

However, when a three-year plan is put together, annual updates require much less time and far fewer resources. At Gillette, we asked each business unit to provide us with a list of strategic issues, which we would subsequently discuss. Only those issues that would markedly change the assumptions and likely outcomes of the initial strategic plan would call for significant revisions of it. Others would be worked into the annual operating plan.

QUARTERLY PRIORITIES: HIGH-WATER MARK FOR SPECIFICITY

The discussion of potential strategic issues also provided an opportunity for me to spend time with a number of people in the organization with whom I would not regularly have contact.

The next important components of my leadership process were the annual operating plan and quarterly priorities, which were so interconnected that they are best discussed together.

As with the strategic plan, my requirements for annual operating plans were more detailed than most CEOs', and I am told that my quarterly priorities set a high-water mark for specificity. Some could call this requirement for detail an effort to micromanage. I view it as just the opposite. You need enough specificity in terms of what is planned and what metrics will be used to assess performance so you can spend little time with those plans that are on track. On the other hand, you will have good and early warning about those plans that are headed in the wrong direction so you can do whatever it takes to straighten things out.

The other reason for full and detailed annual operating plans and quarterly priorities is to help assure complete alignment throughout the company. So many companies are so stingy with shared information that it requires the powers of a mind reader to know what's happening in other areas of the business. You should lean in the other direction. All senior executives should know what's happening throughout the entire company. That knowledge enables them to know what the direct expectations are of them and their group. It empowers them to make recommendations that could improve, revise, or even put a plan on hold. It sharpens their awareness of what's important to the company as a whole and gives them a new perspective on their own role as well as those of others in different functions and areas.

And trust me, sharing information with senior people does *not* dramatically increase the risk of confidential information leaking to competitors. Everyone knows they have a heightened level of responsibility to be certain that neither they nor their people leak anything. They also know that the consequences are harsh if any slipups occur.

ANNUAL PLANS—MULTIPLE BENEFITS

I view annual operating plans from many perspectives.

First, the entire process is a unifying one, since it involves input and participation from all corners of the company.

Second, it is the best indicator of an organization's overall excellence. A company's financial performance—the growth of its sales, earnings, and market shares; the introduction of successful new products; the management of its working capital and assets—all of these metrics and the many others that should be part of a good operating plan provide a real gauge of how good all elements are: its products, people, brands, practices, and systems.

Third, it is a great motivator and team builder. The targets set in an annual plan must be tough enough to be challenging and cause the organization to stretch and grow. But they must be achievable so that everyone is fully engaged in the effort and feels accountable. They must also heighten the awareness that unless the team wins, no individual can win.

Fourth, it reinforces the company's values by stressing the quality and manner in which targets are achieved, not just the end result. Any target can be met if a company and its people are willing to cut corners and bankrupt the future in order to score a short-term win.

Fifth, it is the basis for rewards and recognition. A good annual plan, along with the quarterly priorities that orchestrate it, lets everyone know exactly how they're performing and how well they will be rewarded. Individual annual-performance reviews are no longer a matter of surprise results that spring from a mysterious black box, or of a biased supervisor playing favorites. Everyone from the board of directors on down knows at the start of the year what the rules are for rewards for the entire year.

There are many other dimensions and values that derive from the annual plan, but the point is that the preparation of annual plans deserves a lot of time, and they deserve even more time and attention as you go through the year.

QUARTERLY OFF-SITE MEETINGS—LAY BAD NEWS ON THE TABLE . . . AND DISSECT IT

The time spent on assessing performance against the plan is one of the biggest differences of my approach to management. Every three months, I would get together with my direct reports—the twelve to fifteen people who make up the executive committee of the company, our Operating Committee at Gillette—for a two-to-three-day off-site meeting. The three-day meeting would almost always occur in the first week of the first quarter of the year; that's the time we would review and grade our performance against fourth-quarter priorities and annual objectives and also agree on annual objectives and first-quarter priorities for the upcoming year. Since each of the dozen or so managers presented individual priorities and objectives for fourth quarter, the current year, and first quarter plus the new year, the three days filled up quickly. In addition to the individual presentations, we also would—as a group—grade the company's performance for the last quarter and the year. And finally, each manager would rate the performance of each of the other managers on the team.

People soon learn that these are not show-and-tell sessions. Good news is welcome at the off-sites. But it is the bad news that has to be laid out on the table. It needs to be dissected and discussed. And out of those discussions come clear decisions about new objectives and next steps. It is not always comfortable to have failures discussed openly and candidly. But that's the only way to create solutions. Polite collegiality is good, except when it stands in the way of progress.

All of this represents a lot of time and effort, and some of the content is repetitive, which is the point. If there is *not* a lot of repetition and overlap on the objectives and priorities, the team and company lack proper alignment. When someone in manufacturing feels they know more than they want about the plans of someone in sales, that's success.

Thirty Years Together, but Still Not Cooperating The initial quarterly off-site meeting at Gillette underscored just how far we had to go before repetition and overlap would come into focus. While my senior managers at Gillette all had long tenure—twenty, twenty-five, and even thirty years with the company—and had known one another professionally and socially for much of their adult lives, the concepts of sharing and teamwork were totally foreign.

Business units that relied on commercial-operations sales units to sell their brands to trade customers and then provide the tactical marketing execution to reach consumers were reluctant to share detailed market analysis. Basic data—such as the market share for a particular Gillette brand—were the basis for heated discussions about which numbers were accurate. Timetables for the availability of new products were fuzzy and ill-defined. Long-standing requests from international markets for package changes or product alterations were ignored.

The walls around each of the units and functions were so high that only a crisis could penetrate them, and all too often, as the siege mentality at Gillette grew, not even a crisis would bring units together. At the first off-site, the regional manager from one of Gillette's important developing markets gave a long emotional tirade about the indifference of headquarter-based executives to foreign markets, and their ineptitude in that area. He said his only option was to ignore corporate mandates, develop his own plans and playbook, and operate as an independent business unit! Gillette was supposed to be one of the great global companies of the day, yet it was acting like a start-up outfit run by teenagers.

Agreeing on the Numbers The recollections about the initial off-site meeting by Ned Guillet, then our number two in our human resources department, tell a lot.

"Everyone on the Operating Committee had received a short note from Jim with instructions and templates about preparing annual objectives and quarterly priorities for the meeting.

"The first guy to get up was Peter Hoffman, president of the Blades & Razors Business Unit. He lays out his current market share for North American blades and razors business as he presents his annual objectives and quarterly priorities. As he starts talking about specific plans and activities for the quarter, Jim would say, 'OK, not bad, but I'd like it a little more measurable. Otherwise, how am I going to know how to score that?'

"Peter said Blades & Razors was developing world-class advertising. Jim then asked, 'What does world-class advertising look like? How will I know it's world class? What tests will you be using? What scores are you shooting for?'

"Jim was asking questions to make sure that what we were saying, we were going to do, and it could actually be measured in some way. It was all nice and polite, but it was hard not to get the drift."

No More Two Numbers "Next up was Joe Dooley, head of our North American Commercial Operations. Joe puts up his slide showing the North American market share for blades and razors. And Jim says, 'Wait, stop. A few minutes ago, Peter said market share for North America was going to be 71.1 percent for the quarter. I'm looking at your number saying it's going to be 69.9 percent. How come we have two numbers if it's the same geography? What's with the two numbers?' "

Ned said Joe Dooley gave a murky explanation that Commercial Operations looks at the market differently than the Blades & Razors BU. "So Jim says, 'From now on, we are going to have one number. You guys agree on what that number is and what data backs it up, but no more two numbers.' "

According to Ned, that was the start of everything. "The meeting was really a calibration and alignment meeting as Jim interacted with each of his direct reports. He did two things. First, he immediately spotted mismatches. 'If you are going to do that this quarter, how come I'm not seeing where the support is coming from? Why isn't it on the priorities of the people who have to support you? Obviously, your peers on this Operating Committee don't know you're about to do that. So, you've got to get aligned.' "

"If You Can't Measure It, It's Not Real" "Second thing was all about measurement. 'How will I measure your objective or priority? Ned, you are going to improve employee morale. How will I know if you do it? Do you have a survey? What's the metric? If the answer is nothing, then you don't have a good objective.' "

Ned concluded that the initial meeting was all about "doing really fundamental things." "Jim started to make the point about lack of alignment by showing obvious mismatches in our priorities that we never knew existed. He showed that there was no alignment; that we really had not consulted each other on objectives, and that this meeting was a great way to help us get aligned. And he also taught us the importance of measurements. Jim's bottom line was 'If you can't measure it, it's not real.' We got the message."

Ned was right. The initial off-site, and several that followed, were difficult. If ever a company needed leadership process and discipline, Gillette was *the* prime candidate. Yet there is no getting around the fact that good process with lengthy quarterly meetings takes a lot of time.

I devote a lot of time to it. Prior to each quarterly off-site meeting, I spend at least one to two hours with each of my direct reports. Several days prior to those meetings, the managers submit detailed written self-assessments with scores on how they performed. The meeting gives us the opportunity to agree or challenge specifics in the performance assessment and on a final score for the quarter—or, in the case of annual objectives, for the year.

OLD-FASHIONED RATING SYSTEM: BRINGING BACK REPORT CARDS

These are not perfunctory overviews or gentle pat-on-the back sessions. The amount of time allocated enables lengthy discussions and sometimes lively disputes. Adding to the overall dynamic is the grading system itself, which is as controversial as it is effective.

Conventional management grading systems just don't work. Whether it is an *Exceeds, Meets,* or *Does Not Meet,* or an *A, B, C, D,* or *F,* or a *1, 2, 3, 4,* or *5,* these measures do not grab at an emotional level. They seem too managerial and remote. But the simple substitution of a 1-to-100 scoring system gets everyone involved at a gut level. It is probably the association we all have with our school grades and our parents' reaction of approval, disapproval, or worse that makes the difference. But it does make a profound difference.

Conventional management grading systems just don't work . . . [They] do not grab at an emotional level. They seem too managerial and remote.

Time and again, I've had senior executives who are pulling down seven-figure comp packages fight frantically to keep from losing even a point or two. For some executives, any score under a 90 percent is a personal failure.

And for me, anyone who consistently scores in the low eighties probably isn't long for the team.

Any number of management gurus and organizational psychologists tell me that the scoring system is bad. It denigrates senior-level people by treating them like schoolchildren. It suggests a degree of precision in measuring results that just does not exist. It creates a paralysis of action for fear of low grades. And on it goes. Each of the observations may have a grain of truth. But they miss the point. Thirty years of actual experience demonstrates the grading system really works.

In fact, in addition to each person getting his or her own score, the entire management group sees everyone's score at our quarterly off-site meetings, and the entire company gets a numerical score for its quarterly performance. I should point out that individual manager scores are not identified by name; it is just Manager A, B, C, and so on. But based on the overall quarterly review process, it is not too hard to figure out who is at the top or bottom of the scoring index.

At the end of the year, each one of my direct reports also rates each of the other team members. This process provides yet another performance perspective for me to utilize. A manager may be hitting all of his targets in a quality way, yet if he isn't a team player, if she doesn't support the efforts of other managers, these ratings make that obvious, and he or she may not belong on the team.

Stars Must Also Be Team Players You need individual stars; sometimes you will tolerate them, even if they do not score high on the team component. But you always keep a close eye on them to make sure their net contribution is more positive than negative.

For example, some people always deliver their numbers. You like having them on your team because you can count on them. Regardless of what the competition does, or how much the economic environment deteriorates, they know how to make adjustments and get things done. But in the process, they sometimes run roughshod over their people, making them work all hours under great pressure and anxiety for extended periods of time. In those situations, you must intervene.

The other advantage of the peer rating process is that it encourages managers to get to know all of the units and functions, even those that they do not work with regularly or with which they have only occasional contacts. If you are going to sign your name to an assessment that has the potential to influence someone's future, you take the responsibility seriously. So you often get some good feedback about different functions and units as a result of the homework that precedes the rating event.

WEEKLY STAFF MEETINGS—REAL-TIME INFORMATION

The quarterly off-site meetings provide the necessary periodic check to assure progress and alignment. Weekly postings and weekly staff meetings provide ongoing, real-time information. Every week, each of my direct reports would provide a detailed report that highlighted key business and market data including market shares, sales and profit from operations, variances and analysis, updated data on whatever metrics related to the business unit or function unit, customer issues, competitive intelligence—in short, all the information the manager felt was important in order to understand what he or she was doing, whether plans were on track, and, if they weren't, what was being done to fix them.

As with the quarterly priorities and annual objectives, these weekly postings were shared among all of the direct reports. They were distributed every Friday so everyone would have the weekend to read them and be prepared for my weekly staff meetings, which were held every Monday. Getting through all of the reports with their attachments and appendixes took at least an hour; the time needed to study and analyze the implications would vary, but often could be even longer.

Attendance at the weekly meetings was mandatory, with no substitutions without prior approval and a good reason. We kept them short—two hours or so.

Suggested agenda items were due on the Wednesday before the meeting, along with the time needed and the desired decision or action. The agenda was reviewed and issued by me the next day.

Strict Rules; No Side Conversations Allowed And there were ground rules: strict confidentiality, full participation, total candor, and focus on the meeting. No side conversations were permitted, and I would bring the meeting to a halt if anyone slipped into a prolonged discussion with the person in the next seat. Detailed preparation was expected for the reports that were made by each of the business units, the domestic and international commercial-operations groups, the manufacturing and distribution unit, and the large functional areas such as finance, IT, and human resources. In addition, there was a once-around-the-table process in which everyone got three minutes to discuss issues of general interest to the group. The tight time limit curtailed potential grandstanding.

The detailed preparation required for the weekly reports and staff meetings helped instill a discipline throughout the organization. It required everyone to stay close to their businesses; analyze and understand all variances and misses; and be ready to answer detailed questions about any part of the operation.

It even made Mary Ann Pesce, who was one of the most energetic and creative managers I've encountered, feel that she needed to go all out just to keep pace. Mary Ann, who led our Personal Care BU and became president of New Business Development, Deodorants/Male Personal Care, and Personal Cleansing for P&G, had been with the company for about twenty years. Most of her time had been spent in brand management and development positions with the personal-care business. However, her biggest successes came when she shifted to the Blades & Razors Business Unit. Peter Hoffman, president of the BU, who had hired Mary Ann, put her in charge of development of what was to become the biggest new-product success in Gillette's history—the Mach3 shaving system.

Mary Ann then took on an area that had never before received dedicated resources—the development of new shaving systems for women. In the past, Gillette would extend its latest men's innovation to women by changing the colors, packaging and designating the item a women's product. So the Sensor shaving system became Sensor for Women and Sensor Excel became Sensor Excel for Women. The betting at the time was that while Mary Ann might make a few additional tweaks, she ultimately would launch Mach3 for Women.

Were they ever wrong. Mary Ann and her team utilized the Mach3's advanced three-bladed technology, but surrounded it with more than a dozen attributes and features specifically designed for female shavers—an oval-shaped cartridge for the curved areas on women's bodies, a special ergonomic handle for easy use in the shower, and many others. The result was the Venus for Women shaving system, the most successful new system ever for women.

I then added to Mary Ann's list of "first-evers in the history of Gillette" by making her the first woman ever to become president of an operating business unit—our Personal Care BU. And with that well-deserved recognition, Mary Ann joined our Operating Committee and started participating in all our off-sites and weekly staff meetings, and also began preparing weekly reports.

As she recalls, "The weekly reports begin the week before, say, Wednesday or Thursday, when you ask your whole team—in effect, your entire business unit—for all the current financial information and updates on all their projects. Then you put together three-to-six-pages worth of data on your business—shipments, sales, profits, and market shares. You have to say what happened, why, and what you are going to do about it. Then you report on other things you're doing: We're working on this; we're working on that."

Running Hard Just to Keep Up In Mary Ann's words, "People begin collecting data early in the week. Each team in the business unit must complete it by Wednesday so the finance team can write this stuff up and give the BU president a draft by Thursday. Then the BU presidents spend a good deal of time reworking and finalizing their reports, before sending them to Jim Kilt's office electronically prior to noon on Friday."

The reports were read over the weekend, which meant that either Friday afternoon or Monday morning, Mary Ann and the other BU presidents would prepare, and rehearse, for a fifteen-minute presentation at the Monday staff meeting.

As Mary Ann explains, "It is a lot of work. For a fifteen-minute presentation, you don't get up and filibuster. You have to keep things on point and crisp. So think about it. You start on Wednesday and your group and you devote parts of Thursday, Friday, and Monday. Monday at three p.m. you are done. That means that you have part of Monday, Tuesday, and some time on Wednesday before it starts all over again."

Using the Process at Campbell Soup Process is never a substitute for excellence of actions. But it is such an important element of success that many of the best people who have worked with me consider it one of the most important things they took away from the time we spent together. For example, Doug Conant, the CEO who has turned around the Campbell Soup Company, worked for me twice—once as my top planning person at Kraft; the second time as president of the Nabisco Foods group, comprising all of the noncookie and cracker snack foods, which included such great brands as Planter's nuts and Life Savers confections, and notable condiments like Grey Poupon mustard and A.1. Steak Sauce. Doug is not only a superb executive and manager; he is also a student of management.

Process is never a substitute for excellence of actions. But it is . . . an important element of success.

"You have to introduce discipline and take control of the rhythm of the management of the business. I did that when I went to Campbell Soup as CEO. Weekly postings go every Friday to the CEO and all his direct reports. Every Monday, the staff meeting sets the agenda for the week and assures alignment—you can ask any question you want. On top of that, there are quarterly priorities and annual objectives, which all create a goal-oriented culture. You need a very structured and efficient environment—weekly postings, read them; weekly staff meetings, discuss progress versus quarterly priorities; once a quarter, make sure you are on track to meet your annual objectives. There's just no question about what's expected of you. None. Then, once you establish the process, you get into the content and start questioning what's being done, why, and how."

Dave Rickard, now CFO of CVS, is another executive whom I've had the good fortune to work with twice—first, when I headed Kraft USA; next, when he was CFO of RJR Nabisco and helped recruit me to become CEO of the Nabisco part of the food-tobacco combine. Dave is one of the hardest-driving executives I have ever worked with.

You Don't Want to Look Like a Wimp Dave believes that good process does two things—creates alignment and fosters accountability. Quarterly off-site meetings require you to present your plans for the next quarter in front of your peers. "You don't want to hear one guy saying I can get this advertising copy developed by *November* and another saying we'll break this advertising with a big splash in *September*. Things have to be coordinated and aligned."

You also don't want people shirking responsibility: "It's tough for someone to get up in front of your peers and say, 'Please understand, boss, things came up that really made my job too tough.' You don't want to look like a wimp."

Dave especially likes the fact that "the grading system is public, dispassionate, and linked to reality. Nobody can really object when the boss says, 'You know, Bill, you didn't do that piece, which was twenty percent of your total, so you get an eighty.' "

The approach gives great clarity: "At the end of the day, your rating determines your bonus. So the four quarters added together tell you exactly what you are going to do on bonus day.

"The grading system is public, dispassionate, and linked to reality. Nobody can really object."

"The quarterly process takes time. It takes eight to ten days a year, plus ten days of prep time. But it's a way to make sure that everybody is rowing in the same direction, so it's a worthwhile investment. Those eighteen-plus days tell a lot about what progress is being made. You can see what is being done collectively. You watch what people are doing individually, how they execute, how they perform in front of others, and so forth. It helps keep a good tally of that so you have a good sense at the end of the day of what everybody on his team has done, what is their motivation, and what their energy and enthusiasm are at any point in time."

Uncompromising, Disciplined, and Logical "All this input and involvement makes it possible to be dispassionate and uncompromising. Jim's message to his group is 'Do we all agree on our annual objectives and overall goal? Does anyone disagree? Does anyone think that that is too much to reach for? No, OK, then that is it. Now we are all going to get it done. We all know our pieces. I will see you at the first-quarter meeting to see what you have gotten done and what you are going to do in the next quarter.' Everything is uncompromising, very disciplined, very logical, and a very effective management approach. If it is used dispassionately, if it is not compromised, it is a recipe for success as a general manager."

WAITING FOR THE HEADHUNTERS TO CALL

While not everyone I worked with fully bought into the total process, the number of converts and believers was high. At Gillette, each of my direct reports adopted the same process with their groups—from strat plans all the way down through quarterly off-site meetings and weekly staff meetings. Not too many companies have law departments, public-relations groups, and human resources organizations with fully orchestrated strategic plans. But Gillette did, and it enhanced the quality of each function and increased the value and attractiveness of the people in them.

When I started at Gillette, I told the senior leaders of the company that one of the barometers of success would be that each of them would wind up being badgered by executive search firms, desperately trying to recruit them away to other companies. The other part of the success factor would be their refusal to move because Gillette was such an exhilarating company to work for, and that each day at work was a constant learning experience.

We never did a comprehensive survey of how many managers were approached, but based on literally hundreds of anecdotal reports, we accomplished that mission. Discipline, hard work, and an effective leadership process really do matter.

PROCESS SETS THE PACE OF PRODUCTIVITY

Each company has a culture as well as a rhythm and tempo that define it. Importantly, the leadership process influences both the culture and rhythm of a company.

- Weekly meetings and reports require full engagement, attention to detail, and a rapid pace in order to stay current.
- Quarterly priorities with quarterly off-site meetings mean that performance must be measured daily to assure that plans are on track . . . and stay on track. Even small deviations can significantly affect achieving quarterly targets.
- Annual objectives and performance assessments close the loop for the year and set the stage to achieve the three-year cycle—the strategic growth plan. So concern with the short term must be balanced against achieving long-term goals.
- The corporate vision of being faster, better, and satisfying customers more completely provides the overarching framework that guides all actions.
- Acclimation to each element in the process affects both the individual's attitudes and the overall business output.

I firmly believe that the leadership process sets the pace of productivity.

CHAPTER 9

THE FIRST DAY MATTERS

What are the two most important times to assure success in your new assignment or position? In chapter 3, we discussed how the time spent prior to start-up can give you the unbiased understanding of the challenges and opportunities ahead. In this chapter, we'll talk about day one—that's right, your very first day on the job—and why it can set a course and give you the momentum necessary to make a real difference in your new position.

Your first day of a new job should be like the first hours of the D-Day landing by the Allies during World War II. It should be that intense and that filled with action. It should be the payoff for weeks of thought, assessment, analysis, and planning. And the good news is that the action takes place with your allies—people who will be key members of your management team, plus as many people as you can reach throughout the entire organization.

By the end of day one, you should feel like a presidential candidate who has just completed a cross-country, twenty-city campaign tour. And even if, by the end of the day, your key constituents aren't ready to embrace you fully as their new leader, they should be predisposed to accept you and believe you definitely deserve a chance to prove yourself.

DAY ONE MESSAGE—NO SUGARCOATING

My first day at Gillette started with an early morning breakfast in the Gillette employee cafeteria at the Boston headquarters and finished at dinner with Ed DeGraan, who had served as acting CEO and would skillfully oversee the manufacturing, engineering, and technical operations throughout our turnaround. However, before I even entered the building, every employee who had access to a computer in the United States and around the world received an introductory message from me that was specific about my plans and expectations. There was no attempt to sugarcoat or pretend that all was well with Gillette. It wasn't, and everyone knew it. The former CEO had been dismissed, and I was recruited from outside the company.

My message stressed that few companies have "more powerful global brands than Gillette" and even fewer had its incredible track record of new-product innovation. But I also said that the company's performance during the two preceding years had "disappointed the entire organization as much as it has our shareholders." Gillette's investors were looking for a company that outperforms peers, and I wanted "consistently superior performance . . . from everyone in the company."

I then talked about the importance of building Total Brand Value and said that I was committed to "setting a well thought out, long-term vision and growth management plan" for the company and then would adhere rigorously to it. "I am also obsessive about executional excellence—about doing the everyday things—the essential blocking and tackling—better than anyone else."

I concluded on a note of confidence and understanding: "You have been through a lot in recent years, and . . . we'll face new challenges . . . [but] I am confident we will succeed and have a bright future."

Twenty Questions with No-Punches-Pulled Answers My day one message was far from a onetime event. Within a week, everyone in the organization received a twenty-seven-hundred-word communiqué, consisting of both a message and a self-interview with twenty questions and answers. Again, my message was straightforward: There are "several issues standing in the way of Gillette reaching its full potential." I would be be assessing and addressing them along with my management team and specific plans would be be forthcoming. In the meantime, "I would like to share with you, in an easily accessible interview format, some of my initial observations, as well as my beliefs about the business and a few of my actual career experiences."

My coauthor John Manfredi and I worked hard on identifying those questions that we felt would be top-of-mind with many in the Gillette organization. And we worked even harder on the responses, which we wanted to be consistent with the total communications program that was planned for the first one hundred days and beyond.

Will People Be Fired? We tried not to duck any tough issues. One of the first questions was "New CEOs often replace existing management teams with outside executives. Are you considering this at Gillette?" My response was honest and comforting, I believe, for most of the people: "My track record throughout my career shows that I give employees a chance to demonstrate they can produce results. So changing the Gillette management team is certainly not my objective—getting results and top performance is."

Several newspaper reports alleged that I went to Nabisco with the specific intention of selling it to Philip Morris (now Altria) so it would become part of Kraft. I said: "Let me set the record straight. Nabisco was sold at a premium price to Philip Morris as an alternative to selling it at a cheap price to corporate raider Carl Icahn. I joined Nabisco with the intent to grow it for the long term. External events made that strategy impossible to pursue."

Since I was virtually unknown within Gillette, there was a lot of concern about my management philosophy and style. On management philosophy, I said that in broad terms it was to "*keep things simple.* I want rigorous analysis and thoughtful assessments, but don't want complexity. If strategies and plans aren't easily understood by everyone, they will be acted on by no one. So by keeping things simple, we will be able to act decisively and communicate clearly throughout the entire organization."

On management style, I said that you might call mine "sort of 'management by walking around'. I like to see what's going on in the organization, and I tend to spend a lot of time in the field."

What You See Is What You Get On the need to achieve excellence consistently and also avoid excessive cost, I noted that "you have to manage carefully . . . I believe there is no conflict between low cost and high quality if you get your business systems right and your productivity is high." Eliminating unnecessary costs allows you to "invest in new products and improve marketing. There can never be a compromise on the ultimate product quality, and there needn't be a conflict between quality and cost."

And there was a final question: What might be the most

I believe there is no conflict between low cost and high quality if you get your business systems right and your productivity is high.

important idea you'd like the employees to understand about you? To which I said: "With me, what you see is what you get. And what you get is a genuine belief in building Total Brand Value . . . I've said it everywhere I've been and I really believe it. Our role is simply to build Total Brand Value. That is what we are all about, and everyone at Gillette has a vital part in it."

DAY ONE MEETING—THREE HOURS, NOT THREE MINUTES

My day consisted of more than a dozen meetings with a range of people. But the most important session, and the one that occupied three full hours, was a meeting with all of my direct reports—the twelve members of the Operating Committee, the senior managers who ran the company.

While the time spent in the meeting may seem less relevant than the content, I think they have a shared importance. Most people expect little more than a brief meet and greet on day one. "I'm Jim Kilts. I'm looking forward to getting to know you. As soon as I get settled in, I'll arrange to get together so we can review your business and discuss any issues you may have."

A very different message is communicated when the new boss calls everyone together, dispenses with the meet and greet in three minutes, and spends the balance of three hours going through a detailed agenda of business issues, management process, and personal expectations. This approach tells the group that you're a person of action. You have a sense of urgency and will be engaged and involved. Those elements are essential if you want to get your group's attention and get them on board to implement major change.

While the Gillette meeting that I'll describe dealt with senior-level managers, I have used a similar approach throughout my career in a number of functions, including production, procurement, supply chain, marketing, product development, and general management, both domestically, internationally, and ultimately as CEO of global enterprises. The elements and structure of these meetings have wide application.

This approach tells the group that you're a person of action. You have a sense of urgency and will be engaged and involved.

The Real Deal—A Complete List of Horrors I started my Gillette presentation by reviewing the conclusions distilled from my weeks of research, discussions, and trade contacts. I told the team that the Gillette board of directors would be given the same presentation at a meeting scheduled for the following week. Thus, everyone would know they would be hearing the real deal, not something specially crafted for this initial meeting.

I started by talking about Gillette's formidable strengths—icon brands, high growth, high-margin product categories, unmatched technology and product innovation, and a great global presence. The group nodded its assent. As I went through the weaknesses—flat sales and earnings, consistently missed profit targets, declining market shares, decreasing ad spending, increasing overheads, soaring capital expenditures, and across-the-board weak financial metrics—I could sense both unease and defensiveness.

Always Confront Reality Throughout the discussion with the group, my message was that we would confront reality. There would be no more top-down dictums, no more setting of targets that couldn't be made or making of promises that couldn't be kept. Outstanding performance would be expected from everyone, but we would be working against reality-based, achievable objectives.

I expected outstanding performance from everyone, but we would be working against reality-based, achievable objectives.

We would cut no corners; integrity mattered big time, across the board—morally, ethically, and legally. In all, this day one session gave my new senior management team a total immersion in my views on managing, business, and people. Let me go over some of the areas covered.

MY STYLE

- Open; straightforward; what you see is what you get. I play no games and have no hidden agendas. I say what I mean; there is nothing to read between the lines.

- Action oriented—fair, but somewhat impatient. I value action and accomplishment; I dislike rationalizations and excuses.

- Want no surprises. If the sky is falling, tell me. I don't want to learn about it by reading a newspaper.

NO GOTCHAS, GAMES, OR TRICKS

- Will avoid "gotchas." No games; no tricks. I judge people based on performance.

- If something bothers you, I want open dialogue. I am not a mind reader. Let me know if you think something is wrong.

- Expect excellence, reward the same. I am demanding, but I reward excellent performance—probably at a level that will surprise you.

- Like and accept challenges. I spent my life building brands and running consumer businesses. My greatest satisfaction comes from dealing with tough issues.

- Save a tree. Avoid memos, if you can. When you can't, keep them short.

- Ask my advice early. I've had more than twenty-five years of experience. Give me a chance, and I probably can help you.

OFTEN WRONG, NEVER UNCERTAIN

- Often wrong, never uncertain. I never equivocate. I make quick decisions. So when I'm wrong, let me know . . . quickly.

MY MANAGEMENT PHILOSOPHY

- It's all about building Total Brand Value.

- Superior marketing driven by consumer and customer understanding.

- Competitively advantaged products and cost structures.

- Believe cost and quality are compatible. I want lowest costs, but insist on no compromise of quality.

- Strongly believe in keeping things simple:
    - Organization structures
    - Communications
    - Process
    - Priorities

- Clear and full accountabilities. Believe in matrixed organization. Organizational matrices facilitate performance, but individual responsibility is essential, which means that one person must be accountable for ultimate results.

NEVER OVERPROMISE; ALWAYS OVERDELIVER

- A promise made is a promise kept. Never overpromise; always overdeliver. I've lived by these words throughout my entire career.

- Believe in alignment and linkage—operating managers working together with strong staff input make the best decisions. The eight to ten days spent at quarterly off-site meetings, plus weekly staff meetings, plus weekly reports, are all designed to reinforce and assure linkage and alignment.

- My key function is to set direction; allocate resources; and provide support. Your key responsibility is to get the results agreed upon in objectives and priorities. I want it clear that my managers have a lot of autonomy to act and complete accountability to achieve.

LEVEL THE SILOS, INCREASE THE SHARING

- The more communications, cooperation, and support, the further and faster we will go. If sharing is increased, silos leveled, and alignment improved, great results will follow.

- Innovation must be applied in all aspects of business; innovation must define how we think and act. (I will expand on the concept of Total Innovation in chapter 12.)

GOOD IDEAS ARE EASY TO COME BY

- Good ideas, well executed, make the difference. The two elements must come together in order to be meaningful. Good ideas are easy to come by; they're meaningless unless they are well executed.

- Finally, although not really part of my management philosophy, I feel so strongly about it that I include it: I hate anyone saying, "Jim said" or "Jim wants," or "the board said" or "the board wants," as the reason for doing, or not doing, something. Things are done, or not done, based on rigorous assessments and considered deliberations. I have experienced firsthand how disruptive and demoralizing top-down dictums can be, especially when no explanation accompanies them.

MY EXPECTATIONS OF YOU

- Outstanding performance. Promises must be kept: we make our numbers; we do what we say we will do. This is another precept that underscores the need for excellence and accountability.

- Support decisions once made; contribute before decisions are made. Nothing is worse than someone who sits silently during a decision-making process and then, after the fact, seeks to undercut the action. I don't tolerate efforts that subvert.

- Help one another work out problems. Sometimes it's pride, or fear of losing authority and standing, but peers are often reluctant to seek help from one another, even though they all are part of the same team. I do everything I can to break down that attitude.

UNTANGLING TOUGH ISSUES—THINK BACK TO PARENTS AND TEACHERS

- Integrity—moral, ethical, legal. Integrity is the starting point for all business decisions. I always say that you can resolve the most difficult and entangled issue if you just "do the right thing." Always be guided by the law. But also think back to what your parents, teachers, minister, priest, or rabbi told you. Do what's right and you'll never go wrong.

- Be leaders of your business, your function, and your people. Upgrade your organization continuously. Since I want Gillette to be the best consumer products company in the world, I need a team of top performers—leaders who will be the best at running their business unit or function and in managing and developing their people. Continuous dissatisfaction must characterize the leader, which results in continuous improvement and upgrading throughout his or her operation.

NO ROOM FOR LEAKERS

- Appropriate confidentiality—both internally and externally. Gillette was one of the most porous companies I had ever encountered. I was not used to leaks, which often signal low morale and a disenchanted workforce. While I intended to work on the root causes, I wanted everyone to know that "leakers" would not be tolerated.

- Don't want competition among functions, or the senior staff. Anything that even hints at it is counterproductive. If the top people in the company are sniping at one another, or appear to be, the impact is corrosive throughout.

DON'T MAKE SMART MISTAKES TWICE

- My policy on mistakes:
  - You . . . don't make dumb mistakes.
  - I . . . don't punish smart mistakes.
  - You . . . don't make smart mistakes twice.
  - An omission mistake is just as bad, or worse, than a commission mistake.

  I do not want a risk-averse organization. But I also won't tolerate slipshod preparation and thinking that lead to failures. When the right process and thinking do not succeed, that's fine, but learn from failure. Whatever you do, never say, "I'm not to blame because I didn't know that x, y, or z would happen." You should have known, believe me.

- Appropriate discipline and fact-based analytics must be used in assessing businesses, infrastructures, and growth opportunities. The more facts that you have and the better analysis that you can do, the more likely you'll make the right decision.

GREAT FREEDOM, BUT NOT AUTONOMY

- You should involve me in major strategic and operational decisions. I give my managers great freedom to act, but not complete autonomy. I must be fully consulted and engaged in all major decisions.

- I need enough information and insights, not just data, so I can understand what's happening and why. (One of my first actions at Gillette was to discontinue a series of monthly reports that resulted in several thick binders of data that provided no real insight or understanding about what was happening in the business, or why.) Quality, not quantity matters.

WEEKLY STAFF MEETINGS

- Why weekly meetings?
  - Want firsthand update on the business
  - Business conditions warrant it
  - Helps assure alignment
  - Share what's going on so you can do your job and gain full executive communication

RESISTANCE PRECEDES EXPERIENCE

Resistance to weekly staff meetings almost always precedes experiencing them. Concerns about the time spent is always overcome by the understanding and insight received about other parts of the business, and also about the impact on the individual's own unit.

- Attendance required; on time; no substitution without my prior approval. I want the point understood that I take the weekly meetings seriously, and so should everyone else.

- Weekly, Monday, 10 a.m. to noon; can be extended, as needed.

- Agenda
  - Suggest items and request time needed to CFO by Wednesday preceding meeting; indicate if significant action/decision desired at meeting.
  - Agenda reviewed by me and issued by Thursday.

  Weekly staff meetings provide an opportunity for full executive team review and decision on an issue in a timely fashion; no waiting for monthly or quarterly session.

- Confidentiality
    - No gossip
    - Reinforce with your assistants and others

By underscoring the importance of confidentiality, we had virtually no issues. In fact, a group of about a half-dozen top senior executives managed to keep Gillette's merger talks with Procter & Gamble confidential for several months, a remarkable achievement.

ALWAYS CONSENSUS, OFTEN UNANIMOUS

- Decision process
    - Consensus—all views heard
    - Final decisions by me, as needed

In my five years at Gillette, we always reached consensus on key decisions—often with unanimity. There was no time that I recall having to override a decision made by the team.

- Behavior
    - Pay attention: no sidebar conversations or secondary tasks; really listen
    - Stick to subject
    - Openness
    - Prework: preparation when needed
    - Jokes, fun are OK

Discipline, focus, and engagement are things I expect from all people at all times, and weekly staff meetings are no exception. However, I realize that fun, jokes, and humor are often the best way to create bonds and bring the group together.

MINIMIZING GRANDSTANDING

- Once-around-the-table process
  - Limited to three minutes each
  - Items requiring more time to be on agenda

I like to give everyone an opportunity to be heard; the three-minute limit keeps things focused and keeps anyone from grandstanding.

OTHER HOUSEKEEPING

- One-on-ones; your call. Since I "manage by walking around," I drop in on my direct reports, and many others, plus have lots of telephone conversations. However, I do not have regularly scheduled one-on-ones with my direct reports other than our quarterly review of priorities. If anyone feels the need, I welcome them.

- Only your administrative assistant sets meetings with me through my administrative assistant. A process for scheduling meetings helps keep control of what easily can become a chaotic calendar.

IMPRESS WITH ACCOMPLISHMENTS, NOT WITH NUMBER OF MEETINGS AND MEMOS

- Less is more.
  - Meetings, paper, attendees

  Some managers believe they impress you with the number of memos and plans they send and meetings they schedule. I want to make sure that weekly staff meetings serve their purpose, which is to limit the need for interim communications, meetings, etc.

- No such thing as a "casual meeting" with outside stakeholders—such as investment analysts, bankers, shareholders, etc. Most senior managers know how risky meetings, even supposedly off-the-record meetings, can be with outsiders who easily can misinterpret and misuse the information provided. I believe in having specialists deal with specialists—for example, John Manfredi used as his vice president of investor relations Chris Jakubik, who was an analyst and a portfolio manager before he came to Gillette. Specialists speak a different language and look at things from a unique perspective. Plus the laws covering what can and can't be disclosed keep a lot of lawyers gainfully employed.

In addition to talking about my style, philosophy, expectations and weekly and quarterly meetings, I also reviewed my leadership process for managing, which is shown in the graphic.

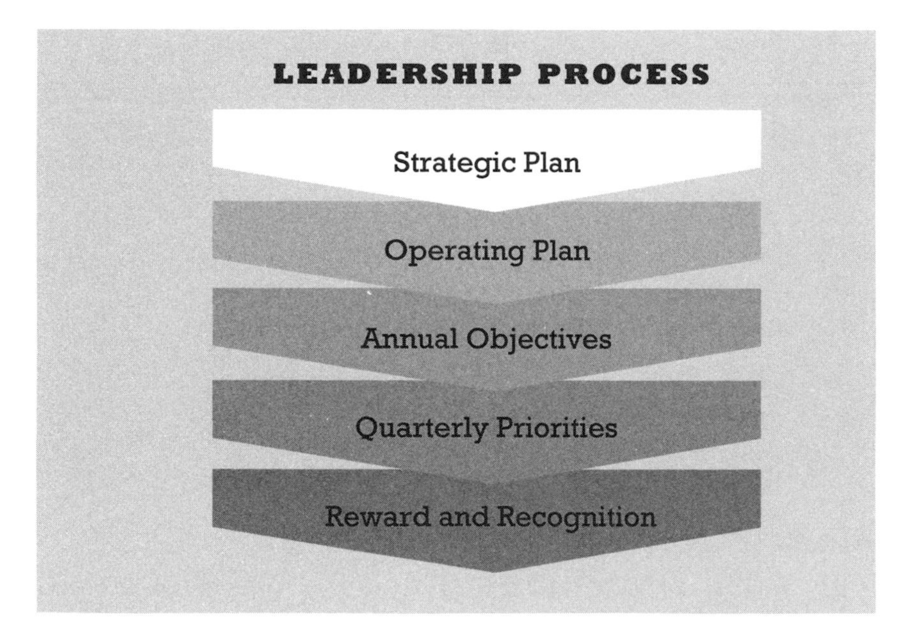

We also discussed the templates for annual objectives and quarterly priorities, which each of my direct reports had to fill in prior to our off-site meeting, which would be held within three weeks. Both templates are shown on the next page.

ANNUAL OBJECTIVES: FISCAL YEAR

Manager: (Insert Name)		Date: (Insert Year)		Approval: Jim Kilts	
Accountability	**Objectives**	**Relative Priority**	**Standard of Performance**	**Manager Self-Rating**	**Kilts' Rating**
Franchise Health	I.e., deliver target shares: • x: +2.1 pts • y: + .1 pts • Etc.	30%	I.e., shares up in business accounting for 80% of operating profit		

QUARTERLY PRIORITIES: FISCAL YEAR

Position: (Insert)	Manager: (Insert Name)		Quarter: (Insert)	Approval: Jim Kilts	
Priorities	**Relative Priorities**	**Due Date**	**Personal Assessment**	**Weighted Rating (0–100%)**	**Comments**
Achieve cost reduction target of $70 million	20%	Quarter End		Total=100%	

+ = Exceed Planned Results
10 = Completed on Plan
8 = Almost Completed (Above 85%) or Completed During the Quarter but Late
6 = Substantially Accomplished (Above 50%)
4 = Partially Accomplished (Between 25 and 50%)
2 = Completed Unsatisfactorily (Objective Not Reached or Less Than 25% Achieved)
0 = Nothing Accomplished on the Priority

MAKE THE MOST OF DAY ONE

Make the most of your day one. Use it to demonstrate that you deserve to be the new leader.

- You have a good understanding of the job ahead. Having done your advance work, lay out the issues, challenges, and opportunities.

Identify not only weaknesses, but the strengths that will serve as building blocks for the future.

- Your leadership philosophy is well grounded. Lay out your equivalent of Total Brand Value, the vision that provides the overarching framework for how you approach business.

- Your management style is fair. You will make people decisions based on performance. Promises made by you—and by all others—will be kept.

- Your leadership process is fully articulated. It's much more than just ideas; your beliefs are detailed and consist of multiple elements—starting with a vision and moving on to strategic planning, annual operating plans, quarterly priorities, and weekly reports and staff meetings.

- Your bias is to act. There is absolutely no mistaking your eagerness to get going and get things done. You want fact-based, quantitative assessments, but you want decisions to act flowing from that process.

- Your personal style is straightforward. You should detail any preferences or idiosyncrasies that characterize your style.

With a day one like that, there will be a lot of other good days ahead.

CHAPTER 10

IGNORING WHAT MATTERS—ENTER THE CIRCLE OF DOOM

When consumers compared the taste of a Nabisco's Chips Ahoy! cookie with a Keebler's chocolate chip, they preferred Keebler's. Same with a Nabisco's Premium Saltine versus a generic, store-brand saltine. The store brand won.

But Nabisco's prices were about 40 percent higher than Keebler's, and as much as 100 percent higher than private label. So most observers weren't surprised that Nabisco's market shares dropped month after month after month . . . for a year and a half.

Nabisco's management, however, was confounded. These were bright, dedicated, diligent managers who had saved the company from bankruptcy when the interest rates on its huge debt soared following the leveraged buyout. But they were deep into what I call the Circle of Doom. Even though the escape path was evident, they couldn't face the reality of their situation. And what existed at Nabisco happens at many companies.

Most business leaders are hardworking and well intentioned. Yet despite their best efforts, they get in trouble because they lack the clarity of vision and certainty of purpose necessary to confront the reality of their business situations. It's often an inadvertent failure to face the truth fully and honestly. It existed at Gillette as well as Nabisco. And from my discussions with other CEOs, I know that this "doomsday" scenario plays out at hundreds, if not thousands, of companies. Although I will describe the Circle of Doom's manifestations at a corporate level, it is prevalent at all levels within companies.

SLIDING INTO THE CIRCLE OF DOOM

In many of these instances, intellectual integrity becomes cloudy and situational and, at the CEO level, reality becomes the latest thing you told Wall Street.

At times, the slide into the Circle of Doom is the unfortunate by-product of success. A company enjoys several years of strong growth and even stronger earnings. Everything is going right—a bright, motivated management team is in place; the leadership process is functioning well; new products are successful; economic growth is robust; and competitors are quiet. Earnings growth of 15 to 20 percent annually seems like a slam dunk. Or at least that's what Wall Street wants you to say, so they can continue to recommend your stock and ride it to new all-time highs.

At times, the slide into the Circle of Doom is the unfortunate by-product of success.

Lulled into Unsustainable Forecasts Even though the CEO knows that 15 to 20 percent annual growth is exceptional and not sustainable, the pressure is strong to go along with the Street. Maybe everything will hit on all cylinders for one more year, and it sure is nice to have everyone sing your praises and have your shareholders making such nice gains. So you continue to forecast record sales and earnings for the future.

Sometimes, the irrational exuberance comes from the other direction—a run of bad luck rather than good fortune. Nothing seems to go right. Several new products were stillborn in the market. Competitive activity hits a new high. And the macroeconomic environment is depressing consumer spending. The result: Your company's share price has fallen more than 25 percent, and there is no floor in sight. Your internal and external advisers encourage you to make a dramatic projection about how bright the future will be. And you are convinced

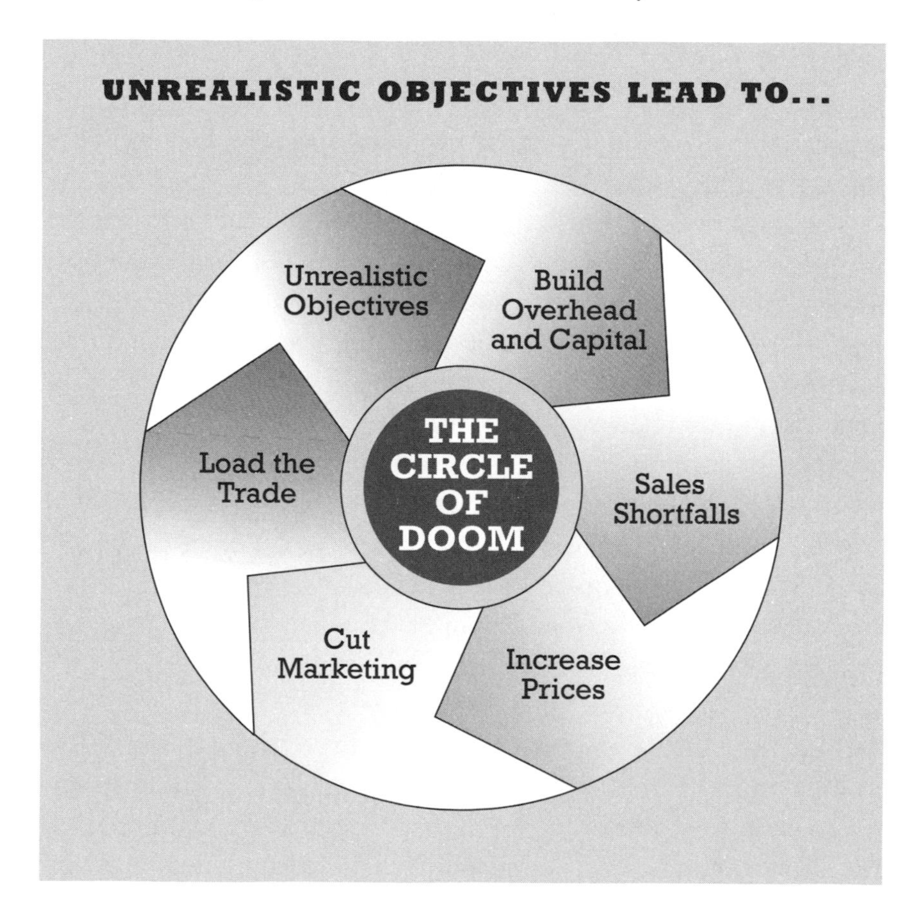

that the worst is over. The economy is improving; your competitors seem more focused on making money than on stealing more of your market share; and you have a pipeline that is bursting with new products. Why not turn things around by predicting 15 to 20 percent growth for the foreseeable future!

THE DOUBLE-DIGIT GROWTH DREAM

It is easy for us to envision a future that we wish would exist rather than one that the analysis and data tell us will exist. A study done by the management consultant McKinsey & Company shows that only 15 percent of the companies in a group of more than one thousand were able to sustain double-digit earnings growth for five consecutive years. For ten consecutive years, the number of companies with double-digit growth dropped precipitously, to less than 1 percent. And for fifteen consecutive years, it is a minuscule 0.003 percent.

So the likelihood of any company putting together back-to-back-to-back blockbuster winning years has such slim odds that you would think most CEOs would know better than to bet against them. But time and again, the wager is made, and lost, and companies start their descent into the Circle of Doom.

It always starts with unrealistic growth targets that are, at best, a long shot to be met. But, investors are pleased. They like high growth, and they are comforted because a CEO is willing to put his reputation on the line.

In order to meet the anticipated growth and keep momentum strong for the future, companies must spend capital and aggressively build overhead structures. Sharp increases in the planned rate of sales mean a larger supply of product will be needed, which in turn means new production capacity will be necessary—a new production line or maybe even a new factory.

Since adding capacity takes lead time, capital has to be allocated in advance of the increased sales in order to start the planning and move the organization into high gear.

Throwing Money at Problems And it's not just bricks and mortar that must be added. A business that will double in four to five years has to add more overhead—more sales people to sell more product; more financial people to maintain controls over larger budgets and an increased workforce; more human resource support to administer the workforce and assist with training, development, and assessment activities. On and on it goes—not just at headquarters, but at locations around the world for a global company. Forecasts have consequences that cascade throughout the entire organization.

When it appears that the unrealistic targets are beyond reach, then the companies throw even more money at their problems. Perhaps some high-value cents-off coupons will stimulate sales. Maybe a pack-on premium will attract new users. The companies realize that if investors are disappointed, reputations will suffer and bonuses won't get paid.

These stopgap efforts may work for a while. But, ultimately, reality comes knocking. No amount of wishful thinking can create sustainable growth. Sales begin to slide, and so do profits.

To increase revenues, prices are raised. But that further erodes sales, and market shares start to drop as consumers balk at the big price gaps between your products and competitive brands.

No amount of wishful thinking can create sustainable growth. Sales begin to slide, and so do profits.

So to prop up the bottom line, marketing budgets are cut. The rationalization goes something like this: Our brand is so strong that reducing the marketing budget by one-quarter and dropping the savings to the bottom line won't even be noticed. We have high consumer loyalty that will carry us through. It is far better to bolster the company's bottom line than it is to have some extra ad impressions.

And when that isn't enough, companies start what's called "trade loading." They jam products into their customers' warehouses at cut-rate prices with special terms and conditions, which again helps to delay reality. Yet the outcome is never pleasant.

Targets Are Missed; Products Pile Up Targets are missed because the business is not being supported. Products that consumers don't want pile up with the customers. And those customers know the company is in trouble, so they wait for even bigger discounts and better terms that are certain to come in the future.

A bad situation gets worse, quarter after quarter, as the company continues to chase unreal promises. At the end of the year, the letter to shareholders in the annual report starts to include comments like "The Company was battered by deteriorating market conditions and unforeseen competitive pressures." Yet for the next year, the new targets are based on the same unrealistic growth premises, and thus the cycle continues.

This was exactly the scenario that preceded my arrival at Gillette. And it is amazing how *similar* Gillette's situation was to Nabisco's. As I noted, Gillette was an icon company that was losing sales and market share to weaker competitors. Its capital spending was spiraling out of control and overheads were substantially higher than peers'. It was a company with sharply curtailed marketing investment, declining net sales, and an ongoing string of missed profit numbers.

And trade loading had become an enormous issue. I had evidence of the magnitude of trade loading and the strong feeling against it within the Gillette organization prior to my first day on the job. As part of my overall research, I had spent several days in the field with Gillette sales representatives. We visited stores in the different channels—supermarkets, drugstores, convenience stores, club stores, and mass merchandisers. We looked at Gillette products on the front ends of stores, their in-aisle share of shelf and positioning, their out-of-aisle displays, and much more.

"IT'S YOU GUYS IN BOSTON WHO MAKE US DO IT"

While personal-care products have a lot in common with the food products that I had spent my entire career learning about, I knew there also would be differences. Many of those differences would be small, but in consumer products, the difference between winning and losing is always a small margin. Attention to details really matters.

Beyond getting a feel for Gillette's in-store presence, I wanted a sense of how the people on the front line felt about the company. You always gain excellent insights by talking with people who know firsthand whether corporate strategies are working or are falling flat in the marketplace. It is easy to become infatuated with your own efforts. It is easy to assume that all the hard work and great thinking that went into a new product or marketing effort just has to meet with great success. Unfortunately, the consumer products world doesn't work that way, and the people on the front line can be an excellent source of reality.

On one of those field visits, I was talking with a young sales rep about trade loading. He said that it happened like clockwork at the end of every quarter. So I asked him why he did it. Why would he sell products in quantities that consumers weren't buying and our trade customers would accept only at greatly discounted prices? I'll never forget his response. He pointed his finger at me and said rather emotionally, "It's you guys in Boston who make us do it. You're the ones." I realized right away that Gillette had people in the field who knew what they were doing was wrong, but were being told to do it anyway.

In fact, when Professor Rosabeth Moss Kanter and her associates at the Harvard Business School researched a case history on the Gillette turnaround, they found managers all over the world who condemned the practice. "I'm absolutely certain there's not one person in the whole company who for one moment thought we should do anything other than get out of trade loading," said Chris Adcock, then the European group director for customer development.

Gillette Had Been Trade Loading for Six Years David Bashaw, who was then a director in our European Commercial Operations unit, was even more emphatic: "We hated trade loading. How can you talk category management with a customer and then three weeks later come in on your hands and knees and say to them, 'Oh please, here is fifteen percent to buy more'?" And this was no short-term, recent phenomenon. Dave said, "We'd been loading for six years . . ."

Gillette was caught deep in the Circle of Doom; trade loading was just one manifestation of it. It took a lot of study, analysis, and brainstorming with a lot of people inside the company and on the outside as well. But, within a hundred days, my team and I had some specific action plans of how we would escape. And when I met with more than two hundred investors, analysts, and financial and business news media in June 2001, I outlined those plans.

Instead of unrealistic expectations, I said that we would set realistic targets and put detailed plans in place and achieve them consistently. Rather than build overhead and spend capital, we would aggressively reduce costs and tightly control future expenditures. Instead of sales shortfalls, we would focus on maintaining and growing share in all our core segments.

Rather than routinely raising prices, we would rigorously assess our consumer value propositions and would manage price gaps in a disciplined way. Instead of cutting marketing, we would reinvest a portion of our productivity savings in advertising, while also upgrading our analytics and spending more effectively.

In the Future, We Would Just Say *No* And as for trade loading, we would just say *no.* We would eliminate excess inventory, once and for all, and would ship only to replace product that consumers were buying.

To give Wall Street and the media an understanding of the depth of Gillette's difficulties, I presented them with an unvarnished look at the company's performance in recent years, which could be characterized as "promises made; promises broken." Not a formula for building trust and credibility.

"Promises made; promises broken" is not a formula for building trust and credibility.

Gillette's sales and earnings essentially were flat since 1997. Worldwide market share was disappointing, with shares gaining in businesses representing only 36 percent of our sales from 2000 to 2001. Shares declined in businesses representing 64 percent of sales, including such core businesses as disposable razors, shaving preparations, and batteries.

This declining market share significantly impacted Gillette's results. I calculated that Gillette's earnings per share could have been 12 percent higher if the company had held market share versus the previous year.

Formula for Failure—Advertising Declines; Sales Promotion Increases Advertising spending was low compared to our peers and was down markedly versus the early 1990s—5.8 percent of sales in 2000 versus 6 to 8 percent in the nineties. An even bigger concern was the fact that sales promotions as a percentage of sales were up dramatically—from the 8 to 10 percent level, all the way up to 13 percent in 2000.

To dimensionalize the size of the decline in advertising, despite the introduction of major new products such as Mach3, Duracell Ultra batteries, and the Oral-B CrossAction toothbrush, Gillette's worldwide advertising spending of $600 million had declined by $100 million versus actual spending in 1995. And that was in an environment in which advertising inflation was running almost 5 percent a year.

General and administrative costs, from 1998 to 2000, were up 15 percent on flat sales. That was $200 million of increased expenses versus zero overhead growth, or an earning-per-share impact of 12 cents versus a zero-overhead-growth standard. As a result, profit margins declined from 24.3 percent to 22.6 percent

In addition, capital expenditures were well above other leading consumer products companies. They had averaged 5 to 6 percent of sales in the early 1990s, and then moved to the 10 percent range in the late nineties, versus a peer group average of 6 percent. Since 1995, that represented about $1.4 billion in excess capital spending.

I expect an incremental return on incremental invested capital. Clearly, Gillette had not gotten one. A pretax return of 30 percent on capital of $1.4 billion should have yielded an annual operating profit of $420 million, an earnings per share equivalent of 25 cents.

Slowest Collector of Debts; Fastest Payer of Bills Gillette's Days Sales Outstanding (DSO) were among the highest across our competitors' group. Yet despite the fact that our Braun business and battery business offered longer terms as industry practice, there still was a lot of opportunity for improvement on DSO.

Gillette's Days Inventory on Hand (DIOH) also was at

the upper end of our peer group. All this combined caused our return on invested capital to underperform. We were down 2.2 points from 1997 to 2000, while our competitors had shown progress.

STRENGTHS TO BUILD ON

These performance issues had driven the fifteen quarters of continuous negative earning revisions that I mentioned. It was not a pretty picture. But I noted that Gillette had many formidable strengths on which we'd build the turnaround.

- Category-defining icon brands
- Leading market shares in our core categories
- Historically, high growth, advantaged categories
- A strong global presence
- A history of high-quality products and innovation
- High margins relative to our peers
- A strong balance sheet

Gillette had some of the best consumer brands in the world, with Mach3, Duracell, Venus, and Oral-B. We had high absolute market shares in our core categories, almost 70 percent in blades and razors, more than 40 percent in alkaline batteries, 23 percent in manual oral care, and 50 percent in power oral care. Importantly, we had strong relative market shares—4.7 times the next leading competitor in blades and razors, 1.6 times in alkaline batteries, 1.2 times in manual oral care, and 3.2 times in power oral care.

We Were in the Right Places Just as importantly, Gillette competed in high-growth advantaged categories, which was the foundation for our long-term growth prospects. We were in the right places. Over the previous three years, blades and razors had grown at a compound annual rate of nearly 4 percent. With batteries and oral care included, the Gillette weighted composite was 3.3 percent, and on a constant dollar basis, the growth rate was much higher at 8.7 percent.

In fact, our categories were among the highest growth in consumer packaged goods. Compared with the growth of a number of other major consumer categories, our core categories represented clear and powerful competitive advantages.

We also had a strong global presence, another substantial pillar for our turnaround. We sold in two hundred countries worldwide, and 57 percent of our sales came from outside of North America. We were strong in developing growth markets, like Latin America and Asia-Pacific.

And we had a history of high-quality products and innovation: in blades, from Trac II to Mach3 to Venus; in batteries, from Duracell Copper & Black to Duracell Ultra; and in oral care, from Oral-B Indicator to CrossAction and the full line of sophisticated power toothbrushes.

Our margins were high relative to peers. At about 23 percent, we stacked up very well against all large consumer products companies. We had a strong balance sheet with superior cash flow, an AA-minus credit rating, and the highest free-cash-flow margin among our peers at over 18 percent.

Those were our strengths. And by harnessing those strengths, we would start on our journey to escape from the Circle of Doom and, over time, transform Gillette into the best consumer products company in the world. There was a lot to do, yet eight months later, at the next major meeting of investors and analysts—the Consumer Analyst Group of New York Conference (CAGNY) in February 2002—our escape from the Circle was gaining traction. I was able to report broad progress on many fronts.

We had said in June 2001 that we would stop making promises we couldn't keep, that we'd jump-start our growth and reverse our market-share losses by investing in our brands.

Reversing Market-Share Declines By early 2002, our promises were being kept. For example, we executed a complete reversal on market share—from losing market share in 65 percent of our global portfolio in 2000 to gaining market share in 64 percent in 2001. In the critically important North American market, where we generated 45 percent of our total revenue, we had made excellent progress. In 1998, we grew share in only 23 percent of our businesses. In 1999, that figure was 34 percent; and in 2000, we increased share in only 24 percent. You can never grow shareholder value when you are losing that kind of market share. By the end of 2001, we turned things around. We grew share in businesses representing 75 percent of our North American sales, a 51 percent increase in one year!

Improving Advertising-to-Sales Ratio In 2000, our advertising-to-sales ratio was one of the lowest in our sector at 5.8 percent. For 2001, our advertising spending increased significantly, and the ratio stood at 7.1 percent. That was still too low, but it was far better than it had been.

No More Trade Loading I had said we would fix our trade inventory issues, particularly in blades and batteries. We did exactly what we said we would in North America, Europe, and Latin America. We were shipping to consumption, as promised.

Improving Cash Generation When we said that we would improve our cash generation and asset management, many investors, and even managers inside Gillette, were skeptical about our ability to manage down accounts receivable and inventory balances. It wasn't the way Gillette had done things for the previous twenty years, so revamping our financial processes would be impossible. Well, few skeptics remained. We had reduced our accounts receivable balance by 31 percent, and lowered our Days Sales Outstanding (DSO) from 68 days at the end of 2000 to 49 days in 2001. That was a reduction of over $600 million dollars! We had reduced our year-end balance on total inventory by 13 percent, with our Days Inventory on Hand declining 15 days, from 123 to 108. Both our DSOs and our Days Inventory on Hand were at their lowest levels in at least 20 years.

This significant improvement in working capital, coupled with lower capital expenditures, generated free cash flow of over $1.5 billion. This was nearly double the level of the year before and was almost four times the average annual free cash flow generated by Gillette from 1996 through 2000. As a result of this performance, we were able to reduce our debt by more than $1 billion during 2001.

We had said Gillette would cut unsalable and nonproductive SKUs, and we had already removed fourteen thousand, or 80 percent, of the SKUs targeted for elimination. We had said we would dramatically cut costs, and we had made good gains on a number of fronts. For example, we were making progress on our Strategic Sourcing Initiative, or SSI, which would harness all our global buying power so we could get the best deals possible in the market place. More on SSI in the next chapter.

ESCAPING FROM THE CIRCLE OF DOOM

So that was Gillette eight months into our escape plan. We had realistic goals, growing market shares, improved organizational discipline, and stronger financial management. And we were committed to the realization of significant cost savings.

But Gillette still was not the best consume products company in the world, and that was our objective. I summed up our position early in 2002 by borrowing from Winston Churchill when he reported on England's progress in World War II. He had said, "Now this is not the end. It is not even the beginning of the end. But it is, perhaps, the end of the beginning." And Gillette was then at "the end of the beginning" in our transformation to become the best.

It took three more years of consistent adherence to our strategies and mission, but we succeeded. Let's fast-forward to five years into our turnaround.

- We had achieved thirteen straight quarters of growth.
- Trade loading remained a thing of the past.
- Our operating results were at record levels. The compound annual growth rate from 2002 to 2006 was 9 percent for sales and 20 percent for earnings per share.
- We increased our market strength in each of our core categories.
- Blade and razor global market share was at a record high.
- Batteries maintained category-leading market share and reached record-high profitability.
- Oral care continued to build its number one position in global brushing.

IT'S NOT REAL IF YOU CAN'T MEASURE IT

To me, if you can't measure it, it's not real. So here are more metrics that measure our performance over the turnaround period. (See appendix, pages 297–301, Gillette's Financial Metrics, 2001–2005, for charts detailing performance.)

- Gross margins improved from 55.8 percent in 2001 to 59.1 percent in 2005.

- Advertising as a percentage of sales increased from 7.1 percent in 2001 to 10.5 percent in 2005.
- Controllable overhead costs dropped by 8 percentage points from 31.3 percent in 2001 to 23.3 percent in 2005.
- Our Strategic Sourcing Initiative generated nearly $500 million of savings.
- Operating profit margins increased more than 5 percentage points from 20.7 percent in 2001 to 25.9 percent in 2005.
- Working capital was dramatically reduced from 22 percent of sales in 2000 to zero in 2004 and 2005.
- The cash-conversion cycle improved by 44 percent from 150 days in 2001 to 84 days in 2004.
- Capital expenditures were reduced from 10 to 11 percent in the late 1990s to 6 percent in 2005.
- Free cash flow more than quadrupled, from $2.1 billion from 1996 to 2000 to $9 billion from 2001 to 2005.
- Return on invested capital more than doubled, going from 16.8 percent in 2001 to 34.3 percent in 2004.
- In all, Gillette moved from the bottom of its peer group in terms of earnings-per-share (EPS) performance rating for the years 1997 to 2001 to the top ranking for the years 2001 to 2005.
- Gillette's share price, which was $27.90 after my initial conference with investors in June 2001, nearly doubled and created $26 billion of shareholder value, outperforming the S&P 500 index by more than 90 percent from June 2001.

That was Gillette's escape from the Circle of Doom. By any metric, it was quite a ride.

AVOIDING THE CIRCLE OF DOOM

Falling into the Circle of Doom happens in all sectors and to all types of businesses, ranging from the blue chips to the start-ups. I've experienced it firsthand with some of the world's best consumer products companies. While escaping from the Circle is long and difficult, there are a number of things that can keep you out.

- Never chase unrealistic, unsustainable growth targets. You must spend the time to identify a rate of growth that is realistic for your sector and business. And not just for a year or two, but for the long run. Setting a sustainable growth target is one of the most important things you can do. Going for a blowout number is a sure way to blowup.

- Regardless of the business, you must control costs and maintain them at a level that gives you a competitive advantage. So benchmark; find out what other companies, your peers, are doing, and then go them one better.

- ZOG (Zero Overhead Growth) should be your mantra, not just for a year, or only in bad times. Always. Let your organization know that ZOG isn't a onetime event or a tactical activity. It's a fundamental strategy.

- Every business sector has a few key metrics that tell you how your business is doing. Learn what they are and focus on them incessantly.

- In consumer products, a rising market share is a critical measure of a brand's health. While competitive activities will cause deviations, the share trends must be heading up over time, or trouble lies ahead.

- Half of all advertising expenditures may be wasted. But you must invest robustly in the marketing of your brands. Determine the right ratio of advertising to sales for your specific product category and then make sure that over time you maintain that level.

- Avoid trade loading and other bad business practices that result in selling more of your product than the market wants or consumers will buy. Selling excess products in order to meet quarterly earnings expectations is a sure sign that you have one foot in the Circle of Doom. Remember, never chase unreal targets. Facing the short-term rebuke from Wall Street is far better than risking an agonizing plunge into the Circle.

SECTION III

THE FUTURE MATTERS

CHAPTER 11

THE RIGHT ROAD MAP MATTERS

One of the toughest things in business is bringing everything together. Putting the right leadership process in place has discrete elements. Compiling a strategic plan involves a lot of input, analysis, and assessment, but lots of good templates exist on the how-to of strategic plans. Assembling the right team takes time to identify the right people and match them with the right positions; but the recruiting process is pretty straightforward.

The road map is useful both strategically and tactically, and it works for first-line supervisors as well as top leaders.

Many managers fail because they have a punch list of all the individual elements, and when they see check marks next to them, they assume the heavy lifting is over. Actually, the opposite is true. The heaviest lifting comes when all of the individual pieces are in place and you must make them work together to drive the company toward its objectives. At this point, you need the right road map.

GETTING THE RIGHT MAP

The road map has multiple purposes. It serves as a high-elevation guide that enables you to see a large swath of the country. It also is like a detailed city plan that shows the side streets as well as the boulevards and avenues. In other words, the road map is useful both strategically and tactically, and it works for first-line supervisors as well as top senior leaders.

Coming up with that road map is a tall order. And it's especially difficult when you're operating in a turnaround mode, where the frenetic pace and high organizational apprehension combine to complicate the normal business situation.

For Gillette, we knew the right road map would be important, and we also knew it would be elusive to develop. We knew, for example, that the company was deep into the Circle of Doom and that a bad practice like trade loading had to go. But we also realized how deeply embedded this practice was internally within our sales organization and externally with many of our customers. Our salespeople relied on loading to make their numbers and get their bonuses; many of our customers also counted on the extra loading discounts to make their own budgets. As much as we wanted to purge trade loading immediately, we understood that everything from our compensation programs to our systems for reporting on retail consumption data would require time to change and implement.

Another aspect of the Circle—the need for increased marketing support—also was easy to identify but tough to implement. Costs had to be cut and asset performance improved in order to make increased ad spending affordable. And simply coming up with the funds wasn't enough. The organization needed the capabilities to know how to spend the funds—how to get the biggest bang for the buck—and the talent to oversee the creation of world-class advertising that would have an impact in the marketplace.

Since Gillette's capital expenditures were tens of millions of dollars higher than its peers' annually, there was an obvious need to reduce the spending. But when the engineering and manufacturing departments of Gillette were producing the most innovative, highest-quality products in the consumer products universe, how do you gain acceptance for the concept that highest quality and lowest cost can be compatible?

Or how do you change a company that has a twenty-year tradition of being the fastest payer and slowest collector of its bills? Especially if your finance group is convinced it can't be done.

What's needed is a multidimensional effort. The company's culture must change. Many behaviors must be unlearned. Reward systems must be modified. New tracking, auditing, and reporting systems must be installed. Capabilities must be upgraded and added. Strategic platforms must be translated into specific action plans. And all of this must be accomplished in the compressed time that is mandated by the exigencies of a turnaround.

Credibility must be quickly established with investors; acceptance for new practices must be sought from customers; employees must have a sense that change is possible and the plans are real. On and on it goes.

The Three Elements Absent a magic wand that brings everything together, you need a road map. At Gillette, ours had three elements. But they were not separately sequenced; they were acted on at the same time.

- **Financial turnaround** was our focus on improving short-term financial performance. Unless you stop the hemorrhaging and get some forward momentum, you'll never be given a chance to do anything more.
- **Strategic turnaround** was our effort to set the business on the right course—to make sure each of our operating business units had a simple, well-defined strategy, not some amorphous high-sounding prose that is meaningless to the people who have to produce daily results. An important part of our effort was a single-sentence, strategic governing statement for each of our core businesses.
- **Functional Excellence** was the process that created an enduring world-class company with an advantaged cost structure and great capabilities. If your costs are too high, if you don't have the right capabilities to get things done with excellence, and if your people aren't top-notch innovators, then nothing else matters. The game is lost.

We began our financial turnaround by moving forcefully on a broad front with a wide-ranging attack on costs and improving asset management and productivity. During the early days, I can recall feeling like the deputy chief financial officer. Every week I would be asking questions about Days Sales Outstanding, finished-goods inventories, accounts payable, and cash-conversion cycles. What should our targets be? Why can't they be better? What are the industry benchmarks? Why are we so far off? Have we worked the new targets into quarterly priorities? What programs are being developed to facilitate change? Why is Italy so strong and Spain so slow? Do we need a new finance team in Latin America? On and on and on.

And sometimes, asking these questions once a week isn't enough. You have to press on them every day. The organization has to know that you are serious, and that you will be persistent. Your focus on change is not going away. They have to get results or get a new position. There would be nothing in between.

Anecdotes that came back to me helped lighten some otherwise grim days. I heard about one of our longtime financial-services managers, who was convinced that his customer would be outraged if pressed for on-time payments. Our man was shocked when the customer responded, "What took Gillette so long to ask?"

How Much for Personal Computers? To assist the organization and accelerate the learning curve, we brought in A.T. Kearney, a consulting group that I have used many times over the years. They know the ropes on everything from identifying and implementing best manufacturing practices to organizing an effective strategic sourcing initiative to how to get timely payments.

One of the things that Kearney does especially well is orchestrate the process of online bidding. At Nabisco and again at Gillette, I asked the purchasing people, *How good are the prices we get on personal computers for the organization?* At both companies, the responses were swift and the same: "The best prices. No question about it."

A few weeks later, the folks from A.T. Kearney ran their session with a half-dozen vendors competing against one another with online, real-time bids. At both Nabisco and Gillette, the results were the same. The prices were 30 percent lower than the previous "best price." Word spreads quickly about an event like that.

At Gillette, the resistance to change was strong in some areas. There was constant pushback from some of our financial people, who said that our terms and conditions were out of sync with our competitors *only* because of the peculiarities of our product categories; industry practice required extended terms on batteries and household appliances. Over time, however, they had to acknowledge that category differences represented only a small part of the issue. The rest could be addressed, and each year for the remaining four years, our working-capital numbers improved markedly. All told, we reduced every element of working capital. As noted, we reduced our working capital from 22 percent of sales in 2000 to 16 percent in 2001, 8 percent in 2002, 2 percent in 2003, and zero in 2004 and 2005.

COLLAPSING SILOS

The trick in the strategic turnaround was twofold—get the strategic plan done in a quality way, and then get it used. All too often, strat plans are more like a library book than an everyday guide to doing business.

All too often, strat plans are more like a library book than an everyday guide to doing business.

The quality way of getting the plan done refers as much to the process as the content. At Gillette, the strategic-planning process helped us attack one of our big cultural and organizational issues—a lack of sharing and interaction among the siloed business units and staff functions.

Gillette had operated with a matrixed organization since the mid-1990s. There were four business units, one for each of the core categories: Blades & Razors, Duracell batteries, Oral-B toothbrushes, and Braun electric shavers and appliances. Shortly after I arrived, I created another—the Personal Care Business Unit—when I separated shave preparations (brands like Gillette Foamy and the Gillette Series), antiperspirants and deodorants from the Blades & Razors Business Unit. The business units were responsible for product development, strategic marketing, market research, and advertising.

Separate Commercial Operations (Com Ops) units handled the selling of products to customers, the servicing of customers, and tactical marketing. In all, there were five regions within Commercial Operations—North America, Europe,

Latin America, Asia-Pacific, and AMEE (Africa, Middle East, and Eastern Europe.) All regions outside North America reported to a group head for International.

The balance of the organization consisted of staff units such as finance, human resources, corporate affairs, legal, and information technology, and a new manufacturing, technical, and operations unit (MTO). When I set up MTO at Gillette, I knew the impact would be big; I just did not know how big. Over the course of Gillette's turnaround, the productivity gains generated by the new MTO organization helped fund much of the increased marketing that powered our growth.

The concept behind the change was simple.

- Centralize all manufacturing, engineering, research, and operations under a single head to facilitate sharing of knowledge and assure best use of Gillette's scale.

- Put the group under the leadership of an expert—in our case, it was thirty-year veteran Ed DeGraan, who had greater knowledge about MTO than any other five people at Gillette. In the prior organizational setup, manufacturing reported to the heads of the business units. Not only did this create separate MTO silos in each business unit, it also put managers with marketing backgrounds in charge of specialized, technical areas. Not a good matchup of talent to need.

Leverage Scale to Lower Costs The consequences of the new organizational structure were extraordinary, and some of them came quickly. For instance, at both Nabisco and Gillette, there were multiple purchasing departments (at Gillette, there were more than a dozen). Often the departments were purchasing the same goods from different vendors at different prices. With a centralized MTO, a single purchasing department would leverage total scale and secure significantly lower prices. Career paths that were constrained by a small number of specialists were enlarged by the pooling of all specialists.

When manufacturing units reported to different business units, sharing was not a priority. In fact, it usually was considered unnecessary: *What does making razors have to do with making batteries?* A centralized MTO found scores of best practices that spanned the different product categories.

The benefits kept on coming as a result of the increased focus, interaction, and sharing within the new group. And more interaction and sharing is what I wanted from the strategic-planning process. In the past, even though the business units and Com Op units were very interdependent, they barely communicated during the planning process. The result was poorly aligned targets and objectives.

Simple Metrics Make Focus Easy The new planning process not only called for more detailed analysis of market trends and competitive forces, it also mandated close coordination by each business unit with all the regional Com Op groups. No plan would be approved unless both the business units and Com Ops had jointly agreed upon the targets.

In talking with a Harvard Business School (HBS) interviewer, I gave the example of an executive in charge of the North American Com Ops group. In the old days, he had to make one North American number. Maybe he was supposed to go from $3 to $3.2 billion in sales. If the sales hit $3.2 billion, he made his number.

But if you looked underneath, he may have sold way above target on blades and well below on everything else. Under the new setup, he had to make five numbers. He had to grow blades by so much, and personal care, oral care, Braun, and Duracell all had to grow, too. He would be measured on how well balanced the delivery was. And this was across all products and all geographic regions. It no longer was possible to just run for glory in one product line, or in one geography.

And the message got through. As Dave Bashaw told HBS: "Seventy percent of my annual rating and bonus is tied to P&L

and market share. This makes it very easy to focus. There's no hiding . . . No, it's 'Here's your budget targets and market-share targets; they're metrics we can measure, so if you're growing over two-thirds of your market shares and you're hitting your numbers, you win. And if you win, I'm going to pay you more in bonus than we have in the past. And if you don't win, you're going to get significantly less.' "

Moving from "Once in a While" to "Every Day" Mutually agreed-upon targets that were part of the metrics for bonuses in both business units and Com Ops helped generate greater teamwork. The second important element in strat planning is *How do you move strategic thinking from "once in a while" to "every day"? How do you imprint the essence of the strategic direction onto the minds of the key players?* That's where the governing strategic statements play an important role.

The governing statement boils down the strategic direction for each business unit. It provides the basis for both broad initiatives as well as daily decisions. Its single-sentence format makes it easy to comprehend and recall.

How do you imprint the essence of the strategic direction onto the minds of the key players? That's where governing strategic statements play an important role.

For example, in the past, our Blades & Razors Business Unit had focused almost exclusively on the premium end of the market, where it had introduced truly breakthrough systems like Mach3 for men and Venus for women. However, in the process, the business unit had given short shrift to the midrange systems market and had treated disposables with benign neglect. As a result, Gillette had limited growth in the mid-price sector, and we lost considerable disposable market share.

The new governing statement said that the Blades & Razors Business Unit would drive market growth and grow our share of the category's economic profits by expanding its focus from just premium shaving systems to a more inclusive approach that included entry and mid-range systems as well as disposables. The strategic governing statement aimed to increase Blades & Razors financial returns so they matched its marketplace successes.

We were the clear market leader in an advantaged category. Our value shares of the U.S. blade and razor market in 2001 had reached their highest levels in forty years. We also had the number one global share at 70.9 percent for 2001, a 1.3-point gain over 2000, with consumer takeaway up 5 points. Driving this growth was the exceptional marketplace performance of our premium shaving systems—Mach3 for men and Venus for women.

Since its launch in 1998, Mach3 worldwide sales had topped $3 billion. Its global market share in 2001 was 22 percent, higher in the United States at 25 percent, and higher still in Europe at 27 percent. Planned for 2002 was an improved version, the Mach3 Turbo. This was an exceptional new product, with thirty-five patents protecting its technologies and features, that we were confident would drive category growth and further increase our share of the men's premium shaving segment.

Our top-of-the-line Venus system was the most successful shaving product in the history of female shaving. In the ten months since its launch in 2001, Venus sales had topped $300 million. In the United States, it captured an incredible 10 percent of all wet-shaving dollars and 71 percent of the female razor market. Planned for 2002 was Crystal Clear Venus, which would give women another attractive variety.

EXTENDING THE FORMULA FOR SUCCESS

Yet this powerful performance in the marketplace had not yielded equally impressive financial returns. Part of the problem related to the timing of new products and investment decisions.

Gillette had just completed expanding its manufacturing capacity for the premium Sensor Excel shaving system when we started allocating nearly $100 million to build new capacity so we could launch Mach3. The rationale for spending funds to add capacity for a brand that was about to be made obsolete with the introduction of Mach3 was hard to understand. For the future, we were committed to capturing top returns from each product cycle and to assuring disciplined capital expenditures that would help enhance our total economic profitability. If Sensor's growth cycle could be extended, then new capacity should be added, but the planned launch of Mach3 would be delayed. If Sensor had peaked, new investment in it should be avoided and instead the focus and spending would be on Mach3.

Along those same lines, we would expand our focus beyond premium shaving systems so we could raise the category's performance to a higher level. We would focus on two major areas: stabilizing and then taking back share in disposables, where we would use our superior technology to improve our products and renew marketing investment to support them, and more aggressively trading up consumers in developing countries to our better, higher-margin products. We would expand our entry-level systems product, Vector, which more than doubled the size of this segment in China. In 2002, Vector would be moved into other key developing markets.

Our Oral Care Business Unit also had focused on growing the premium end of the market and primarily in developed countries. As a result, midrange products were underdeveloped and emerging markets were a low-level priority. And the entire battery-toothbrush segment had been ignored. Oral Care's strategic governing statement called for a growing share of the profit pool of both power and manual toothbrushes.

The Oral Care business was built on a clear formula for success: clinically proven superior performance, powerful equity with consumers and the dental profession, and a full product line that allowed consumer trade-up.

One of our key objectives for 2002 was to build share in the battery-powered-toothbrush segment, which we were very late in entering, and grow in the high-opportunity kids segment with a new line. We also would promote the replacement of power brush heads at regular intervals because, like blades, this was a highly profitable business.

Fewer Products, More Profit Our Braun Business Unit had suffered from an opposite problem. Rather than a narrow focus, it had operated too expansively. In the past, Braun was run as a small appliance company, seeking to broaden its product line and extend its geographic reach. The strategic governing statement gave Braun a narrowed charge. It would focus on dry shaving, ensure that each product line minimally returned greater than its cost of capital, and restrict distribution to profitable geographies. That strategic change made all the difference. In just one year, profits from operations went from $94 million in 2000 to $120 million in 2001; operating margin rose by three percentage points to 11.6 percent; and return on assets increased from four percentage points to 14.8 percent.

Our Personal Care Business Unit was newly launched after having endured years of inattention. Its costs were high. Its profit margin was low—considerably lower than peers'. Its powerful brands in both antiperspirants and deodorants (AP/DEO) and shaving preparations needed to be refreshed and relaunched to stop the ongoing erosion of their market shares.

The AP/DEO category was one of the toughest in consumer products. Global heavyweights like Unilever and Procter & Gamble engaged in dogged battles that yielded little market growth. So our direction for our Personal Care acknowledged the realities of the marketplace: Personal Care would achieve modest share growth and increase profit margin to the industry benchmark level.

Duracell—Climbing the Steepest Mountain The battery category was bigger and more important to Gillette than Personal Care. But it suffered from some of the same issues—competition among the top alkaline battery makers was intense and Duracell's costs were high and out of control, which had depressed its operating margins.

As noted, Duracell had battled the competition with the wrong segmentation approach, which resulted in serious share loss. Therefore, Duracell must grow share and significantly improve margins. Its strategic governing statement said that Duracell must grow volumes slightly greater than the category, while generating industry-leading margins.

Governing statements were fine-tuned as needed, but the essential directions stayed constant.

These governing statements were fine-tuned as needed, but the essential directions stayed constant throughout the entire turnaround.

While each of the business units had remarkable successes, Duracell had the steepest mountain to climb, and its strategic turnaround is especially instructive. Guided by its governing statement, the Duracell management team drove out costs and improved productivity, taking profit margins from unacceptable to unexcelled. They used marketing intelligence to develop a positioning for the Duracell batteries that resonated with consumers and differentiated it from all competitors. And they slashed inefficient promotional spending and invested heavily in equity building advertising that resulted in record-high market shares. The centerpiece of Duracell's success was its discipline.

Historically, Duracell had been a great business in an advantaged category. However, its successful track record came to a halt in 1998. Following its acquisition of Duracell, Gillette pursued a flawed trade-up strategy that resulted in twenty-one straight months of market-share declines.

Getting Back to Basics So I worked with Mark Leckie and the new management team on conducting a thorough review of the business. In 2001, we decided that Duracell must get back to basics in order to reverse its share erosion. We restaged our bestselling, midrange battery, Copper & Black, renamed it CopperTop in the United States, improved its technology and performance, gave it new packaging, and launched new advertising.

The impact was immediate. We reversed our share declines and posted eight consecutive periods of share improvements. However, the overall category environment was still unstable with hyperpromotions and costly deals. In 2002, over 50 percent of alkaline-battery volume was sold on promotion; the average discount offered was more than 35 percent off list price; more than $80 million in sales were lost through cell giveaways; and price deflation accelerated to almost 7 percent.

So we went to the next phase of our turnaround plan: Duracell implemented a price-deal realignment to introduce some sanity to a category that had become addicted to promotional spending. We wanted to slash cell giveaways, reduce volume sold on promotion, and stabilize pricing.

We had success on all three. Duracell led the industry by eliminating free cell giveaways. Others followed, as total-category free cells were cut by 60 percent. Volume sold on promotion decreased to 44 percent in 2003 from 49 percent in 2002.

We stabilized net pricing, with Duracell's average price per AA cell remaining steady in 2003, the first time in four years that our prices did not decline. While these initiatives led to some unit-share loss, Duracell's dollar share was flat and profit rose a hefty 49 percent.

New "Trust" and Savings of $200 Million Advertising was our key differentiator for the brand. Our "Trusted Everywhere" campaign was the centerpiece of a 30 percent increase in worldwide media spending. Our ads portrayed the feelings of trust that consumers have for Duracell. The campaign has been highly effective. Our research showed this campaign, which has run for several years, is 30 percent more effective than any we had run.

In a category that is always under competitive pressure, cost reductions are critical. And the Duracell team was aggressive. We divested two foreign businesses that used the outdated carbon zinc chemistry. We closed an alkaline plant in India, where the market at the time could not support our higher-priced alkaline batteries. We gained nearly $100 million in savings through our Strategic Sourcing Initiative. We cut manufacturing headcount by 36 percent and administrative and professional headcount by more than 25 percent. In all, the savings totaled well over $200 million.

We also built revenue from new sources. For example, in 2003, Duracell acquired Nanfu, China's leading alkaline-battery company.

From its low point in 2000 to its high point in 2005, Duracell tripled its profit from operations while also improving its global value market share by two points.

FUNCTIONAL EXCELLENCE = SUSTAINED COMPETITIVENESS

The first two elements of the road map—the financial turnaround and the strategic turnaround—were aimed at immediate needs. The third—Functional Excellence—bridges the gap from the immediate needs to long-term performance. I view Functional Excellence as an ongoing process that gives lasting differentiation to a company. It is a broad-gauge initiative to achieve best-in-class capability and performance at the best possible cost.

At Gillette, our benchmarking showed that we spent significantly more on overhead than our competitors. Therefore, we had great opportunity to improve our performance and reduce our costs.

Some improvements, the low-hanging fruit, were quickly harvested. Within six months, we made our global supply chain more efficient by closing down thirteen unneeded distribution centers, and we made it more effective through a special focus on customer service that improved our fulfillment of customer orders for first-time fill rate from the 70 to 80 percent range to the 84 to 93 percent range. Our new universal target was moved up to 95 percent.

In some functions, we estimated our opportunity would yield large cost savings as we introduced new ways of doing business. New systems, processes, and structures would greatly enhance our efficiency and increase our effectiveness all along our value chain. These savings would fund further cost-reduction activities, increased brand-building investments, and, over time, help drive greater profit growth.

To recap, a road map serves many purposes. The financial element helps stabilize the business. The strategic portion makes the most of your strengths, addresses the critical issues, and provides clear direction to create profitable growth. And Functional Excellence provides the foundations of change that will create a culture of continuous improvement with top capabilities and the best cost. In the next chapter, we will take a further look at the role of Functional Excellence in shaping the long-term future for your company.

ROAD MAP TO EXCELLENCE

Whether you are high in your company, or on your way up, you need a road map that guides you for the short term and also lays out a direction for the future.

- Jump-starting financial performance provides the base you need for all future actions. If you don't get the numbers early, you won't be given a chance to do anything later on.

- Search out opportunities for "quick wins" that will create buzz among your people. The online bidding for our PC business not only cut our costs, it also became the talk of the organization. Instructing people on how to collect bills quickly and go to term on payments is another exercise that gets organizational attention as well as financial results.

- Leveraging scale to lower costs has a positive ripple effect. For example, when a single purchasing unit buys something like cardboard, there's pressure to harmonize and reduce differences in specifications. Unexpected operational efficiencies often accompany scale savings.

- Articulate your strategy clearly and precisely. No need for lengthy discourses, filled with high-sounding business terms. Keep your strategic governing statement simple, preferably a sentence or two, so everyone can understand and follow it.

- Let people know what they *shouldn't* do. While a strategic statement must provide clear direction on where the business should go, there is value in identifying a counterpoint of where people shouldn't be going, such as *"Do focus on profitable, innovative widgets; don't seek geographic expansion and worldwide distribution."*

- Securing a long-term competitive advantage must drive all efforts. Your road map needs initiatives to achieve both lowest costs and top capabilities. One without the other isn't enough. Low cost plus top capabilities are true differentiators.

- Long-term advantages require ongoing programs that ultimately define and shape your culture. Onetime or short-term initiatives aren't enough. Seek out programs that can be as enduring as the competitive advantage you're pursuing. For example, a focus on innovation isn't enough. You need a comprehensive, inclusive effort that empowers all people and lets them know that innovation can range from revolutionary "big-bang" changes to small, everyday, continuous improvements.

- Avoid one-size-fits-all approaches in drafting strategic governing statements. Some products and groups need to be more expansive and open in their actions; others need to be channeled and focused. Broad, generalized corporate strategies can cause unanticipated problems.

CHAPTER 12

THINKING FOR THE LONG TERM MATTERS

Everyone likes to believe that they're committed to long-term thinking. But when it comes right down to it, few people really are. The CEOs of the largest companies talk about the importance of thinking and acting for the future. Yet most of them are practitioners of quarterly earnings guidance that focuses both Wall Street and the internal energies of their companies on short-term targets.

Young, fresh-from-grad-school product managers believe they want to shepherd the long-term health of their brands. But given the choice between a short-term spike in results, followed by a sharp fall off in future years, versus moderate but sustainable growth for the long term, most youthful managers opt for the sharp rise that they think will propel their bonuses as well as their careers.

So does long-term thinking and planning really matter? It does. That's why it's part of my road map for success and why a company's short-term successes cannot be the main factor in assessing its long-term prospects.

In terms of the road map, long-term means building Functional Excellence (FE) because it will separate your company or unit from all others. It gives you great capabilities at the lowest cost. And it gives you the added plus of Total Innovation (TI), which is the fuel you need to keep growing.

Long term also means planning and thinking out far enough about your company or unit to know what you have to do to meet the future on your own terms. Our strategic plan gave us the changes we would make at Gillette and how we would achieve them. But it didn't tell us how the rest of the world would change. Specifically, what would happen to our competitors and our retail chain customers? How would they change as Gillette was changing? And could we see Gillette thriving in that future?

FUNCTIONAL EXCELLENCE—DEFINING AND CHANGING CULTURE

We started talking about the role of Functional Excellence in the last chapter. The best way to frame the discussion here is to say that FE starts as a number of projects and activities that have specific purposes, but ends up changing and defining the entire culture of the company. That doesn't happen overnight. But over a period of years, the more that FE thinking takes hold, the more it molds future thinking.

FE (Functional Excellence) starts as a number of projects and activities that have specific purposes, but ends up changing and defining the entire culture of the company.

When we started FE at Gillette, the organization's primary focus was on just one part of the FE proposition: Achieve the lowest possible cost. If we had polled the Gillette organization during the initial year of FE, I'm certain that an overwhelming majority—including a significant number of senior managers—would have said that FE was a euphemistic way of describing layoffs and cost reductions.

People at Gillette had done enough background checking on me to know that at both Kraft and Nabisco I had insisted on ZOG (Zero Overhead Growth)—across-the-board productivity efforts and the elimination of all unnecessary costs. And my focus on costs was not a onetime thing.

Year after year at Kraft, I was told that ZOG had run its course. ZOG had wrung all of the excesses out of the system; there was no more to be had; it was time to let up. When I left after ten years, I was getting the same admonitions, and the costs were still coming out.

So the Gillette organization knew that costs would be my focus. And it was right. I mentioned it in my letter to the organization on the day that I arrived. I followed up with a letter on ZOG within two weeks. And the message started cascading through the organization as a result of my meetings with my direct reports.

My back-of-the-envelope calculations told me that costs were too high across the board. General and administrative costs had grown by 15 percent over the previous three years despite the fact that sales had been flat. But I realized that generalized statements about "too-high costs" were not going to resonate with anyone in particular; everyone was going to look to his or her right or left and say, "The problem is not with me; it's with them."

With generalized statements about "too-high costs," everyone would say: "The problem is not with me; it's with them."

So to avoid the finger-pointing and gain individual responsibility and the acceptance of the need for action, each of my direct reports and their organizations went through the exercise described in chapter 4.

First, each business unit and function

had to get benchmarks to identify best costs, best practices, and capabilities for comparable operations.

Next, they had to compare their costs versus benchmarks. And for best practices and capabilities, they had to take three cuts at determining their relative rank versus benchmarks. First was a self-assessment of how their own organization felt they compared. The second was an internal polling of how their unit was viewed by others in the company. And third was an external view of how a consultant or industry expert viewed Gillette capabilities versus benchmarks.

The final part of the exercise was to determine where Gillette should be. What should our targets be on cost? On capabilities? On cost, we would always want to have the lowest cost for the value delivered. Often that would mean relative costs that were the lowest among our peers. But not always.

While our research costs, for example, *weren't* the lowest, they were highly efficient and effective, delivering great benefits—blockbuster, differentiated products that set Gillette apart from our competitors. And while our target for advertising spending was high as a percent of our sales, the impact further differentiated Gillette and built the equity of our icon brands.

On capabilities, we often would want to be the best, but again, not always. For example, we would want the best capability on research and technical expertise so we could make the best use of the resources needed to achieve marketplace superiority. However, on payroll administration, being the best might be nice, but being average might be the right place, if lower costs were possible as a result.

Instilling a Sense of Purpose and Urgency This process took more than six months to work through, but the time spent was worthwhile. It drove home the need for reduced costs in a real and dramatic way. It was one thing for our human resources group to be told that their costs were too high; it was different for Ned Guillet and his team to go out on their own and find their costs were 30 percent too high, and their capabilities were mired about twenty years behind the times. Ned, his leadership team, and the entire group came away with a great sense of urgency to get on with the change efforts. They had a sense of purpose and commitment to become the new standard setter for the function in all industry. And they had a desire to become a catalyst for change for the entire company.

Similarly, when Chuck Cramb and his finance group found that their costs were 40 percent too high, the mandate for change became real and immediate.

For information technology, the results were similar. Our chief information officer, Kathy Lane, worked tirelessly with her team on some massive issues that had enormous cost impacts. Kathy was a new hire, whom we recruited for my executive team from General Electric. I remember vividly Kathy coming to my office one day, stunned after she learned how much Gillette had spent, year after year, for consultants, who were performing routine maintenance activities at top-dollar hourly rates. When Kathy had inquired about what competitive bidding was involved in these long-term arrangements, she found there was none. And that was one of her easier, more tractable issues.

I've talked about our initiative to eliminate SKUs. When our managers started to work on SKU reduction, they found that IT systems were not yet there to support them. In preparing its case studies on Gillette, Harvard Business School learned from our people that each business unit had a different system and set of codings. "In some cases, it was difficult to generate profit information that could be used to guide decisions. In one region, the same SKU was sold in four markets that shared a language, but not a database; for the regional decision-maker to determine what the SKU was earning required calling four different people representing each market to identify the P&L of the SKU, which he would then add up to determine what the SKU was worth—a tedious process for a base of several thousand SKUs. And there was no system in place to cross-reference an SKU, which required another tedious process of translating code numbers." A global product catalog to track SKUs and their financial performance online would not be up and running for several years.

I will not go through each of the functions and units. But I will analyze a few of the projects to give you some sense of how profound the change was and some understanding of the type of change that affects the culture of the company.

The structure of our human resources department practically defined a siloed organization in a decentralized global company. Every operating unit and staff function had separate HR specialists for recruiting, staffing, compensation, and benefits. Each of the specialists functioned separately within an operating unit and separately from all the other operating units. There was virtually no identification or sharing of best practices. These specialists were working within the same company, but there was little about their work that identified them as being part of the same company. Among several of the specialists, the differences in doing the same work was extreme, and for no particular reason.

No More Sitting on the Sidelines Although the concept of shared centers that pooled specialists who could service either the entire company or a major geographical area—such as North America, the European Union, South America, or Asia—was in fairly wide use, it had never penetrated Gillette. However, once they studied it, our people quickly saw the benefits for the individual specialists, who could enjoy greater career growth within a larger pool of workers with similar backgrounds, and for the company through reduced costs, a more universal set of practices, and a higher caliber of programs.

It took two years to implement, but HR's service centers and centers of expertise around the world saved tens of millions of dollars, resulted in double-digit reduction of the workforce, and upgraded HR services, systems, and programs. In the process, HR went from a relatively passive, disengaged group of individual practitioners to a true business partner that could add value throughout the organization.

Finance traveled a similar path. Our studies showed that some things the finance group should have, it didn't have. Hard to imagine though it might be, we found that Gillette had functioned without a corporate controller for two years. And finance also had far too many things that it shouldn't have. As with HR, finance had many hundreds of siloed specialists attached to operating units and staff functions. There were no centers of expertise; there were no service centers; and there were scores of different systems, but little compatibility among them.

Change took longer within finance than HR for two main reasons. Many of the changes were tied to IT system changes that were being separately managed; leadership changes within finance went more broadly across the top level of the organization and also to the next layer down. However, within four years, Chuck Cramb and later Joe Schena had totally transformed the finance group. Joe eliminated unnecessary layers and positions and assembled the most talented group of finance managers I had ever worked with. Whenever we did succession planning with our board, I would say we had so many people with CFO potential that it would be tough to select one.

The function had gone from one that was told to "stay away from the operating units" to a hard-charging group that was thoroughly engaged and helping to make both tactical and strategic business decisions throughout the company.

MOVING TO AWARD WINNING FROM BACK OF PACK

Functional Excellence helped us leverage scale, share best practices, and reduce headcount.

Functional Excellence changed processes throughout Gillette. For example, it guided the total reorganization of our procurement function, which delivered $500 million in savings. It helped us show a whole new scale to suppliers, helped us leverage that scale, share best practices, and reduce headcount.

FE also helped us totally rework our value chain, creating a global line of sight from procurement to the retail shelf. And that, in turn, drove dramatic improvements in customer service, inventory management, and cost-to-serve. In fact, Gillette went from back of the pack to among the best in those measures. We went from a company that Wal-Mart used to consider a troubled supplier to receiving its vendor-of-the-year award.

FE got at the root causes of trade loading, led by Joe Dooley, our senior vice president of North American Commercial Operations, and Ernst Haberli, and then Ed Shirley, our senior vice presidents for International Commercial Operations. Their efforts focused on reorganization and retraining that permanently exterminated trade loading at Gillette, and they also introduced new analytic tools that reduced trade spending year after year. It is safe to say that during the five years of our turnaround, Gillette was the only consumer products company in the world that consistently decreased trade spending while increasing advertising spending. All the industry trends were headed in the opposite direction.

Trade spending, which sometimes amounted to little more than price discounts, was rising markedly as the power of the retail chains increased and competition became more intense. Joe, Ernst, Ed, and their teams used funds for trade promotions with proven ability to increase sales and drive profitable growth. So while Gillette's spending was going down, it wasn't at our customers' expense; they were benefiting in a big way.

Those trade marketing tools were part of our Integrated Marketing Intelligence (IMI), which is another example of Functional Excellence. The IMI effort identified the best marketing practices and best tools around the world, which we then used to deepen our understanding of our consumers, customers, and competitors. We put the analytical tools in place to make fact-based marketing decisions. Through our IMI database, Gillette marketers around the world could access vital information like market structure and segmentation research, price-elasticity analysis, marketing-mix modeling, and consumer-insight data.

Realizing a Dream—Marketing Intelligence Online The high quality of this IMI information and analysis enabled us to act with confidence. With IMI, when we placed a commercial or did a promotion, we weren't gambling. When John Darman activated the initial phase of the IMI online database, I said it marked the realization of a dream of mine that was more than twenty-five years old. As a young product manager at General Foods, I would wish for access to information that could help inform and guide my marketing decisions. Unfortunately, the data was paper-based and stored in scattered locations, and, at best, it was difficult to get at even small portions of it in a timely way. With the Internet, IMI provided instantaneous access to a treasure trove of data for all Gillette people—anytime, anywhere in the world.

With IMI, when we placed a commercial or did a promotion, we weren't gambling.

IMI played an important role in the development of Duracell advertising. Battery marketing had become mainly an exercise in dueling claims. One company said, "My battery lasts longer than yours," and the other company said, "No, it doesn't." IMI showed us that consumers were saying, "We don't care." The reason: It was virtually impossible for consumers to put claims of long life to the test in everyday use.

So, guided by IMI, we rethought the advertising for our Duracell batteries to build on the trust people have in our brand, and the "Trusted Everywhere" campaign emerged. While this superb campaign was only a part of Duracell's successful turnaround, it was a key driver. As noted in chapter 11, despite rampant, competitive giveaways, excessive trade promotions, and a substantial price gap between Duracell and the low-end price brands, we increased sales, regained market shares, and boosted our profits and margins to best in the category.

IMI also helped reshape our marketing in Oral Care. For example, Oral Care president Bruce Cleverly and his marketers gained a better understanding of the strength of the Oral-B brand, which led them to place all our oral-care products under that name, including our power toothbrushes that previously used our Braun branding. With one brand name, our marketing for Oral-B would benefit both our manual and power toothbrushes.

We also gained a better understanding of the power of dentist recommendations when consumers are making a toothbrush purchase decision. Combining that understanding with our strong support among dentists, we created the powerful positioning "Brush Like a Dentist," which became an important element in Oral-B advertising. Again, marketing alone was not the sole driver of success, but it was important. And Oral-B was the only global player that increased market share in the total toothbrush market for several years running.

TOTAL INNOVATION—MORE THAN PHD'S IN WHITE JACKETS

There are hundreds of examples of change that were driven by Functional Excellence. But the most important point is that it went beyond a way to fix problems. It became the way that Gillette worked. It gave us a continuous dissatisfaction with the way things were and provided the sense of position and direction that drove meaningful, measurable change.

About two years into the initiative, I felt the time was right to introduce the third and final element of FE, something I called Total Innovation (TI).

TI served to increase the connection of FE with Total Brand Value, our overall vision, which said Gillette would continuously innovate to deliver consumer and customer value faster, better, and more completely than our competition. It also provided a broad-based organizational thrust to drive our growth.

It's almost a cliché to say that innovation is the life blood of consumer products. But it's true. If the growth of most consumer products' categories roughly tracks the population growth of 2 percent annually, you can see why, without innovation, the sector would lack vitality. If you combine innovation with top capabilities and best cost, you have a surefire formula for success.

The issue was to convince the organization that innovation was everyone's responsibility. The company had been so successful with our mega new-product launches—products like Sensor, Mach3, Venus, Oral-B CrossAction, Duracell CopperTop, Braun Activator, and more—that people had a great sense of pride in Gillette's innovative prowess. But they also felt that innovation was the exclusive domain of the engineers, researchers, and chemists. After all, Gillette had more than 160 people with PhD's and hundreds more with master's degrees, who populated our laboratories in the United States, Europe,

Convince the organization that innovation is everyone's responsibility.

and Asia. They spent all their time thinking up and developing the great new products of the future. The task of the rest of the organization was not to innovate, but to implement; to get the new products to the customers and consumers without a glitch.

The organization had to think about innovation, and their roles as innovators, in a different way, which is why we introduced the three-tiered concept of TI.

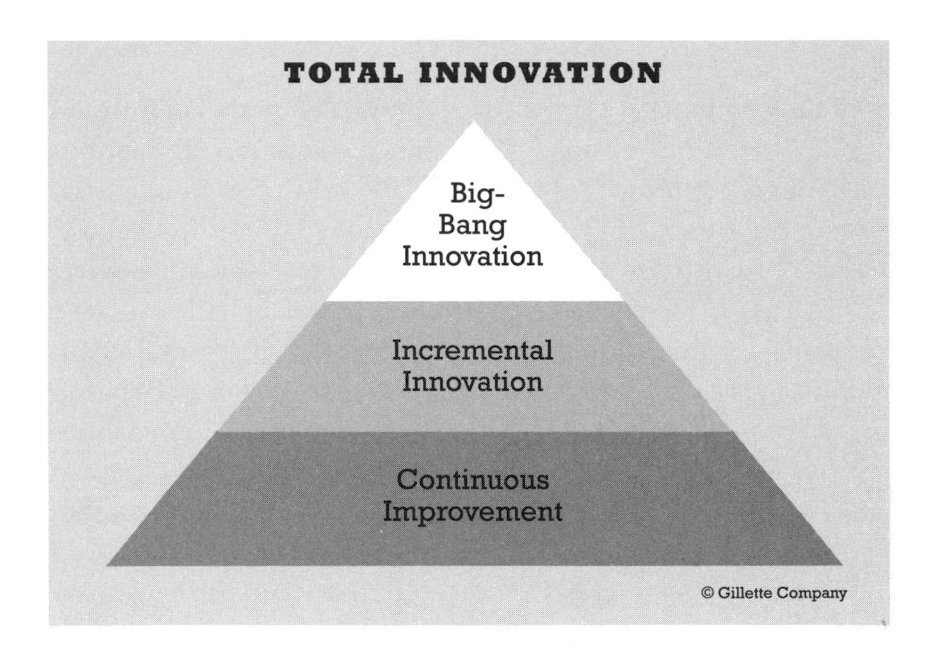

New Acronym on Everyone's Lips It took us more than a year to work on the communications and implementation program that would launch TI. But the time was worth it. TI became as well known throughout the organization as ZOG. Within a relatively short time, we had hundreds of teams working on innovation projects and programs throughout the company.

Our approach was to launch Total Innovation by doing a retrospective exhibit, called the Innovation Challenge, on what the organization had achieved during the past year, without having any name or focus put on the TI concept. I would make a speech to our senior leaders defining and describing TI and its benefits, then we would open the Innovation Challenge exhibit, where initially the senior leaders, and then, over a three-day period, the bulk of the Massachusetts-based Gillette organization, could see examples of TI. They would view TI in action, what it meant, and how it worked. In the end, more than five thousand Gillette employees toured the exhibit, so the impact was immediate. As I said, TI became the talk of the company.

Accelerating Growth to "Bring Home the Bacon" Let me describe how I talked about TI to the organization and then give a brief description of some exhibits on view in the Innovation Challenge.

Since I always like to establish the need for something before getting into it, I discussed Wall Street's commentary on Gillette, which by 2004 was giving us enthusiastic reviews on our turnaround efforts. One influential analyst, who consistently praised our performance, had written about us: "We believe further multiple expansion [*the price-to-earnings multiple that is one factor in setting the valuation of a stock*] is unlikely, and [*we*] think Gillette needs to grow into its current multiple, in other words, bring home the top-line and earnings bacon, before we can get excited about the stock at current levels."

That was a tough review, but not one you could disagree with.

We did have to "bring home the bacon," and to do it we had to find a way to unlock even more of our potential. We had to find a way to accelerate our future growth.

And the best way of doing that was to create a capacity throughout Gillette for TI. TI would be a new approach to the way we did our jobs. It would mean that everyone in the organization would take responsibility for generating ideas, which would then translate into action and improve the way we did business.

TI means everyone takes responsibility for generating ideas, which then translate into action and improve the way we do business.

A good way to think about Total Innovation is to think about a pyramid.

At the base is continuous improvement. And continuous improvement is important because it enables a company to improve a little every day. It could involve such things as a change to our packaging graphics or an improved product formulation. But continuous improvement alone would only keep us an average company, because our competitors would be making the same small improvements at the same time we were.

Big-Bang Innovation Still Essential At the top of the pyramid was big-bang innovation. This kind of innovation focuses on big new breakthrough products like Sensor and Mach3, or big changes in process like Gillette's Strategic Sourcing Initiative, which was delivering those hundreds of millions of dollars in procurement savings. Big-bang innovation is essential for success, but it no longer was enough.

We needed to increase our focus on the middle of the pyramid—what we called *incremental innovation.* And that meant the many smaller innovations that in the aggregate and over time would help us achieve the big step, which was to accelerate our company's future rate of growth.

One good example was our Mach3 Turbo Champion razor, which went from concept to rollout in only seven months. As described in chapter 1, we were able to use the color red to reinvent our Mach3 Turbo razor. Armed with exciting new packaging, effective advertising, and a high-impact retail program, Turbo Champion became an important weapon in Gillette's arsenal against the Quattro introduction from Schick.

Incremental innovation would create the success necessary to outperform the competition on a consistent basis.

That was Total Innovation: a combination of continuous improvement, incremental innovation, and big-bang innovation. Achieving TI would make the difference between Gillette being a very good company or being the best company. Another way to look at TI was with the analogy of a missile launch. Liftoff gets you off the ground and on your way. It allows you to break the gravitational pull of the Circle of Doom. But you need to fire the booster rockets to go into orbit to continue to resist the pull of gravity. It was time for Gillette to fire those booster rockets, and TI would do that for us.

Innovating Faster, Better, and More Completely As an introduction to the Innovation Challenge, I gave a précis on some of the twenty-five exhibits and described the categories into which the entries were divided. Those categories matched up with our Total Brand Value statement of performing *faster, better,* and *more completely*. I explained that we had chosen a winner within each category and an overall grand prize winner.

Within the *faster* category, the innovation was a classic example of problem solving. Significant increases in demand for Gillette's PowerStripe form of antiperspirant that was used in the Gillette Series and Right Guard brands required a rapid manufacturing response to ensure enough product was available to meet the demand. Mike Cowhig's manufacturing team took an innovative approach to create step-change improvements on the production line to manufacture product faster and more efficiently. They leveraged computer simulation technology to reduce the time needed; they engaged shop-floor personnel throughout the process; and they executed with excellence. They made major improvements in capacity, speed, output, and cost. And, they avoided a capital expenditure of $18 million for a new production line. They did it fast, and they did it on their own.

Champion of Incremental Innovation In the category of *better* was the work on the Mach3 Turbo Champion launch. Mach3 Turbo Champion epitomized incremental innovation. The Mach3 team came from a number of different units—Peter Hoffman's Blades & Razors Business Unit; Joe Dooley's Commercial Operations group; Ed DeGraan's Development and Engineering group; and John Manfredi's Corporate Affairs unit. They focused not on breakthrough technology, but on a red razor. They also challenged existing procedures and then created an innovative way to do things. Their plan included every element in the marketing mix, from themed packaging to displays and consumer PR programs. And the results were outstanding. Mach3 Turbo Champion was the catalyst for a 40 percent quarterly increase in consumer sales of Mach3 razors. As important, Turbo Champion went from concept to rollout in only seven months, beating the Schick Quattro to market.

In the category of *more completely,* a training initiative by Ned Guillet's human resources people working with the Blades & Razors manufacturing unit called Peak Performance was the top incremental innovation, which helped the manufacturing organization become significantly better. Their basic problem was fragmented training. There were different criteria for operations from plant to plant within Blades & Razors. And, typical of Gillette at the time, there was no baseline for what was best in class. The training process was also paper-based, inefficient, and unnecessarily complex. A cross-functional team attacked the problem by building a Web-based training model that centered on information mapping, Web-based documentation and assessment, constantly updated procedures, and streamlined certification. The results were outstanding. For example, technical knowledge increased tenfold and reporting of training data improved, as did communications within departments and among organizations. The process became a global benchmark for training.

New Culture Emerges We also chose one innovation that stood out above all the rest—an innovation that captured the creative thinking, collaborative approaches, and commitment to find a better way. It was the product development effort that led to the M3 Power razor.

M3 Power demonstrated the capability of DeGraan's engineering, technical, and manufacturing organization to utilize resources across their unit, and across several operating businesses, including the Blades & Razors, Braun, and Duracell divisions at more than a dozen locations around the world—in the United States, Germany, and several different sites in China. This team implemented new processes to handle significant complexity and delivered an innovative, best-in-class product all at a record-setting pace. The exceptional collaboration brought M3 Power to market in only thirteen months. Most important, the lessons learned from the M3 Power efforts would continue to be leveraged and optimized to support other new-product programs.

With Total Innovation, innovation would move from being the exception to becoming the rule. It would go from being outside the norm to defining the new culture of our company. And over time, TI did just that. Gillette became a culture of total innovation, and each layer of the pyramid—continuous improvement, incremental innovation, and big-bang innovation—got stronger.

One striking illustration was the development of the Gillette

Fusion system—a unique premium shaving system that defines big-bang innovation and places Gillette into a totally different realm than any of it shaving competitors. Fusion combines the most advanced engineering, technology, and manufacturing know-how to deliver the best-performing shaving system in the world. And that's not just a proud, former CEO talking; it's fact based.

At the risk of having this appear like a blatant commercial for Fusion, let me list some of those facts.

- The brand name utilizes the term for the physical reaction in which nuclei combine and release enormous energy; it's the imagery that describes Fusion's combination of breakthrough technology on the front and back of the shaving cartridge.
- The five spring-mounted blades on the front of the cartridge are configured much closer (30 percent closer than the Mach3 blades) to create a "shaving surface" that shaves closer by engaging more hairs more times with each successive stroke.
- On the other side, Fusion has the first ever Precision Trimmer, a patented single-blade trimmer that allows men to easily shave under the nose, trim sideburns, and shape facial hair (beards, goatees, and the like).
- Fusion comes in both manual and battery-powered forms that are protected by seventy patents.
- Results from independent consumer-use tests are impressive, to say the least: Fusion is preferred by a two-to-one margin over what were the best products on the market—our Mach3 Turbo and M3 Power.
- Fusion was preferred on all thirty-seven performance attributes, including "closeness," "comfort during and after shaving," and "less irritation."
- And another noteworthy and extremely important dimension was a big win on "worth paying more for." The consumers' overwhelming

willingness to pay a premium price for the added performance and benefits of Fusion is the critical factor that drives Gillette's one-of-a-kind history of trade-up successes—from Gillette Blue Blades all the way through Trac II, Atra, Sensor, Mach3, Venus, and now Fusion.

The teams that worked on Fusion—headed by Ed DeGraan and Mike Cowhig in Global Technology & Manufacturing and Peter Hoffman and Sandy Posa in the Blades & Razors Business Unit—devoted years to the effort. In all, hundreds of people were involved in a massive, matrixed initiative, including people throughout the Duracell and Braun divisions, who worked on various elements of the battery-powered Fusion razor.

Will Fusion be a long-term, blockbuster win for Gillette? At this writing, Fusion has been on the market less than a year, so I won't violate my mantra by making a prediction. But I will make some suggestive observations: Most consumer products are considered home runs if they ever generate $100 million annually in revenues. Fusion reached that level in three months!

So Functional Excellence, with the unique TI concept, is the long-term initiative that gives your company the enduring ability to win. It takes time, but it provides an unbeatable competitive advantage.

ACTING TODAY TO ENSURE STRENGTH TOMORROW

The other aspect of long-term planning is to know whether you will be able to be a player even after you accomplish your strategic objectives and have the full benefit of FE. What's your best estimate of how the external environment will change? And what can you do beyond organic growth to put your organization in the best position to prosper? What are your best options for external development?

Perhaps the best way to get into long-term planning and options is to talk about the Gillette merger with Procter & Gamble. As we have acknowledged and the media have reported, it wasn't Procter & Gamble who came knocking at our door asking to acquire Gillette. We initiated the discussions with P&G. We felt that bringing the two companies together made sense.

Yet people still ask, "Why did you merge *when* you did? You were doing so well. Your turnaround was in high gear and you had incredible momentum."

To answer that question, I quoted President Dwight Eisenhower, who said, "Our real problem is not our strength today; it is rather the vital necessity of action today to ensure our strength tomorrow."

Overreliance on One Category The questions the Gillette board and I had to answer were: Would there be greater potential and opportunity for Gillette as a stand-alone $11 billion company that was dependent on one product category, blades and razors, for two-thirds of its earnings, in a world increasingly characterized by global customers that are vastly larger and more powerful and by competitors that were rapidly consolidating?

Or would Gillette be best served by joining with a company with a similar vision, values, and culture and the scale and resources that would enable both companies to grow our brands and go head-to-head with the most powerful competitors and customers?

And that is what the merger was and is about. Alone, Gillette was then an $11 billion company, heavily reliant on one product category. With P&G, Gillette became part of a $70 billion company with a broad and well-balanced product portfolio. With Gillette, about half of P&G's business comes from health, beauty, and personal care, while the other half comes from baby, family, and household products. This balanced mix is a great combination of large, steadily growing household categories and faster-growing, higher-margin health, beauty, and personal-care businesses. And what an incredibly powerful brand portfolio it became—definitely the best in consumer products and arguably of any company in the world. More than twenty brands with a billion dollars or more in annual revenues. And not just any brands, but true icons: Tide and Ariel laundry detergents; Crest toothpaste, whitening strips, and mouthwashes; Pampers disposable diapers; Pantene, Head & Shoulders, and Wella hair and beauty products; Iams pet products; Mach3, Sensor, and Gillette blades and razors; Duracell batteries; Oral-B toothbrushes; and Braun electric shavers and appliances.

Driving International Growth As we looked to the future, we saw that P&G had the strengths to drive growth in areas that would be difficult for Gillette. P&G had unsurpassed distribution capabilities, particularly in international regions. China is a good example. We realized that in about a decade there would be more people shaving in China than in the rest of the world combined. The challenge was to capture that opportunity. Gillette was distributing shaving products in about sixty Chinese cities, with the majority of sales in the four largest cities.

P&G, on the other hand, had a distribution network that encompassed two thousand cities and more than eleven thousand towns throughout China. As a result of this merger, China's huge consumer market became almost immediately accessible to Gillette.

Another core strength is P&G's outstanding customer relationships.

In surveys of customers, P&G is consistently ranked as one of the top marketers in the consumer products category. P&G has what retailers want, especially the biggest retailers. For example, Wal-Mart derived about 17 percent of its revenue from P&G products in 2005, up from 12 percent only five years ago.

And as good as Gillette's relationship was with Wal-Mart, the merger with P&G made it stronger. The combined presence of Gillette and P&G products at retail is probably the single most important advantage of the merger. Even with the largest retailers in the world, P&G and Gillette are now key players in an elite group of working partners. And in the land of the giants, that is the way to drive consistent growth.

Selecting a Partner—Opting for Choice, Not Necessity For Gillette, the question was not whether we could execute our strategic plan and FE initiatives. We had proven our executional excellence. The question was, would that be enough? If the consolidation trends within the consumer products sector continued, would any $11 billion company be viable? Or, put another way, aren't you better off initiating the merger process with your partner of choice when you're working from a position of strength rather than waiting to be picked off by someone not to your liking when something has gone wrong and you are operating from a position of weakness?

By Any Measure, a Dream Deal From a vantage point of securing top dollar for shareholders, there is no question that working from strength and choosing your partner is the preferred course. For example, we received the highest price-earnings multiple for a consumer products company since 1997. The price was a remarkable 5.5 times our sales. It was the highest EBITDA (earnings before interest, taxes, depreciation, and amortization) multiple at 18.8 and the highest cash-flow multiple. In fact, it was the highest sales and EBITDA multiple paid for any public company with sales over $2 billion in any industry for the preceding eight years. The price was almost double where the stock was in our darkest days of 2001. And the dividend payout also rocketed.

Importantly, because it was a stock merger, Gillette shareholders were able to roll their investment into P&G shares on a tax-free basis. Finally, while Gillette represented only 16 percent of the combined companies' total sales, Gillette shareholders received 29 percent of the equity of the combined company. By any measure, it was an excellent price.

However, long before we even considered a possible merger, we had looked at all other options. Beginning in 2002, we had a thorough review with our board of all the strategic options, including mergers, acquisitions, and joint ventures.

Pursuing Growth in Oral Care Those board discussions and subsequent reviews led to two acquisitions in oral care, an area that exhibited advantaged growth. One was the Rembrandt company, which was the leader in the premium segment of tooth whiteners and pastes. The other was Zooth, a company that used licensed cartoon characters for toothbrushes for the kid segment.

Our corporate development group maintained a full list of potential acquisition candidates. In an average year, this group would screen more than twenty-five companies against a set of hurdles and criteria; the board would receive periodic updates.

At two different times, we had discussions with Colgate Palmolive. We wanted to build scale, and the combination of Gillette with Colgate, which had been considered but abandoned by Colgate and past Gillette CEOs, represented a good option. The combined companies would have increased revenues, an expanded global presence, and a larger pool of resources to fund future growth. In our first discussions, we explored the possibility of a merger of equals, but Colgate was not interested. In our second contact, we discussed an acquisition, since our share price had increased while Colgate's had declined.

Those discussions also did not work out, so we asked our board if we could study Procter & Gamble. Our board was involved every step of the way. We knew that our board was not interested in a merger just to get bigger; neither were we. But as we studied P&G, we realized that there were very few opportunities where everything fit—the finances, the scale, the business philosophy, the product portfolio, and the culture. Our objective was to become the best consumer products company in the world; this merger would create that company. We wanted to do something that would make a fundamental difference. This would do it.

Unanimous Agreement—Right Deal, Time, and Company All of our senior managers and all of our board members agreed that P&G was the right partner. But we had to have the right price, and the long process, with several false starts, that led to our final agreement gave me, our senior leaders, and the board an opportunity to reassess the certainty of our decision. During one period when talks had broken off, I spoke at length with Ed DeGraan, Chuck Cramb, John Manfredi, Peter Klein, and general counsel Richard Willard, the Gillette executives involved in the negotiations. I asked each one: "If P&G comes back, should we go forward with another round of negotiations? Are we absolutely certain that a combination with P&G is the right thing to do?" I told each of them, "If anyone says no, we shut everything down permanently."

These managers, most of whom had been at Gillette for almost their entire careers, felt this was a dream merger. When I went to our board in January 2005, our directors also knew that any one of them could stop the deal. I told our board the same thing, "If anyone doesn't want to do this deal, we won't do it." The board voted unanimously in favor of the merger. They voted yes because they knew the deal was right, the company was right, the time was right, and, most important, it was right for the long term.

. . .

To recap, two elements are important for long-term planning: an FE initiative that will differentiate your company by giving it the lowest costs and best innovative capabilities, and a long-term perspective that enables you to see your company's real prospects for the future. Neither one is enough by itself; together, they can make all the difference.

SUSTAINING YOUR ADVANTAGE—FUNCTIONAL EXCELLENCE MATTERS

How do you keep your success from being a flash in the pan, a onetime burst of excellence that shifts into undifferentiated mediocrity? That issue faces all individuals and businesses . . . and pursuing Functional Excellence is what I think makes the difference.

- Functional Excellence (FE) has three equally important elements—lowest costs, top capabilities, and across-the-board innovation.

- Eliminating all unnecessary costs provides you with the funds you need to invest in growing your business by increasing marketing, adding to research efforts, or accelerating product-development activities. Cost reductions must become part of your way of thinking throughout your career.

- Engage your organization in setting targets by having them get benchmarks to identify best costs, best practices, and capabilities for comparable operations. Then ask for comparisons versus the benchmarks.

- Require three separate cuts at determining the relative rank of your unit or business versus benchmarks. First, a self-assessment of how the unit feels they compare—usually, it will be *too high* versus reality.

Second, do internal polling of how the unit is viewed by others in the company—often, this will be *too low* versus reality. And third, an external view of how a consultant or industry expert views the unit—hopefully, a quantitative-based assessment that *gets it right.*

- Multiple perspectives will confirm the need for action and also underscore the importance of acting with urgency.

- Cost reductions and capability upgrades put you in a position to deliver on the third element necessary for long-term success—innovation that differentiates your products or services from competitors.

- To fully engage your entire unit or business, you need to use Total Innovation. Remember, this also has three parts—*continuous improvement* (day-to-day gains that keep you current with your competition), *big-bang innovation* (periodic blockbuster innovation that enables you to leapfrog your competitors), and, perhaps most important, *incremental innovation,* which gives you more than just day-to-day productivity gains, but less than a big-bang home run (perhaps a double rather than a homer, something similar to the concept for the Mach3 Turbo Champion, our "little red razor").

- Consider using an *innovation fair* or an *innovation challenge* to focus attention on the importance of unit-wide involvement. Reward your innovators with public acknowledgment and awards. Celebrate success.

SECTION IV

DOING THE RIGHT THINGS MATTERS

CHAPTER 13

POLITICIANS AND MEDIA MATTER

GALVIN IN LATHER OVER DEAL
Demands to know: Did CEO sell out Gillette?

The biggest question: Did [James Kilts], Gillette chairman and CEO, and other board members get improper payments in return for agreeing to the takeover by Crest-to-Pampers household goods giant Procter & Gamble? "We're very interested in this transaction," [William F. Galvin, Massachusetts Secretary of State] said, noting that Gillette board members and other executives "have a fiduciary responsibility to . . . shareholders."

—Brett Arends, *Boston Herald,* Feb. 2, 2005

Among the top business leader scoundrels of 2005, there's James Kilts, CEO of Gillette, who truly rode the gravy train of excess, making more than $185 million for his short four years of service at Gillette.

—Gretchen Morgenson, *New York Times*

> With this one, Kilts' take is estimated at $153 million. . . . Suggest that this is capitalism perverted, and you are labeled a socialist—a bigger sin than overt, conscienceless greed, which chief executives like Kilts like to define as "success."
>
> —Joan Vennochi, *Boston Globe,* Feb. 1, 2005

> There's a lesson here for [James Kilts]. His impending $162 million payoff from Procter & Gamble is new, thus dirty. In two generations, the Kilts fortune will be suitably laundered, and his grandson will be able to drown a young woman in a car and then run for president. Or his granddaughter can marry a gigolo, and the gigolo can then run for president, on your dime.
>
> —Howie Carr, *Boston Herald,* July 13, 2005

These quotes are just a few from the dozens of stories that followed in the wake of our announcement that Gillette would merge with Procter & Gamble. Were they predictable? Did we know there would be great furor in Boston because the city would lose the world headquarters of its last corporate icon? Did we know that several Boston politicians, noted as being among the most business-unfriendly in the nation, would attack me, my management team, and the Gillette board in order to push their personal political agendas? Did we know I would be pilloried day after day in the local press as a world-class, villainous, greedy capitalist? Of course we did.

So the questions we faced were: *Should we move forward with the merger? Or should we avoid the attacks by putting things on hold, and hope that something else would come along?* For me, there never was a question. But faced with such unpleasant consequences, not everyone would make the same call. Since similar scenarios are not unusual, you really do have to understand the media and politicians, and know what to do when your path intersects with theirs.

Throughout my career, I've had good relations with the news media and with politicians. Good, but limited. With the news media, I have never sought publicity. As a matter of fact, I have turned down many requests to participate in stories or features. At one point, John Manfredi and his people in our Gillette Corporate Affairs group kept track of the media requests. During the first year following my election as CEO, more than a hundred media groups—newspapers, business magazines, and radio and television stations—asked for interviews. We turned them all down.

LOOK BACK WITH PRIDE, NOT FORWARD WITH ANTICIPATION

The rationale for turning away the media was not a dislike or aversion. It reflected my belief that stories about CEOs tend to give the impression that one person is responsible for all of a company's accomplishments, or all of its mistakes and failures. The CEO has an important role. But a company's accomplishments reflect the efforts of thousands of managers and, in a global company like ours, tens of thousands of people throughout the organization. That acknowledgment of a broad-based group effort is not what makes for good stories.

My other belief that kept me from the media is my mantra of "Never overpromise; always overdeliver." Said another way, I don't want to talk about something that's on the come. I want to have it planned, orchestrated, and successfully implemented before I discuss it. It's far better to look *back* with pride on accomplishments, not look *forward* with anticipation of what might be. That approach is the antithesis of the way the news media operate. They want to have a scoop; get the story first; provide the reader, listener, or viewer with a glimpse of what might be coming.

> **I don't want to talk about something that's on the come. . . . That approach is the antithesis of the way the news media operate.**

So why do I say that I've basically had a good experience with the media? Because with a few notable exceptions, most of my contacts have been positive. I do my homework in advance of getting together with reporters. I know what the media want; I know how far I can go in giving them what they want; and I tend to be very direct with them.

A number of CEOs and others in business say they can't stand dealing with media. Reporters are arrogant, deceitful, ill-informed, poorly prepared, and biased against business, wealth, and the establishment, they say. You name it, and the media are accused of it. They are tarred with a broad brush.

I'm not naive. There are some bad apples and biased reporters. But the truly bad ones are relatively few and get weeded out by their own organizations. And bias often is another way of saying that most reporters are Democrats and liberal in their politics, versus businesspeople who are Republican and conservative. But the overwhelming majority of reporters are professionals who work hard to keep their political beliefs out of their reporting on business stories. They strive for objectivity, at least in the nontabloid press. (I think of the tabloids as being TV entertainment programs in print, not news reported by journalists.)

Sure, the real journalists misquote you from time to time, or use a quote out of context. And the limitations of space and time make it difficult for the news media to give stories a lot of texture and nuance. But by and large, when I have worked with the news media, the experience has been positive.

For example, on joining Gillette, I spoke with reporters from the *Wall Street Journal, Dow Jones,* the Reuters and Bloomberg newswires, and the *New York Times,* as well as the daily newspapers in Boston, Gillette's headquarters' city. The reporting was fair and balanced.

Once a year, after our major presentations to investors and

analysts at the CAGNY conference, I would be the exception among CEOs at the event by spending time with each of the reporters covering the conference. Most CEOs kept the reporters as far at bay as possible. Several times during the year, I would talk with members of the trade press about specific issues or industry trends.

Approximately three years into our turnaround efforts at Gillette, we agreed to cooperate with *Fortune* magazine for an in-depth profile on Gillette. That experience was as good as it gets, and I don't think it was atypical. The reporter was Katrina Brooker, a senior writer, who had worked several years with *Fortune.* I told her at the start that Gillette still had issues, but I felt there was a good story to be told about the progress we had achieved. She said that she had heard good things about what was happening, but would spend several weeks researching and investigating to find out whether people knowledgeable about the company would affirm it or had a different perspective.

I was as open with Katrina as I could be. After the fact, some people said I had been too open. I asked her to accompany me on a NetJet flight from New York to Boston. Since I'm a white-knuckle flyer, she observed it and reported it in her piece. I invited her to attend a practice session that preceded a meeting the next day with the senior leaders of Gillette. My day had been long and tiring, and the late-evening rehearsal was tough. As I mentioned earlier, I spend a lot of time and effort preparing for meetings—regardless of whether it is for an internal or external audience. If the top managers of the company are taking several hours of their day to be with me, then I better have something worthwhile to tell them and communicate it clearly and with a feeling, force, and conviction that make an impact.

"Being Treated Like Naughty Schoolchildren" As a result, with a fully scripted presentation, it's not unusual for me to go through thirty, forty, or even fifty different versions and drafts before arriving at the final copy. Each version is not a total rewrite. But the changes can and do range from reordering to rewording to major cuts and/or additions.

Once the script is final, then the read-throughs start. Something may look good on paper, but until you hear the words coming from your mouth, you cannot tell if it sounds like you, or like the person who worked on the draft with you. So the read-throughs and rehearsals are important to refine both the language and the meaning. Are you giving too much emphasis to a failed initiative? Are you giving enough credit to a cross section of business units? Are your specific expectations for the next six weeks clear? For the next three months? Next half year? Are the remarks too long? Too short?

Well, a part of Ms. Brooker's story dealt with our late-evening rehearsal, with comments both on my obsessive need to be prepared and the difficulty my associates had in coaching me. I opened the window too wide, some of my friends thought. To me, the flight, the rehearsal, and the time spent with Ms. Brooker in a variety of settings was the right thing to do when you've agreed to work with a major publication on something they say will be a major article.

For her part, Ms. Brooker did cast a wide net. She spoke with more than a dozen of my former associates—people who had worked for me or whom I had worked for; she spoke with customers and competitors; she spoke with analysts and investors; she spoke with current and former Gillette employees. She really did her homework. And the final article reflected it. While I didn't like everything in the piece, it did provide an excellent understanding of what we had done at Gillette and where we seemed to be headed.

". . . the company had gotten in trouble trying to keep up with increasingly unrealistic sales growth targets. In many ways, Gillette has been a victim of its own success during the

1990s. Its biggest seller—razor blades—is arguably the most profitable consumer product in the world. And nobody markets razors better. . . . It sells five times as many blades as anyone else. . . . The profit margin on all those razors is close to 40 percent. That's astounding when you consider that other grocery products, such as deodorants, yield margins of 7 to 9 percent. . . .

"Naturally, Kilt's new discipline has been hard for some Gillette old-timers to swallow. The company has long had a gentle, paternalistic culture, and until Kilts arrived all its top managers had been with the company for decades. Kilts' grading system—which he's implemented throughout the company—made some feel they were being treated like naughty schoolchildren.

"Not that the company is out of the woods yet. 'The question is: How far is this turnaround going to take us? That's what most people are wondering,' says Keith Patriquin, a buy-side analyst for Loomis Sayles. . . . By his own estimation, Kilts is just halfway through his turnaround. He believes the company needs to go further to cut costs. . . . Kilts, however, has no intention of changing the plan. 'Basically you are training the army. We were in basic training. Now we're getting out of our basic training,' he says, the tiniest of glints in his eye. 'The next step is taking this army to war.' "

GOING FROM WHITE KNIGHT TO PRINCE OF DARKNESS

So if the media are fair, do their homework, and strive to be professional, what explains the negative headlines and stories that appeared about me for a period of weeks following our announcement about the Gillette–Procter & Gamble merger?

Overnight, I went from someone who was doing all the right

things to restore Gillette to someone who was intent on destroying the company. I went from someone who wanted to create value and refused to cut corners or engage in bad business practices to someone who was indifferent to the plight of the average Gillette employee and retiree and was driven strictly by greed and self-interest. If the headlines and stories in the Boston papers were to be believed, I went from white knight to prince of darkness, with no stops in between.

There were several forces at play. While I did not enjoy the nasty labels and invectives that were coming at me during that time, I do understand why and how it happened. Let's look at three factors.

First, what preceded our announcement?

Second, what did others say at the time of the announcement?

Third, what kept the story alive?

The first element is straightforward. Going back in history, Boston had rivaled New York as *the* center in the United States for business and commerce. Through the nineteenth and middle of the twentieth centuries, Boston was headquarters for more major corporations and financial-services companies than virtually any city in the country, with the exception of New York and Chicago.

Gillette + P&G—Not a "Dream Deal" for Boston However, with the passage of time, companies consolidated, went out of business, and moved. By the late 1990s, Boston had a handful of financial services companies and only one major manufacturer, Gillette, with world headquarters in the city. Within a decade, it had lost such prestigious names as the Bank of Boston, John Hancock, Polaroid, Digital, and Wang.

Since Gillette had a hundred-year history in Boston, and both our world headquarters and largest factory were based there, our roots ran deep. Gillette was a part of the lives and family history of tens of thousands of people who had worked either in the manufacturing center, in the headquarters as part of the managerial and administrative group, or with one of the hundreds of companies that supplied goods and services to Gillette.

So announcing an action that would alter the relationship between Gillette and the city was bound to ignite considerable apprehension. We knew it, and we told the Gillette board of directors that regardless of what we said, the initial community reaction would be negative.

It is important to note here that unless you lived in Boston and read the daily press, you would never have been exposed to negative press about the merger. Within the financial community, among analysts and investors, and, consequently, in the financial and business news media—newswires, newspapers, and magazines—the merger was received with universal approbation and delight. Warren Buffett's characterization of it as a "dream deal" was widely shared.

And with good reason. The price paid was among the highest ever in consumer products history. So Gillette shareholders were being nicely rewarded.

The fit of Gillette with P&G was exceptional. The management philosophies and values were compatible. The product lines were not overlapping. Even the geographies were well matched. Places where Gillette had strength, such as Europe, were areas where Procter & Gamble was less strong. Places where Gillette had a presence, but could benefit from a more developed distribution infrastructure, such as China, coincided exactly with what P&G had in place.

Employees would be perhaps the biggest beneficiaries. P&G was rock solid and universally acknowledged as one of the best and most ethical employers in the world. It had received honors from *Fortune* as being on the list of the "most admired companies" for more than a decade; it also had been selected as one of the "best places to work." Gillette employees would become part of an organization that valued people, treated them very well, and placed their development and growth as one of the company's highest priorities.

P&G's treatment of its workforce extended to its vast retiree population. So Gillette retirees also could feel a great sense of comfort. Not only did the actual terms of the merger assure a continuity of their pensions and benefits, but the P&G corporate culture would also make anything other than the highest ethical conduct unthinkable.

Importantly, Boston also would be a beneficiary of the merger. Yes, there would be some job loss as redundant functions were consolidated and high-level executives were released, but the South Boston manufacturing center would be expanded, not cut. And P&G contributions and support of the community would be increased.

Viewing Political Office as a Lifetime Occupation Those were the facts. And that's what was reported across the country and around the world. However, the headlines that hit in Boston on day one and in the days following were more along the lines of *Gillette sells out to Ohio-based soap maker P&G; headquarters will be lost; jobs eliminated.*

The second part of the news-media reporting involved what others said about the merger. Here things get interesting due to the politics of the situation and are complicated due to the lawyers and regulatory restrictions that surround a transaction of this size and global scope.

While I have high regard for many in the news media, it is hard to say the same thing about politicians. There are thousands of honest, principled people who serve as elected officials at all levels of government. Unfortunately, there seem to be many more who view politics as a lifetime occupation, and though they may not be corrupt or dishonest, they will not hesitate to do and say the most outrageous things in order to protect their positions and prolong their time at the public trough.

It's a sad commentary that we have so many within our political leadership who serve the public so poorly. It is pervasive. I experienced it in Boston. But, fortunately, not at the highest levels—not by the mayor of the city or the governor of the state. Mayor Tom Menino, the four-time mayor of Boston, is someone I have known since my first days in the city. He is a hardworking, totally dedicated politician who has no pretense and no desire to do anything other than serve the city of Boston. He doesn't want to be governor or U. S. senator. He doesn't want to run a company or retire to the Riviera. If everyone in Boston politics emulated Tom Menino, the city would be attracting new business in droves.

Former governor Mitt Romney is another dedicated leader who was committed to working on behalf of the people of the state. He comes from a family where public service has a tradition, since his father, George, was governor of Michigan and also a presidential candidate.

However, other politicians, most notably the secretary of state, William F. Galvin, used our announcement for utterly ulterior political motives. And he did so with a callous indifference to the concern, worry, and anxiety that he caused thousands of Gillette retirees.

Within a matter of days, Secretary Galvin seized on a way to exploit our announcement, manipulate the news media, and sway public opinion for his own political advantage. Democratic contenders for the then upcoming gubernatorial election were attempting to push their candidacies, and Galvin desperately wanted to be in the race.

Since his position as secretary of state gave him few real responsibilities, Galvin had a tendency to reach far beyond his purview in order to grab headlines. And that's exactly what he did with Gillette. His initial charge: Gillette retirees were at risk of losing their pensions when Gillette merged with P&G. And the next day's headlines in the papers and newscasts on radio and television dutifully reported on the outlandish allegation.

As I said, P&G is no financial raider; it would never renege on pension obligations; and we had written protections into the merger agreement. So the charge was totally baseless and irresponsible.

Distorting Facts for Personal Gain But imagine countless retirees being confronted with a headline that says Gillette is being sold and the acquiring faceless company will take away all pension and health benefits. Our Gillette switchboards lit up with panicked calls. Our people provided the facts, but our retirees found it hard to believe that a public official would deliberately distort facts for personal gain.

Galvin did not stop with his charges about potential defaults on pensions. And this gets to the third factor of how stories are kept alive. There has to be someone in power who stokes the story. Galvin's next attack was directly on me, claiming that the entire merger was carried out single-handedly by me, with virtually no involvement of the Gillette board of directors, solely for personal gain. I wanted to cash out and make big dollars, so I somehow beguiled and duped our board and Warren Buffett, and made a deal with Procter & Gamble.

Another barrage of headlines and new stories ensued. Kilts is a greedy capitalist who is jeopardizing pensioners!! Fast-forward another few days, and Galvin is back again. This time he claims that the investment bankers colluded with me to give a lowball estimate of Gillette's actual market value so that Procter & Gamble could buy Gillette on the cheap, and Gillette shareholders would be cheated—they wouldn't get full value for their shares.

This is a charge being made by a state official despite the fact that Wall Street universally has applauded the deal, and the price being paid is among the highest ever in the sector, based on any relevant metric.

I said that the injection of politics into this situation made it "interesting." The insertion of lawyers—the outside lawyers who were advising us and guiding us through the extensive global regulatory procedures—complicated the situation.

Suffering Silently Through a Barrage of Charges It would seem evident that if the news media are filled daily with false charges and accusations that are poisoning the attitudes and feelings of employees, retirees, and the public, in general, the company should go public with its story. Gillette should speak out and say here are the facts: *Pensions are safe; the price is among the highest ever paid; P&G is one of the best companies in the world and will be great for our employees and for Boston.*

It seems simple and obvious. But not to the lawyers, whose main responsibility was to get a nod from the Securities and Exchange Commission that everything was in order to proceed with a vote by shareholders on the transaction, and an OK from the Justice Department in the United States, the Office of Fair Trading in the United Kingdom, the Monopolies Commission in Brussels at the European Union, along with more than fifty other regulatory entities around the world, that there were no restraint of trade or other complicating issues.

To the lawyers, our saying anything was forbidden. Even repeating previously published information, public domain materials, or unembellished factual information was verboten.

Their logic was unassailable given U.S. regulations that were written in the pre-Internet era. The regulations say in effect that no information about a transaction can be distributed once a prospectus has been filed, otherwise the SEC can require the issuance of a new prospectus, which could delay the transaction by weeks or even months. The regulations' concern, when initially promulgated, was that companies could issue new, material information altering the terms of a transaction and that it would never reach shareholders. Twenty-four-hour all-news television was an unknown concept then, and the SEC rules have not yet caught up with reality. So a company like Gillette, which found itself barraged with false and misleading charges and accusations, is forced to suffer silently or risk long and potentially deal-breaking delays.

The final chapter of this saga played out in several parts. First, the shareholders, even those in Boston, where Secretary Galvin received considerable visibility for his spurious charges, voted overwhelmingly in favor of the transaction. The total shareholder vote in favor was more than 96 percent.

Second, Gillette retirees are very much whole. There has been absolutely no change to their pensions or benefits.

Third, the Gillette manufacturing center in Boston continues to have new money invested in it. As a matter of fact, we completed a total investment of nearly $1 billion in ten years, upgrading equipment and adding new capacity. This South Boston facility is the largest shaving factory in the world and the source for all of our new Fusion blades and razors in North America.

Fourth, Secretary Galvin was told by a state court that he had overreached his jurisdiction in claiming a right to make charges about excessive compensation and retirees' issues. His sole area of authority was to determine if Gillette had been given any wrong information during the lead up to the merger, not whether Gillette had done anything wrong itself.

Piling on Big Business Fifth, Galvin pulled out of the gubernatorial race early, realizing that despite all his grandstanding charges, hearings, and headlines, support for his candidacy was slim, to say the least. At this writing, Galvin has never issued any findings as a result of his investigation.

Let me backtrack now to answer more fully one of the questions I raised at the start of this discussion: What gave this story life beyond its normal news cycle?

The role of politicians—and especially Secretary Galvin, in

this instance—cannot be overstated. Galvin's charges, his staged hearings, his steady stream of news-media leaks all pumped great interest and life into this story. Unfortunately, he had a malleable news media that was all too willing to play along with him. I know it's hard for a beat reporter to openly question the motives of a high-level elected official, but the Boston media was, by and large, totally compliant.

The business-news reporters had a long and symbiotic relationship with Galvin. He was in a position to provide a steady stream of business- and finance-related stories that could fill the pages of their business sections and sometimes give them front-page bylines. So it was difficult to ask provocative questions of a good and steady source, even if his charges seemed rather thin and attenuated.

The second factor providing the story with longevity was the role of the columnists, editorial writers, and those writers who considered themselves feature reporters and would write with a heavy overlay of opinion and color. For this group of the media, the story had all of the elements necessary to write endless pieces without risking reader fatigue. The charges included greed, corruption, and malfeasance that would result in job loss, pension loss, loss of prestige for Boston, and much more. Given all of the corporate bad news that preceded our announcement, this was an ideal time to pile on a big business and its leaders. And most of the editorial writers did just that, not once, but several times.

For example, shortly after the merger proposal was announced in January, the *Boston Globe* ran a thousand-word piece on its op-ed page by a man named Jack Falvey, whom the *Globe* identified as "a former Gillette executive." Mr. Falvey took a number of shots at Gillette's past and current management teams and gave his perspective on P&G's plans for Gillette, which included the closing of our South Boston manufacturing center, he said.

The *Globe* failed to check Mr. Falvey's credentials. If they had, they would have discovered that he was a sales training manager, not an executive. He worked for Gillette for six years in our South Boston facility, not corporate headquarters. And his employment was terminated in 1978, more than twenty-five years before the proposed merger was announced. Falvey's "opinions" on what senior executives were thinking and his assertions on what P&G might do with Gillette were unfounded and untrue.

To this day, I find it inconceivable that the *Globe* would give such prominent op-ed space, and attendant credibility, to a person who worked for Gillette for a few years in a lower-level management position from which he was removed nearly three decades ago! And I say this, even though I am a member of the board of directors of the New York Times Company, which owns the *Boston Globe*.

Reporting to Godless Wall Street On July 14, months after the announcement, one of the *Globe*'s top columnists devoted her space to the merger and concluded: "The corporate behemoths that emerge from these transactions owe their shareholders, not their neighbors. They report to godless Wall Street, not to any higher moral authority, and certainly not to the citizens of any commonwealth, city, or community." She was convinced Gillette employees and Boston would be shafted. Once again we responded to the column, and once again the *Globe* edited out much of the content.

Serving the Community The final factor contributing to Boston's piñata-like treatment of Gillette was its long-standing culture of distrust toward and, to some extent, dislike for business. This antipathy is obvious in its taxes, which are among the highest in the nation; it is obvious in restrictions and encumbrances on business that want to invest and expand in the city. It is obvious across the board, even though the administration of Mayor Menino is trying to change the attitude.

I consider the Boston flap that surrounded our merger announcement to be an aberration. By and large, my relations with the media and politicians have been low key, but positive. I believe that businesses have a duty to act responsibly within their communities and to observe all laws and support initiatives that help its citizens. I personally am a big supporter of the United Way. Back as a child growing up in Illinois, some of my relatives received assistance from a predecessor organization to the United Way. That outreach had a big impact on me, and I have led fund-raising efforts at every company that I've been associated with.

As a matter of fact, when I started with Gillette, employee support for the Boston United Way campaign had withered to a participation rate of between 30 and 40 percent. I had just left Nabisco, where our participation rate ran about 95 percent, so I was horrified and dumfounded by Gillette's poor showing. As we dug into the causes, we realized it was a manifestation of a dispirited employee workforce—a Gillette organization that had lost its winning ways and was sinking into broad-based feelings of self-doubt and disengagement. Over the next four years, Gillette's participation rate more than doubled, and we received the United Way's highest award for the creativity and energy of our campaigns.

I also believe that it is the responsibility of top managers to provide the leadership for their sectors, especially as it relates to the business-government dialogue about public policy. Despite everything we had going on at Gillette, I served as chairman of the Grocery Manufacturers Association (GMA), the main trade organization for our business, which is noted for its influence on Capitol Hill. GMA is our leading industry lobbyist, which I mean in the best sense of that word. GMA is empowered to let the government know when proposed legislation, regulation, or treaties would work well for the consumer and food products sectors, when they would not, and what compromises are possible. Over the years, led by Manly

Molpus, one of the top trade association leaders in the country, GMA has played a positive role both for its member companies and also for the country through its stands on the elimination of trade barriers and the liberalization of trade.

Several other Gillette leaders also held leadership positions. My coauthor John Manfredi served as head of the International Food Information Council, an organization that provides science-based information about widely misunderstood food issues, and chairman of the Advertising and Marketing Commission of the International Chamber of Commerce in Paris, which is the global leader in preparing codes of conduct that are used by hundreds of thousands of businesses around the world to self-regulate their advertising.

The list of our involved managers was lengthy, and it underscores the point that leaders must lead within their companies and in appropriate areas outside that will benefit the company and will be good for the sector and public at large.

SETTING THE PUBLIC AGENDA AND ATTITUDES

So what's the relative importance of the news media and politicians? How much do they matter? They are not the make-or-break forces that keep CEOs and others awake at night *most of the time.*

As public institutions, however, corporations depend on public opinion and public sufferance in order to survive and prosper. And the news media are not only "messengers" who convey stories, they also are "influencers" who shape the public agenda as well as attitudes. I think company leaders should be open and aboveboard with the media. They are doing an important job, and usually do it well.

Regarding politicians, the good ones really need our help because there are more than enough bad ones causing problems.

A corporation has a social responsibility and leadership obligations that it should fulfill. And the bigger the company and the higher its profile, the greater its responsibility.

So the news media and politics definitely belong on the list of things that matter.

DEALING WITH MEDIA AND POLITICIANS—BE GUARDED BUT HONEST

- Be prepared. There's no such thing as a casual or informal meeting with the media or a politician. They will have an agenda. You must have an objective and plan.

- Agree in advance on subject matter. Open-ended interviews and discussions are never a good idea. Know the ground that will be covered and keep the discussion channeled to those topics. Wide-ranging discussions almost always lead to oft-regretted, unintended comments.

- Remember that the media person is a trained communications professional; you're an amateur. As good as you are in your position, you're not as skilled at responding to questions as a broadcaster or reporter is at asking and pursuing them. So keep your answers brief and simple. Be direct. If you try to evade or dance around issues, you're likely to be misunderstood or have your responses used out of context.

- Prepare key messages and stick with them. Whenever you're talking with the media or politicians, know what you want to communicate. Think about them. Distill them to a few essentials. Then make sure you deliver them with precision and clarity.

- Remember that reporters want news; forecasts and predictions make for interesting stories. Obliging them can lead to commitments you can't deliver. Beware of entering the Circle of Doom.

- Rehearse long and hard. Until you hear a question and experience the emotions of responding, you're not ready to go near the media. Work with someone who can assess and critique you. Better yet, videotape the rehearsal and force yourself to go through the painful process of watching it—preferably a few times—so you can see what's working and what's not.

- Less is more. Unless there are very good reasons for agreeing to an interview or media placement, you're better off taking a pass. There's more downside risk than upside potential anytime you go into the public arena without an objective.

- Be guarded but honest with the media. They have a job to do. It's an important one, especially in a free-enterprise democracy. So understand their role and how they work.

- Realize there's no such thing as an off-the-record comment with the media, so be careful. But never try to deceive or prevaricate. That's not only bad ethical behavior, it also never works.

CHAPTER 14

LEARNING MATTERS—REFLECTIONS ON A CAREER OF BEING CONTINUOUSLY DISSATISFIED

This final chapter will circle back and talk about some things previously discussed, but do it from a different perspective or in a context that reinforces some points.

It will also cover some lessons learned over a thirty-plus-year career that didn't fit neatly into the principles and practices previously discussed. Much of this learning has helped form one of my lifelong mantras: *Continuous dissatisfaction with the status quo is the best way to keep growing as an individual and an organization, or company.*

Some knowledge came from experiences early in my career, when I was trying to understand how the business world worked. And much of it came from my contacts with some truly notable figures in the business and investment communities—people like Warren Buffett and Henry Kravis, to name just two.

The observations range from aphorisms such as "Easy access to money causes undisciplined decisions" and "Bad businesses will beat good managers every time" to some anecdotes that drive home the importance of relationships and how career-long associations with your business cohorts can help with your success. In short, this chapter is a grab bag of things that have been useful in guiding my daily actions.

MENTORS—RELATIONSHIPS THAT MATTER

Let me start with relationships. At some point in their careers, I think every successful leader has a mentor, someone who has a close relationship and profound impact on the person's future. For me, it came relatively early in my career at General Foods. I was thirty-two at the time, and reporting to Bob Sansone, who was then president of the Beverage Division.

Every successful leader has a mentor, someone who has a close relationship and profound impact on the person's future.

Bob was a bright but rough-and-tumble guy from New York City. He had street smarts plus a great education that he received at Columbia University, where he earned both his undergraduate degree and his MBA.

It was the combination of common sense, book learning, and a serious dedication to applying management concepts that made Bob an exceptional leader. He was the total package.

Many of my management approaches to strategic planning, annual objectives, quarterly priorities, and weekly reports and meetings had their genesis with Bob. He was organization personified. But he was also much more. Bob had great self-confidence that permeated from him and affected everyone in his group. There was never a question in Bob's mind or anyone else's about whether he would succeed. It was always a matter of how quickly and how much above and beyond targets he would be. That self-confidence led some people to look on Bob as self-centered and arrogant. And he may have had some of that in his personality. But what made him rise above that characterization in my opinion was the absolute faith and confidence he placed in his people.

Once Bob got to know and trust you, he would back you to the hilt, regardless of the circumstances. He would stay close to you when the situation required it, but he would give you incredible leeway and latitude to do your own thing within the agreed-upon objectives and priorities. Working with Bob was being given a unique opportunity to grow as an individual and as a manager.

Not surprisingly, Bob had a rapid rise at General Foods, including a stint as president and general manager of the company's large Brazilian operations. In that position, and at that time in the mid-1970s, Bob had almost total autonomy. Heads of international subsidiaries had carte blanche to manage as they saw fit. And the roller-coaster, up-and-down economic swings in Brazil, which was then being governed by a military junta, gave Bob lots of opportunity to practice and hone his management skills.

Bob returned to the United States with General Foods, but ultimately was lured to Mattel in California, where he had a very successful stint as its president. Unfortunately, Bob died while in his forties from cancer. However, he had made such a positive impact on the company that when Mattel was in trouble in the 1990s, it felt comfortable recruiting another General Foods/Kraft executive, Bob Eckert, who also had the talent, temperament, and background necessary to lead the toy company's turnaround.

Loyalty—Staying True to Those You Know Everyone should have a Bob Sansone in his or her career. People like him make a big difference. For example, in addition to his expertise in management process, Bob's loyalty and belief in his people had a major influence on me throughout my business career. They're one of the reasons that so many people have worked with me more than once.

All too many managers forget everyone who stays behind when they move to a new position. I'm just the opposite. I know who contributed to the success that made my move up possible and want them with me for the next chapter.

All too many managers tend to forget everyone who stays behind when they move to a new position.

I have mentioned that my coauthor John Manfredi worked with me at General Foods in the 1970s, and again at Nabisco in the 1990s, at Gillette throughout the turnaround, and now on this book. And John is not the exception.

I first worked with my other coauthor, Bob Lorber, when I was at Kraft in the 1980s. And again while at Gillette, where Bob counseled our HR and finance groups as they worked through their transformations.

Peter Klein is perhaps my longest-term associate. He worked with me at General Foods and Kraft as a marketing consultant. He left his successful consulting practice and worked for me full-time at Nabisco, and again at Gillette. We still share office space in Rye, New York, so the relationship continues.

Joe Schena, now an associate at Centerview Partners, the private-equity company that I cofounded, is also someone I knew from my days at General Foods and Kraft. We recruited Joe to Nabisco, where he headed up planning, and then to Gillette, where over time he became the chief financial officer.

Mark Leckie worked with me at Kraft and then went off to Campbell Soup and Heinz. But I lured him to Gillette to run Duracell, and then he became head of the Gillette businesses for P&G.

Doug Conant and Rick Lenny are both Kraft alumni who wound up with me again at Nabisco. Doug was already at Nabisco; I brought in Rick Lenny to run our biggest division, Nabisco Biscuit. I worked with Roger Deromedi at both General Foods and Kraft and helped to launch his ascendancy to CEO. While we haven't worked together again, we stayed close, and our Gillette board asked Roger to become a member.

Dave Rickard, the chief financial officer of CVS, the giant drug retailer, is another career-long associate. We've worked together twice—at Kraft and Nabisco. We still stay in touch and share perspectives on the industry and general business issues.

The list goes on, but the point is evident. Loyalty and long-tested relationships really matter and make a difference. Why anyone would want to take a chance with a total stranger if a past associate is available and qualified for a position is beyond me.

Fortunately, the people whom I have felt good about have reciprocated the feelings. They have enjoyed and benefited from the relationships, and to this day, many of them have indicated a desire to do it again. There is no greater compliment to a leader than for their people to say, "Let's do it one more time."

PERSONAL MOMENTS MATTER . . . THROUGHOUT A LIFETIME

Another thing about relationships has struck me recently. In reading the transcripts of the interviews with my associates, I realized that some of their most vivid recollections involved personal moments with me that affected their careers and our ongoing relationships.

For example, Doug Conant, now CEO at Campbell Soup, recalls the time that we went out for a hamburger at McDonald's. We talked through a number of tough issues he faced in managing Nabisco snacks, condiments, and other foods—a mixed bag of superstar and also-ran businesses. But we also spent a lot of time on his feelings and mine about what was going on in the office and in our own lives.

Betsy Holden, who became co-CEO of Kraft, recalls a lunch we had early in her career where she was convinced, because of her struggles with the pizza business, that she was headed for a sort of last supper—her termination meal. Actually, I wanted her to know that I trusted her and would work with her to succeed.

Bob Eckert speaks of the time spent in the basement of my suburban Chicago house where we bonded through the crucible of figuring out how to deal with a cheese crisis for Kraft.

Genuine, real relationships really do matter.

These recollections and so many more come from incidents that were unplanned in terms of the effects that they had, but were totally genuine and real in terms of the feelings I had toward each of my associates. It is something that also makes you feel good. Genuine, real relationships really do matter.

I have many of these same feelings about my relationship with Warren Buffett. From my first meeting with him, there was a sense of comfort, trust, and closeness. Over the years, that relationship grew as I looked to him as a board member for advice, counsel, and guidance. Warren never said much, but his words were always full of common sense and wisdom.

Warren Buffett—Turning Off the Raiders At Warren's parting luncheon from our Gillette board, I reminisced about how he had saved the company. It started in the 1980s, a time of great turmoil in American business. Ivan Boesky and Michael Milken were becoming notorious, playing fast and loose with the rules and making millions from shady deals. The corporate raiders were riding high.

The takeover frenzy was in full swing, and it didn't take long for Gillette to become a target. From the fall of 1986 through the summer of 1988, Gillette fought off four takeover attempts. Three were tender offers by Revlon chief Ron Perelman. The fourth was a tough proxy contest against a group called the Coniston Partners.

It was a close fight, and Gillette won by the narrow margin of 52 percent of the shares voted. Gillette's defense was led by the then chairman and CEO, Colman Mockler.

As Gillette fought back against the hostile takeover attempts, the company was forced to borrow heavily to repurchase shares. About $1.5 billion in equity was replaced with debt in the years between 1986 and 1988.

By the time the smoke cleared in late 1988, Gillette had a negative net worth. But not for long.

In the spring of 1989, a friendly investor called, wondering if the company would be open to a proposal. A few days later, Colman Mockler and Warren Buffett met in Omaha. Over a lunch of hamburgers and Cokes, they roughed out an agreement that was finalized a few months later.

Warren's $600 million stock buy was a clear vote of confidence in Gillette's future and a strong signal that raiders should look elsewhere.

The company gained the cash it needed to reduce debt and the breathing room to focus on its strategic growth plan. More important for the longer term, it gained Warren as an outstanding addition to the board.

In preparing for the farewell luncheon, I came up with some comments of Warren's that demonstrate both his wisdom and wit. The first two were mentioned earlier in the book, but they deserve repeating.

On the dangers of forecasting, he said in 2001: "For a major corporation to predict that its per share earnings will grow over the long term at, say, fifteen percent annually, is to court trouble. . . . The problem arising from lofty predictions is that they corrode CEO behavior."

And on the same subject, he later said: "Be suspicious of companies that trumpet earnings projections and growth expectations. Managers that always promise to 'make the numbers' will at some point be tempted to 'make up' the numbers."

"Bad Businesses will Beat Good Managers Every Time" On Gillette's blade business: "It's pleasant to go to bed every night knowing there are two and a half billion males in the world who have to shave in the morning."

Here is a Warren story about trade loading. It goes like this: "At noon on the last day of the last month in the quarter, the foreman at the warehouse is asked, 'How's the quarter going?' He replies, 'The quarter's only half over. Ask me at five.' "

Warren on spending: "Easy access to funding tends to cause undisciplined decisions."

On integrity: "It takes twenty years to build a reputation and five minutes to ruin it. If you think about that, you'll do things differently."

On buying a business and unsuccessfully trying to turn it around: "Bad businesses will beat good managers every time."

And finally, a story that is one of my favorites. It is on motivation, and Warren is speaking about one of his managers, Jack Byrne. "Byrne is like the chicken farmer who rolls an ostrich egg into the henhouse and says, 'Ladies, this is what the competition is doing.' "

SECRET TO SUCCESS—DO SOMETHING YOU ENJOY

Back to mentors. Bob Sansone was a mentor early in my career, and Mike Miles played that same role in the middle of my career. Mike was CEO of Kraft, and I came in as his vice president of strategy after having worked at General Foods, Oscar Mayer, and Kraft International.

Mike is one of the brightest, hardest-working, most self-effacing people I've ever met. When asked why he was so successful in business, becoming the CEO of the Philip Morris Companies (now Altria) as well as Kraft, he says, "I've thought a lot about that and the only truthful answer is *pure luck*. Being at the right place at the right time."

Why were so many of Mike's people so successful? "They would have turned out to be top-notch, first-rate managers whether they had ever worked with me or not. My management style is that you don't overmanage your people. You don't second-guess them. You let them make mistakes. You hold them accountable. And you try to instill the right values." He did all that and much more. He had a view of business and life that helped to shape my career.

His number one teaching is to do something you enjoy. If you like what you do, and are excited by the challenges, your passion will show in the quality of your results. He also favors thoughtful, quality work over large quantities of mindless activity. Too many people, he says, believe they are judged on the amount of work they do; they learn too late that it is how well they do their work that makes the difference.

In a similar vein, Mike feels strongly that the quality of products matters. In a world that is filled with things that don't work, Mike says that you will be rewarded if yours do work.

If you like what you do, and are excited by the challenges, your passion will show in the quality of your results.

And finally, Mike always advises that you surround yourself with the best people. Fairly or unfairly, Mike says everyone always credits the bosses for the successes of their people and blames bosses for their failures. So it's wise to hire and promote people who are better than you are, and fire the slackers and troublemakers promptly.

TERMINATIONS—CONFRONT REALITY, AVOID JUDGMENTS

Making the tough decision to fire someone, and doing it promptly, is something that I took to heart early on. Terminating anyone is tough, but it doesn't get any easier if you put it off. Once you make the decision to fire someone, you start sending out signals, consciously or unconsciously, that are difficult to ignore. The intended employee's time on the job may be prolonged, but it will not be quality time, to say the least. If you level with someone, a termination or separation can be positive. Unless you are dealing with a bad actor, people lose their jobs because their position has become redundant or unnecessary, or because the person's individual skills are a mismatch for the position.

Terminations should not be judgmental. They should be an attempt to help the person find something he will enjoy doing and will do well. There are many people whom I have counseled out of the company whom I still maintain contact with. Almost all of them have gone on to rewarding and successful careers. On the other end of the spectrum is a former CEO I worked with whose phobic inability to terminate anyone was legendary. As a result, separations were infrequent and a lot of deadwood accumulated. When a firing was absolutely essential, this CEO would schedule a business trip—at least a week long and often out of the country—to absent himself! Consequently, those in the know always were a bit apprehensive when they heard that the boss had a long trip planned.

We have spoken a lot about off-site meetings because of their value in aligning objectives and cementing bonds among colleagues. One off-site meeting stands out in my memory over all others. It was our first Gillette off-site, the operations committee's first exposure to how Gillette would be run in the future: no more silos, lots of sharing and collaboration, individual objectives and priorities that tied to company objectives and priorities, rigorous accountability, and promises made and kept. It was a full list of changes.

As noted several times before, one of the important roles for every leader is to be a careful listener and observer. And it became obvious to me within a matter of an hour or two that one of the executives was not likely to make the transition from the old to the new Gillette. He was bright, energetic, and knew his business from A to Z. But he was not a team player. He did not want to share and collaborate; he did not want to have his performance tied to any others. He wanted to excel on his terms in his own way.

I kept my promise to base decisions about retention on performance, so I filed my observations away. However, it was no surprise when not long after the off-site, the executive came to my office and retired. He said that he loved Gillette and thought we would be successful with the turnaround, but the new approach was not for him. We had a full and frank discussion, and it was obvious that he made the right decision, so he left. If we had not had the off-site meeting, this executive would eventually have come to the same realization. However, the concentrated action and focused format of the off-site accelerated the process for him, just as it did for the others.

CLEAR DIRECTION—LOOK TO YOUR CHURCH GROUP

I always like to keep things simple and give clear direction. You get much more from people when they know what you want and are free to act, than when their first action in times of doubt is to schedule a meeting with you. But when you're dealing with areas of judgment, especially with areas involving changing standards and tastes, it's not easy to know how to frame your guidance.

For example, when we were developing our plans for TAG body spray, several of the initial marketing approaches stepped over the line of good taste and decency. That was to be expected, since we were trying to reach teenage boys and young men with a product—body sprays—that they viewed as a surefire way to get girls.

There's nothing much in business school curricula or business books that's helpful when you are dealing with issues of changing mores, tastes, and the new media environment. So I finally reverted to a variation of something that I had used in the past. My direction was: *If your marketing approach wouldn't pass muster with your church group, it won't be OK with me.*

I tell my people: Always do the right thing. When in doubt, think back on what your parents and clerics told you when you were a kid. You'll have a good moral compass for how you should be acting.

GAUGING DISCIPLINE AT GUT LEVEL

The importance of discipline in business is hard to overemphasize. Since winning is measured by small margins, especially in consumer products, paying attention to details and executing with excellence really do matter. But focus and extra effort aren't things you can expect from an organization that lacks discipline.

So in addition to underscoring the importance of discipline in my meetings, presentations, speeches, one-on-ones, and off-sites, I found an effective, backdoor approach that made the point, literally at a gut level.

Focus and extra efforts aren't things you can expect from an organization that lacks discipline.

Many years, usually at the off-site that followed the Christmas holidays, I would invite my direct reports to participate in the *Jim Kilts Weight Loss Challenge* so we could shed the extra pounds gained over the holidays.

The Challenge clearly had health advantages. Who wouldn't benefit from losing the ring around the middle! And it also served as a bonding experience, as team members compared notes on how their weight-reduction efforts were going. The rules were simple. Those people who wanted to participate would wager $100 that they could beat the Challenge. Participation was voluntary, but out of a group of direct reports that usually ranged around twelve to fourteen people, it was rare to have more than one or two who didn't join in.

We would agree upon a Challenge amount to be lost—say, fifteen pounds for men; ten pounds for women. Everyone would be weighed by the company doctor, who would keep the records confidential; at the end of three months, prior to the next quarterly off-site meeting, everyone would be reweighed. The doctor would then give me the names of those who won and those who didn't. There would be no other info, such as how much weight each person lost, or their absolute starting or ending weights. The purpose of the challenge wasn't to embarrass anyone or surreptitiously compile data.

The winners were announced at the off-site, and they would then split the pot of money collected from those who didn't make it and had to surrender their $100 wagers. More often than not, we would select a charity that would receive all the winnings.

The whole thing was good fun. But it also made the point that discipline extends to all areas of our lives, and that it brings rewards. Perhaps the most interesting aspect of the Challenge was what it told me about the individual participants.

Discipline extends to all areas of our lives, and it brings rewards.

RETHINKING THE APPROACH TO WINNING

Some—let's call them the *hypercompetitors*—wanted to prove they were better than all the rest. They wanted to beat everybody else to the weight-loss finish line. Our ex-football star at Gillette, Ned Guillet, fell into that camp. Ned not only cut off virtually all food intake, he also started exercising two to three hours a day. Sure enough, he dropped about ten pounds in four days, but on the fifth day he nearly passed out, and decided to rethink his approach.

Others, the *hyperconfident,* decided that fifteen pounds wasn't much of a challenge. So there was no need to suffer through three months of deprivation; they could do it all in the last two to three weeks. I don't recall anyone in that group ever actually winning.

There were a few—the *fatalists*—who would enter the Challenge assuming they would never win. They did nothing, and they never did win.

And, of course, there were *winners,* those who did the mental homework necessary to figure out how they would change their regimes and what foods they would avoid over the entire three months to meet or beat the goal. Needless to say, more often than not, the disciplined weight losers won the prize.

Yes, I did compete. While I usually won, I can vividly

remember each time that I didn't. They were self-learning experiences.

SOME SIMPLE CONCEPTS

Let me end this chapter where we began. As someone who likes to keep things simple, I would summarize my thinking with a core belief that a continuous dissatisfaction with the status quo is the best way to keep growing as an individual, an organization, or a company. Constructive discomfort with yourself, your business, your people, and your products, systems, and services will fuel ongoing change and progress. However, never allow your dissatisfaction to become negative or dysfunctional. That's because you will find over time that some other simple concepts—such as relationships, loyalty, shared moments, and loving what you do—are things that also really matter.

THINGS THAT REALLY MATTER

On a day-to-day basis, there are literally dozens of things in business that seem important. Often in the whir of action, with loads of conflicting advice and mountains of information to sort through, it's difficult to know what matters. Well, after more than thirty years of a full and challenging career, here's my list of some of the things that have really mattered to me.

- **Growth matters.** Continuous dissatisfaction with the status quo is the best way to keep growing. Without an ethos that assumes you are *never as good as you will become,* you will stall out and your people will put their performance on cruise control.
- **Relationships matter.** Mentors can be the difference between your having to struggle and learn entirely by trial and error versus

profiting from the sage advice and past experience of someone who is older and wiser.

- **Loyalty matters.** Staying true to associates and subordinates creates the credibility and trust you need to be a leader. And loyalty cuts both ways. You benefit by retaining the support of smart people who know your style and want to meet your expectations.
- **Small moments matter.** Expressions of concern and interest in an associate's career and struggles must be real and genuine, but they don't have to be large, orchestrated events. Small things—a hamburger at a fast-food restaurant, a hot dog at a roadside stand, or a meeting at your home—can create a lifelong remembrance. Be honest with your people about your expectations and don't sugarcoat any shortcomings, but take the time to support them when they need your help.
- **Timely decisions matter.** One of the toughest things in business is firing people, which usually results in delays that hurt everyone. Remember that someone who's a poor match for a position in your business may be a star elsewhere. At any rate, putting off a tough decision never makes it easier. Timely decision making helps your business, your associates, and ultimately the displaced person, who can get on with a new life.
- **Doing what you enjoy matters.** It was true for me when I started my career. More than thirty years later, I can't think of a better lifelong mantra: *Find something you like to do, and then find someone who will pay you to do it.* If you don't like what you're doing, every day seems like an eternity. If you're absorbed and consumed with your work, a career of decades seems short. I believe the more you like what you do, the better off, the more successful, and the more satisfied you'll be over time.
- **Life's early lessons matter.** In an age of such great change and tumult, what better mooring could you have for your values than the lessons learned at your mother's knee! Everything from *play fair* . . . to *be on time* . . . to *work hard* . . . to *tell the truth* . . . to *don't blame*

others, and on and on. Warren Buffett says: *Don't do it if you wouldn't want to read about it on the front page of your newspaper.* I agree, and would add: *Don't do it if your parents or clergy wouldn't approve.* Doing the right things always matters.

- **The right team matters.** As Mike Miles says, surround yourself with the best people. Fairly or unfairly, you're credited for the successes of your team and blamed for their failures. So get the best and the brightest people and keep many of them with you throughout your career. If you do that, you're probably doing what matters.
- **Confronting reality matters.** Often the challenge is accepting the fact that change is needed to make things better. But equally important is the wisdom to know when no amount of change will work. As Warren Buffett notes, you have to acknowledge that there are those "bad businesses," and bad business situations will beat "good managers" every time. There's wisdom in knowing your limitations and accepting those things you can't influence.

APPENDIX
Gillette Financial Metrics, 2001–2005

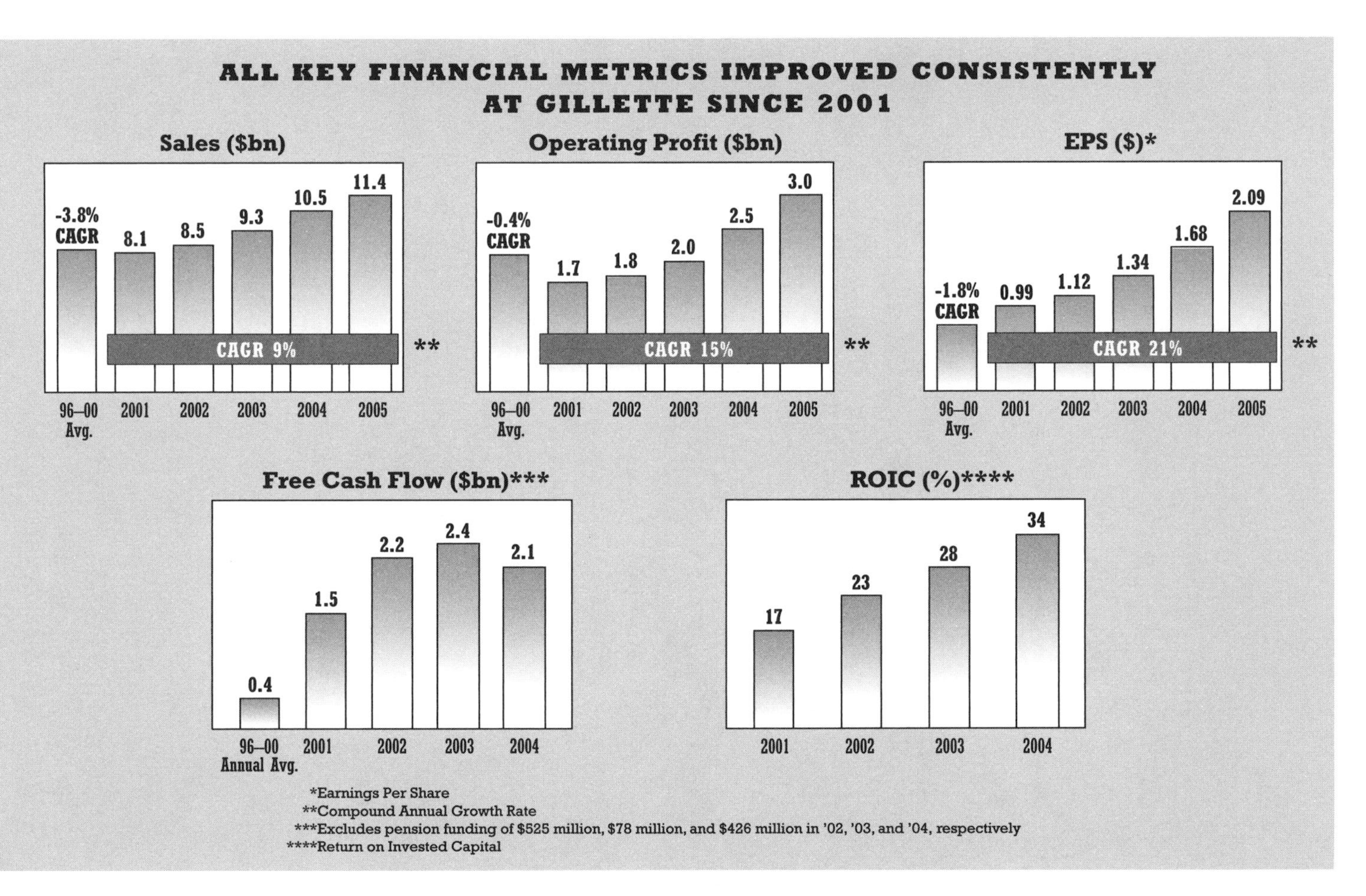
ALL KEY FINANCIAL METRICS IMPROVED CONSISTENTLY
AT GILLETTE SINCE 2001
Sales ($bn)
-3.8% CAGR
8.1
8.5
9.3
10.5
11.4
CAGR 9%
**
96–00 Avg.
2001
2002
2003
2004
2005
Operating Profit ($bn)
-0.4% CAGR
1.7
1.8
2.0
2.5
3.0
CAGR 15%
**
96–00 Avg.
2001
2002
2003
2004
2005
EPS ($)*
-1.8% CAGR
0.99
1.12
1.34
1.68
2.09
CAGR 21%
**
96–00 Avg.
2001
2002
2003
2004
2005
Free Cash Flow ($bn)***
0.4
1.5
2.2
2.4
2.1
96–00 Annual Avg.
2001
2002
2003
2004
ROIC (%)****
17
23
28
34
2001
2002
2003
2004
*Earnings Per Share
**Compound Annual Growth Rate
***Excludes pension funding of $525 million, $78 million, and $426 million in '02, '03, and '04, respectively
****Return on Invested Capital

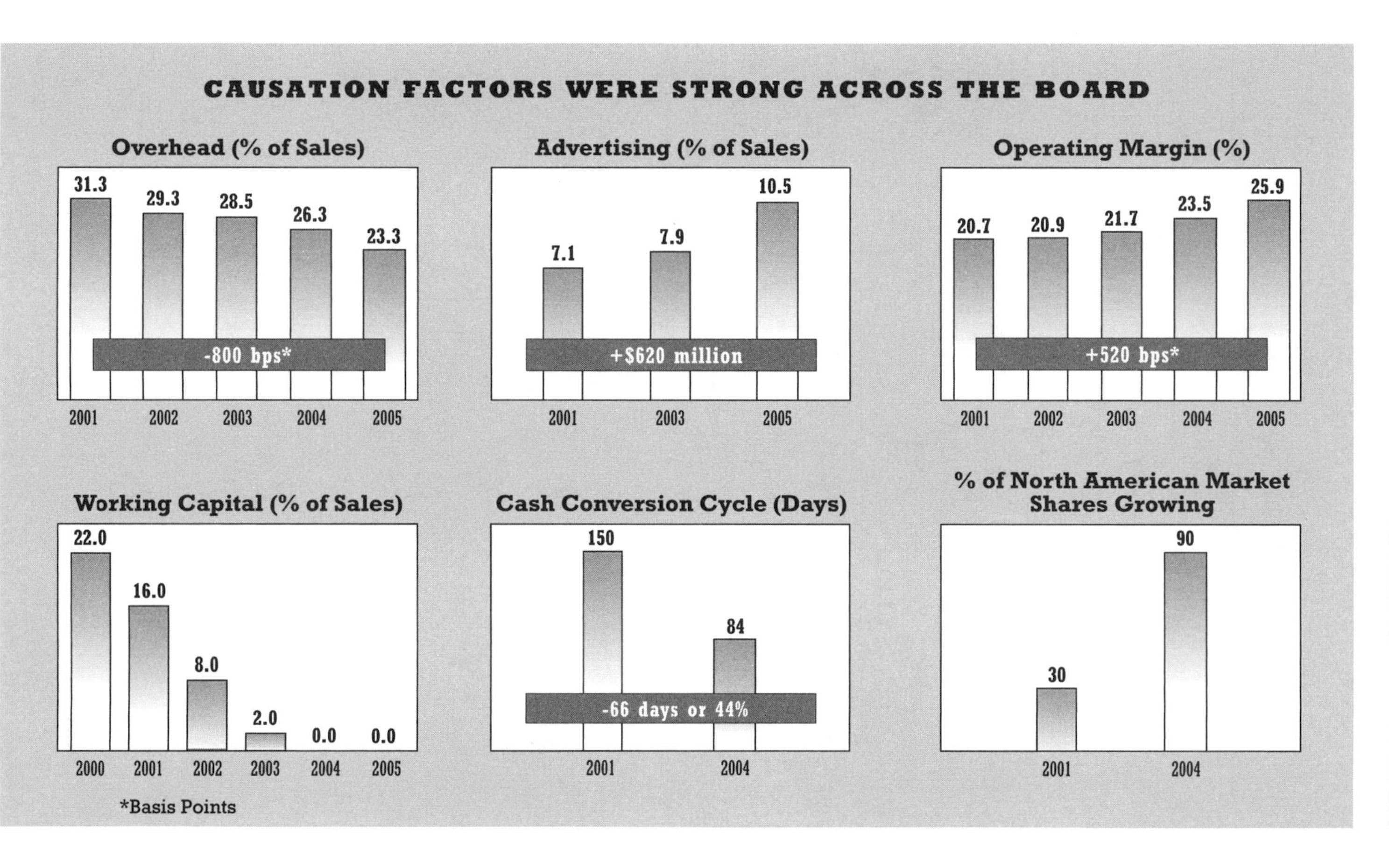
CAUSATION FACTORS WERE STRONG ACROSS THE BOARD
Overhead (% of Sales)
31.3
29.3
28.5
26.3
23.3
-800 bps*
2001
2002
2003
2004
2005
Advertising (% of Sales)
7.1
7.9
10.5
+$620 million
2001
2003
2005
Operating Margin (%)
20.7
20.9
21.7
23.5
25.9
+520 bps*
2001
2002
2003
2004
2005
Working Capital (% of Sales)
22.0
16.0
8.0
2.0
0.0
0.0
2000
2001
2002
2003
2004
2005
Cash Conversion Cycle (Days)
150
84
-66 days or 44%
2001
2004
% of North American Market Shares Growing
30
90
2001
2004
*Basis Points

PROFITS IMPROVED ACROSS EVERY GILLETTE BUSINESS UNIT

SEGMENT	FY2001 EBIT* ($mm)	FY2005 EBIT* ($mm)	CAGR** (%)
Blades & Razors	1,141	1,888	13%
Duracell	218	548	26%
Oral Care	240	362	11%
Personal Care	68	131	18%
Braun	98	133	8%

*Earnings Before Income Tax—excludes corporate overhead
**Compound Annual Growth Rate

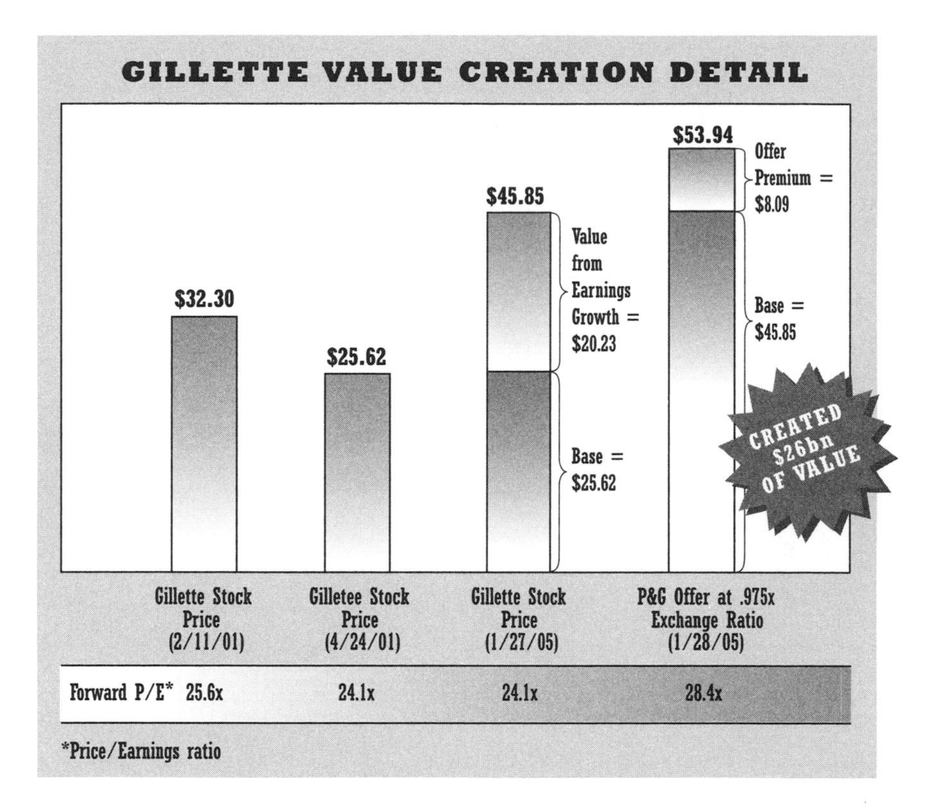
GILLETTE VALUE CREATION DETAIL
$32.30
$25.62
$45.85
$53.94
Value from Earnings Growth = $20.23
Base = $25.62
Offer Premium = $8.09
Base = $45.85
CREATED $26bn OF VALUE
Gillette Stock Price (2/11/01)
Gilletee Stock Price (4/24/01)
Gillette Stock Price (1/27/05)
P&G Offer at .975x Exchange Ratio (1/28/05)
Forward P/E* 25.6x
24.1x
24.1x
28.4x
*Price/Earnings ratio

ACKNOWLEDGMENTS

In many ways, this book is a tribute to the tens of thousands of associates who worked at General Foods, Kraft, Nabisco, and Gillette where the principles and precepts of *Doing What Matters* took shape and were applied. Business practices never emerge fully formed. There is always trial and error—cutting and fitting. Many of our associates were direct participants in that process through the years. All of them have our thanks and a share of the credit for shaping the *Doing What Matters* approach.

In describing accomplishments and achievements, our book may make it sound like just two or three people thought up the strategies and also did the heavy lifting to get things done. Nothing could be further from the truth. Leading and running businesses is a total team effort. In today's matrixed organizations, each team member and group reinforces the others. Critical participants include the members of the boards of directors—and at General Foods, Kraft, Nabisco, and Gillette, they were outstanding and storied people, who made all the difference in guiding and enabling our accomplishments.

Next is the senior leadership, and as you have seen in our book, as individuals and in groups, our leaders devoted their intellects, emotions, and countless hours to helping accomplish many things—small and large.

And as we have said, the efforts, thoughts, and enthusiasm

of all the organizations also truly mattered each step along the way.

Two associates deserve special credit. Joe Schena, who worked at each of the four companies mentioned, participated throughout the formative period. Joe also was a big help in securing and vetting financial data throughout this book. Peter Klein also was present at the beginning, and throughout the growth and creation, of *Doing What Matters*. He served as a marketing and brand consultant at General Foods and Kraft and then as an executive staff member at Nabisco and Gillette.

Pivotal in drafting the messages that communicate the *Doing What Matters* approach to the organizations at Nabisco and Gillette was Bill Ruffin, who worked on many speeches and presentations that brought our concepts to life. At one point, Bill worked within the communications function at RJR Nabisco, but decided that the vicissitudes of freelancing were far preferable to the preleveraged buyout environment of RJRN.

Special acknowledgment also goes to each of the people whom we interviewed in preparing the book. The thoughts and observations of some of these friends and associates are part of the book. While many others are not directly referenced and included, their words influenced our thinking as we put the book together.

John Mahaney, our Crown Business editor, was with us each step of the way as we went from concept through outline onto drafting and rewriting. Always encouraging, John also knew when to push, challenge, and demand. He enabled us to see where a little more energy and effort could yield a lot more interest and insight. He also knew when cutting and eliminating would result in more, not less. John is a rarity. He gave it to us straight, but in a way we could move ahead, not wither and wonder what to do next.

Also with us each step of the way was our literary agent, Margret McBride, whose entire office joined in to fashion our preliminary thoughts into a cogent book proposal that was the springboard for what has become *Doing What Matters*. Margret was a source of knowledge, support, and energy throughout our journey.

Finally, we would like to thank our loving families—Sandy, Jimmy, and Sarah; Doreen, Kendre, Hadley, and Nicole; and Sandy, Tracie, Lindie, and Kaylie—for their support and encouragement. Doreen worked diligently and patiently on each chapter. She provided gentle, but extensive constructive criticism and editing throughout. Without her tireless efforts, deadlines never would have been met.

INDEX

ABOUT THE AUTHORS

JAMES M. KILTS was, until recently, the chairman and CEO of Gillette, a position he held from 2000 until he merged the company with Procter & Gamble. He was widely credited with turning around a once iconic company in serious decline.

As CEO of Kraft Foods, he was in charge of a $20 billion plus company that had operations all around the world. As CEO of Nabisco, his portfolio included some of the world's best-known consumer products.

Between his time at Kraft and Nabisco, Jim Kilts was a visiting lecturer at the University of Chicago. It was while teaching some of the best and brightest that the idea for this book started to gel, as students asked him about what happens in the real world of business.

Jim Kilts is now a partner at Centerview Partners, a private-equity firm. He is also on the Board of Trustees of the University of Chicago, is chairman of the advisory board of the University of Chicago's Graduate School of Business, and has endowed the James M. Kilts Center for Marketing. The Center's purpose is pushing the boundaries of analytics and research through the ongoing exploration of advanced applications.

JOHN F. MANFREDI was one of the executives who turned around Nabisco and then Gillette. As executive vice president in charge of investor relations and many other units for Nabisco, John Manfredi helped raise the funds necessary to finance the huge LBO that resulted from the famed assault of the "barbarians." He then worked with Jim Kilts to jump-start Nabisco after its shaky IPO.

Moving with Kilts to Gillette, John Manfredi reestablished the company's credentials with Wall Street and the media and was one of the few executives to deal with Procter & Gamble on the megasale of Gillette, the largest in the consumer products sector.

Manfredi led a number of industry initiatives in the United States and worldwide as the longtime chairman of the global marketing commission of the International Chamber of Commerce in Paris and of the International Food Information Council in Washington, D.C.

His community and professional activities include more than a decade serving as chairman of the U.S. Olympics Committee in New Jersey and as a member of the boards for United Way of New England, the Foundation for Teaching Economics, and the Arthur Page Society.

Manfredi attended Yale College and Columbia University where he received his B.A. and did graduate studies in English.

DR. ROBERT L. LORBER is president of the Lorber Kamai Consulting Group, a firm formed in 1976. The organization has implemented productivity improvement systems for companies on five continents. The Lorber Kamai Consulting Group's client roster has included Kraft Foods, Santa Fe International, Teichert Inc., Occidental Petroleum, Gillette, Sutter Health, American Express, Mattel, AlliedSignal, Raley's, VSP, Maxtor, ETS, Wells Fargo, Pillsbury, Pfizer, Kaufman and Broad, Tower Records, and many other medium-sized and Fortune 500 companies.

Dr. Lorber is an internationally recognized expert and published author on executive coaching, performance management, leadership, teamwork, culture, and developing strategy. He is one of the leading resources worldwide on executive coaching with chief executive officers and senior executives. He is the coauthor of the *New York Times* bestseller *Putting the One Minute Manager to Work,* which he created with the renowned management consultant Dr. Ken Blanchard; *One Page Management,* coauthored with Dr. Riaz Khadem; and *Safety 24/7* with Greg Anderson. Dr. Lorber is an established professional speaker who has delivered presentations for profit and nonprofit audiences throughout the world.

Dr. Lorber works with numerous boards of directors on governance and effective board participation. Currently he serves as chairman of the Dean's Advisory Council for the Graduate School of Management at UC Davis, the UC Davis School of Medicine's Board of Visitors, and many other corporate and not-for-profit boards, including Tower Records, The Blanchard Companies, Basic American Industries, The Hugh O'Brian Youth Foundation, The Sacramento Region Community Foundation, Sukut Construction, Sacramento Entrepreneurship Academy, LeadershipTraq, J&M Realty, and the Board of Governors of the Ukleja Center for Ethical Leadership.

In addition to his executive coaching, consulting, writing, and speaking pursuits, Dr. Lorber is an associate professor at his alma mater—the Graduate School of Management of the University of California at Davis—where he teaches two courses on leadership. Dr. Lorber received a master's degree in sociology and a PhD in organizational psychology. He resides in Davis, California, with his wife, Sandy, and their three daughters, Tracie, Lindie, and Kaylie.